"I Should Be Sc ____,

The Story of My Life

BY

Roy Cook

To Bob with best wishes

Roy

GROOVESIDE PUBLISHING

British Library Cataloguing in Publication Data.
A catalogue record for this book is available from the
British Library

ISBN 0-9553153-0-1
ISBN 978-0-9553153-0-5

Grooveside Publishing
12 Groveside
Great Bookham
KT23 4LD
Tel: 01372 452583/01483 202270

Printed in Great Britain by Lightning Source of Milton
Keynes

All profit from the sales of this book will go to the
Alzheimer's Society

I SHOULD BE SO LUCKY – List of Chapters

This book is dedicated to my wonderful wife Jean who was an inspiration to everyone she met for a very large part of her life.

During her last years I owe an overwhelming debt of gratitude to Penny Weaver and Deirdre Etherton, both of the local Alzheimer's Societies for helping me to look after her at home for so long and enabling me to write this book.

Finally, thanks are due to my son Gary and son-in-law Colin for their patience in dealing with a computer illiterate.

A DEDICATION BY RUSS ABBOTT

Elizabeth Laing was truly an elegant lady. She left her home in Scotland at the age of 16 to work in service for the Duke of Westminster's family. She met Don Roberts, married and raised 6 boys - me being no.5.

She passed away at the age of 74 but sadly never remembered her latter years due to Alzheimer 's Disease.

My brothers and I have such treasured memories of a truly great lady and a wonderful Mother. She was my No.1 fan. Sadly at her last visit to one of my performances, when asked if she enjoyed the show, she didn't know me, which you can imagine was very sad for me, but alas not for Mum. The cruel thing about this illness is that it takes away all dignity from the men and women who have, all their lives, given so much to family and friends. Only we are left to remember.

We must pursue a cure for this terrible disease and also support the friends and relations who have to endure the heartache and help give them strength and courage, but above all – understanding.....

Jean as we remember her.

INTRODUCTION

If a certain amount of luck is necessary for a person to have a very happy life, then I reckon I have been more fortunate than most. My parents, Alick Ambrose and Marguerite Edith, were two of the most kind and gentle people it is possible to meet. Dad came from Ipswich in Suffolk where his father, my Grandfather, was a highly respected train guard, working for the London & North Eastern Railway, as it was then called. During holidays with him, we would often go walking in Gippeswyk Park which was a stone's throw from his house overlooking Ipswich Station in Ranelagh Road.

From time to time, as trains passed us by, he would take out his pocket watch and announce that the 4.40 to Norwich had just gone through. I fear today he would not be able to be as accurate as he was then. Many's the time I have travelled up and down in the Guard's van and as I recall, I believe the journey only took a little over one and a half hours. My understanding is that it takes as long even today.

Dad had three brothers, Jess, Ernie and Jim and two sisters, Edie and Ciss. Edie became known as "little Edie" because Uncle Ernie married her namesake, who thus became "Big Edie". It would be quite indelicate of me to explain why!

Uncle Ernie was the only member of the family to possess a car during my youth and I well recall the many trips to Shingle Street on which he took us. Uncle Jess was the elder statesman, a Civil Servant who ended up taking over the function of best man at my wedding, but that's a story for a later chapter. Uncle Jim worked at Ransome's factory in Ipswich which was famous for lawn mowers.

1

Auntie Ciss married Uncle Wilfred who was a very fine stonemason and examples of his later work are to be seen in the modernisation of Bury Cathedral. There is a special book locked inside a glass case inside the Cathedral listing all the craftsmen who worked on this project, but on the two occasions we have visited Bury, they were unable to locate the key for us.

Last but by no means least, Little Edie married Uncle Cecil, a printer and the two of them were to become a very important part of my life when the war broke out whilst I was on holiday with them and I remained in Ipswich for the next three years as an evacuee. My mother, Marguerite Edith Shimell, was born in 1897 as was my father. Because of her unusual surname, a very keen distant relative has spent a tremendous amount of time, energy and money in producing the most comprehensive family tree which begins in 1786 with a JAMES SHIMELL in Devon. The main chart itself is crammed with names but in addition, this is backed up by no fewer than 19 separate sheets listing their descendants.

He has provided a separate record of all the Shimell weddings listing the dates and places commencing in 1837 and totalling 538 in all and they appear to cover the length and breadth of the country.

Mum was one of 10 children of the second marriage of my grandfather and there were 4 other children by his first wife and I cannot understand how he turned out to be such a miserable so and so. No hobbies I suppose – although he was a very fine master carpenter by trade. Seven of his children died at a very early age, the oldest having reached 5 years. Of the remainder there was a fairly strong musical element in that Uncle Arthur played the cello, Uncle Walter the violin, my mother played the piano and before he lost an arm during the war, Uncle Dick played the banjo.

I understand that on Sunday evenings they had concerts in the front room at Laitwood Road which frequently attracted an outside audience. This was always of a fairly classical nature and much later whenever we visited Uncle Arthur I was invariably made to accompany him with Chu Chin Chow – not my favourite type of music. Perhaps this was the catalyst that made me eventually turn to jazz.

Mum and Dad were married in Wandsworth in September 1922 and lived for a short time in Hazelbourne Road which featured in more recent times in discussions on the poll tax as on one side of the road was Lambeth – the other in Wandsworth and the difference in rates was phenomenal.

My grandfather on my mother's side suffered the loss of his wife – my grandmother, Jane Voice, in December 1923 and shortly after this my parents moved in to look after him in Laitwood Road, Balham until his death on the day after his birthday 17 years later at the age of 89. My earlier comments about him may have raised a few eyebrows but I assure you they are entirely justified. From my own personal point of view it is a fact that all the time I was living with him, he only ever gave me 2 separate shillings and on each occasion this was for doing something Dad had refused him. Outside he was looked up to by most of the neighbours but he was far from easy to live with. Nevertheless he was an exceptional craftsman and we still have a mahogany case, originally made to house an early radio, which I now use to store music. This brings to the mind the fact that I often had to take the accumulator down the road for charging in my early youth. He also panelled the walls of the dining room up to waist level and when the ceiling of the same room gave way when the upstairs bath overflowed he replaced it with zinc.

This he panelled in a most intricate design – so much so that every time the Doctor called he insisted on viewing it! When we had to clear the house after Mum died we had to dispose of a very fine china cabinet which must have been about 6 foot long x 5 foot high and I often wonder what that would have been valued by the Antiques Roadshow – we got £30 for it. Just after granddad died all the relatives came round to share out his remaining property and his tools and to this day I find it hard to conceive that his magnificent collection of planes was actually split up into several lots – talk about divided we fall!

My grandfather's brother Charles also had two wives and a very large number of children and in course of researching the family tree one of his sons and later his grandson, Ronald Shimell, came across a cutting from the Daily Sketch dated September 1st 1915 which reads like a follow up to the Four Feathers and would certainly never see the light of day in today's world. A copy of this document is shown later in this chapter.

Both brothers were cabinet makers and master carpenters and William Shimell, my grandfather, was a foreman carpenter involved in the building of houses in Laitwood Road and he eventually bought No.43. The two brothers were only 5ft 2 and 1/2 inches tall and so alike that their children would mistake their uncle for their father form behind. With this information it is easy to understand why my mother was a mere 4ft 10 and 1/2 inches in height. She was far from pleased with this and she found it almost impossible to obtain size 2 shoes and invariably ended in the children's department.

Mum was known as Maggie or more affectionately as Dimples and she was extremely good looking and despite the problems she had with Old Bill, I can only recall seeing her upset on two occasions – why I shall never know! Everyone liked both her and dad. Their next door neighbour was Welsh – a Mrs Williams whose son lent me his dress suit when I was 17 to enable me to appear in a Jazz Concert at the London Coliseum one Sunday afternoon – but that again is yet another chapter for later. There is an amusing tale concerning Mrs. Williams during the war years when the milkman's horse provided some very useful garden manure right outside her house. Before she could return with a shovel and bucket, the woman opposite beat her to it only to be upbraided with the words "you're not even registered with this milkman".

Gwyn, her son, was an amazing character who worked for some considerable time for the railways and then joined the R.A.F. eventually becoming a Wing Commander in India where he met his wife Menna and they had a son called Clive. After returning to Civvy Street, Gwyn ultimately became a senior consultant to a well known firm through whom he produced a text book video on the art of consultancy which was translated into many languages.

When I first contacted Ronald Shimell regarding the family tree, he realised he had actually worked for Gwyn and we were able to invite them both to our 40th wedding anniversary to talk over old times.

When Gwyn died in October 1999 there was some delay in arranging the funeral and when Clive told me the details he commented that Gwyn would have been tickled pink as the cremation was to be held on Guy Fawkes Night.

Unfortunately the name of Cook does not lend itself to deedy investigation and as I failed to ask the pertinent questions at the right time, my information on my father's early life is somewhat sketchy. As I understand it, he worked for Marconi originally and during the First World War he became a wireless operator on a hospital ship.

After the war he became an electrician and we have a large photo of him on top of the Shredded Wheat factory at Welwyn Garden City somewhere in the house. On another occasion I recall going as a family to the grand opening of The Gaumont Cinema in Kings Road, Chelsea, where Dad had been working for some time, to see Jack Hulbert & Cicely Courtneidge in a film called "The Camels are Coming".

Uncle Tom was also an electrician and he eventually became chief electrician at one of McCorquodale's premises in the Euston Road. Amongst other items the company printed bank notes and at one time were very famous, although the company has seemingly disappeared following a big takeover battle some years ago. Eventually Dad took over from Uncle Tom and during his time there he was able to take on two of Uncle Frank's sons, my cousins Douglas and Gerald who became qualified electricians. Their father had died at the very early age of 43 when their sister Kathleen was only 8 years old and this placed an enormous burden on her as Gerald was only 5 years old and she also had to look after another brother who was born just after his father died – he was actually given his father's full names! Unfortunately both Gerald and young Frank died at the ages of 56 & 39 respectively but Douglas lives in Douglas on the Isle of Man and has passed on his electrical business to his son Bernard.

Whilst the company name has gone, the name of McCorquodale most certainly lives on and at one time Raine McCorquodale was married to the Earl Spencer – Princess Diana's father. Last year we took up an offer in the Daily Telegraph to visit Winslow Hall in Buckinghamshire, reputed to have been built by Christopher Wren which it stated had previously been occupied by one of the McCorquodales. I thought there might be some evidence of their stay but could see nothing. During our tour of the house I was told we would be meeting the current owner on the way out where he was collecting ticket money. I mentioned my particular interest and that Dad had often been to their houses to carry out repairs and he told me that there were none of their possessions in the house and furthermore that he had been compelled to renew the wiring before being allowed to move in. I have a feeling he quite enjoyed that conversation! I later established that this could not have been one of the family houses that Dad worked on. There is one intriguing matter that remains a mystery. Dad's middle name was Ambrose and it was only in the last few years that I found out that Auntie Lily who married Uncle Dick, my mother's brother, had the maiden name of Lillian Ambrose and furthermore she, like my father, came from Ipswich. I also believe that at one time she and Mum worked together in the West End – possibly at Debenham's but I have no means of verifying this now.

My early childhood was spent in Laitwood Road which in those days was virtually a playground as there were very few cars to worry about. We would play all manner of games and skate up and down with impunity. One of my earliest recollections is that on Derby Day, always held midweek in those days, we would stand by the traffic lights at Balham Station and shout "Throw out your mouldies" as the returning coaches passed by – a very early form of begging.

In those days we always celebrated Empire Day at school and I wince when I recall an early photograph of me festooned with small display cards covered with apples advertising Whiteway's Cider. These had been sewn together somehow and I was wearing a hat of satin like material with an enormous feather on top. At the appropriate age I started at Henry Cavendish Infants from which I progressed to the Junior School. Much later in life after I married Jean she was to become a teacher there and our two children Linda & Gary were both pupils.

When I first met Jean she was working at the Cavendish Hotel in Jermyn Street still run at that time by the famous Rosa Lewis about whom the television series "The Duchess of Duke Street" was produced – another chapter for later!

Reverting to my early childhood I can recall Kenny Lucas and Peter Jones (no not that one), Billy Shoebridge whose father worked in the undertakers and was quite a source of unusual stories (you have to have a sense of humour to do the job at all!!!) and there was poor Terry Dignum who was electrocuted tragically on the railway line.

I met Jean at Ken Lucas' wedding where I was best man and she was chief bridesmaid and we have a photograph of the two of us emerging from the church from their wedding looking for all the world like the Bride & Groom.

When we were well established at school we were allowed to go to Tooting Bec Common on our own for hours on end – or so it seemed. There we played cricket, rounders, tennis against the brick wall surrounding the railway lines and anything else we could think of. I doubt whether many parents of today would or indeed should allow such freedom. Dad taught me and most of my friends how to swim both at Elmfield Road Baths and later on at the open air pool on Tooting Common.

At the age of eight it was decided that I should learn to

play the piano and I was put in the charge of a lady teacher who operated above a bakery in Bedford Hill just beyond the railway bridge on the way to Tooting Common. Frankly I was never very impressed with her but nevertheless she managed to get me to a standard where I could take exams and play in festivals and I ended up with several certificates some of which were adjudicated by Alec Rowley – quite a famous name at the time. Mum used to complain that I was far too wooden and lacking in expression and I suppose she was quite right. However, I firmly believe that a major part of the luck which I have enjoyed throughout my life came about when the outbreak of war marked the end of my piano tuition at the age of 13.

On many occasions I was allowed to ring the bell to call the children to school. The bell was high above the school and required considerable force on my part to operate it. I had to brace one foot against the wall and hold onto a short wooden bar attached to the end of this very long chain. Unfortunately there was a join in the chain near the bottom which on occasion would part so dumping me unceremoniously on my backside and making a ghastly sound at the same time. Overall I have a general sense of having enjoyed my time at Cavendish School. The only girl I can recall was a Sylvia Knowles who lived in Sistova Road and who was highly involved in dancing and I cannot recall how I came to get to know her although possibly our parents were friendly. Many years later when I used to attend the Feldman Jazz Club in Oxford Street (now known as the 100 Club) I found out that she was running a Dancing Club about fifty yards down the road on the opposite side.

Eventually I qualified to go to the Bec Secondary School in Beechcroft Road, Tooting where I learned to play rugby and joined Rodney House for whom I played cricket. I was a fast bowler and developed my own style of delivery by sending my arm round twice before letting go of the ball. I do not know how this came about but it worked quite well as on many occasions the bat would come up before there was anything to hit. On house meetings I recall the house master saying "The sight of Cook bearing down on the wicket is enough to put the fear of God into anyone". Years later the school produced a very fine rugby player - name of Hillier I believe – afraid I cannot remember his first name but I do know he kicked a very large number of points during his career. I also believe Jimmy White and Tony Drago came from the school although I doubt that much credit for their abilities could have been attributed to their education. Possibly the Temperance Billiard Hall in Balham High Road would be more appropriate. Dad and I had the occasional game there later in life and when Uncle Tom lived in Balham he had a half size table in one room and we would often spend Sunday morning there.

Every year the school played cricket at the Oval against Sir Walter St.John's School who overlooked the ground and on one notable occasion the Williams twins from the Bec each scored a century in a total of something like 261 for one wicket. As a direct result they both received a trial for Surrey.

In those early days in Laitwood Road all the power was provided by gas, mainly via gas mantles, but in the very small kitchen just above the mirror there was a plain jet of gas coming out of the wall making it possible to have a shave and a singe at the same time! As I have already indicated my grandfather was not particularly communicative but he once commented on a popular song of the day called "I guess I should have seen right through you but the moon got in my eyes" by saying "She must have had bloody big eyes".

We used to go fairly often to the Hippodrome Theatre at the foot of Balham Hill which was on the main music hall circuit and we saw people like Max Miller, the Western Brothers, Florence Desmond and many of the famous names of the period. For some reason I found the antics of a mad piano player called Herschel Henlere particularly appealing.

When I was eleven years old Peter Jones and I were running down Laitwood Road holding his younger sister by the hands when I hit a raised kerbstone and landed face first on the pavement. This took a piece out of my upper front tooth and I have lived with it ever since. I have to say it is far less obvious than it was and the basic tooth is still quite healthy. This is another area where luck has been kind to me. During my early childhood most of the dental treatment I required was carried out under gas and I was quite happy with this. However when they started using injections I was not at all keen. Fortunately I discovered that my teeth were very strong and when I was in Palestine in 1947 I was treated in a mobile unit just prior to being demobbed and it was not until 1966 that I next visited a dentist and the time after that was in 1986. I always had a vivid imagination when dental matters arose – or perhaps I should say I'm a complete coward in this respect. Mind you, when treatment was essential I had several unpleasant experiences in the chair, which is probably the flip side of having strong teeth.

During the pre-war days most holidays consisted of trips to Ipswich to stay with Edie and Cecil or Grandad Cook and when he was still in Clacton we would stay with Uncle Jim and Auntie Elsie but other than this I do not recall much else.

Money was tight and my father had, in common with others, experienced unemployment during the depression in 1926 – a fact which influenced him for the rest of his life. He was absolutely horrified when Jean and I first became involved in hire purchase – how times change!

These days no one thinks twice about going out for meals but for him and his contemporaries I honestly believe it was quite a painful experience.

Of course the major difference between now and then was the lack of cars on the road and the profusion of trams and buses and also the excellent reliable service on the Underground. When I was going to the Bec School I had the choice of running for the bus or tram I could see ahead of me or waiting for the one I could see approaching in the distance – they were so plentiful. The Tube was so reliable that if you were planning a journey it was only necessary to allow two minutes per station plus an allowance for changing lines to be sure of arriving on time – try doing that now!

We used to visit the Science Museum quite frequently and the main attraction was the hands on children's section where I first came across the door that opens as you approach. Every time we go to a major store I am reminded that I once thought it was very clever but who on earth was likely to put it into production considering the costs involved!

Of course there was no television in those days but there were three cinemas in Balham and we were allowed to go to suitable programs and most of them were quite O.K. I do remember seeing Richard Dix in "The Tunnel" which was quite scary but I cannot say how old I was at the time.

When it comes to food I have always been difficult as my mother would have confirmed. I never liked or would eat salad and that goes for today too – but you try getting a sandwich without it. Similarly I would not eat greens, I hated onions and as for garlic!!! Mind you garlic did not feature in my youth. That does not mean I was given an alternative but rather than eat the stuff I would go without – much to mum's dismay. You must also bear in mind there were not too many alternatives in those days – exotic foods were not being flown in out of season from all over the world, of course a chicken WAS just for Xmas.

Having a birthday on Midsummer's day June 24th means that nobody has any excuses when it comes to present giving – another bit of luck! After my 13th in 1939 I went to Ipswich to stay with Auntie Edie and Uncle Cecil as had been the custom for many years and we had a marvellous time. We had the permanent use of a beach hut on the front at Felixstowe and used to cycle there frequently. As I recall I had a Hercules Bicycle which cost the princely sum of £3 and nearly everyone in Ipswich had a bike of some sort. We lived in Fairfield Road which was on the outskirts of town close to the airfield and most of the industry in those days was situated near the centre of town and to get there you had cycle down Bishop's Hill, which was very steep and extremely long. It was only possible to walk up on the way back from the factories and offices and I cannot recall anywhere that I have seen more bikes at one time.

One weekend we went on an excursion by train to Southend on Sea. The adult fare was two shillings and sixpence, (12 1/2 pence today) and I went for half fare. We spent most of the day enjoying amusements & rides at the Kursaal Amusement Park and had the company of a friend of theirs from Oswestry who was also staying with them.

I believe they had met her and her husband some time before when holidaying in Shropshire and the husband had since become very ill and was unable to accompany her.

Now Cecil and Edie were unable to have children but they knew how to enjoy life and being with them at this age was great fun. My mother often described them as being nothing more than a couple of kids themselves.

As the holiday progressed the news of what was happening on the continent gradually got worse and worse until on September 3rd we listened to Neville Chamberlain, the Prime Minister, announce on the radio that "This country is now at war with Germany". After discussions with Mum and Dad it was decide rather than return to London to go with the Bec School to Lewes, where they were being evacuated they would look after me and it was arranged that I would continue my education at the Northgate School for boys – the local Secondary School. Now if that isn't luck I don't know what the word means! This was a major turning point in my life.

Mr. Charles Shimell has six sons serving.   William Shimell has five boys fighting.

FATHER WHO RECRUITS BY LOOKING AT SLACKERS.

Man Who Has No Sympathy With Lamp-post Supports.

11 SONS AND NEPHEWS IN KHAKI.

Roland, H.M.S. Raglan.   Percy, Royal Field Artillery.

Dick, Royal Fusiliers.   Tom, Royal Fusiliers.

" When I see them supporting lamp-posts or lolling about with girls, I just look at them!

"I can do no more, but as long as the war lasts I shall continue to look at them! If I have shamed some of them into proving their manhood—well, then my looks have not all fallen on waste ground."

So said Mr. Charles Shimell, of Graveney-road, Tooting, to the *Daily Sketch* yesterday. He and his brother have between them eleven sons in the Army and Navy, and, failing other means of persuading other people's sons to join their own, Mr. Shimell employs the gentle art of looking at the slackers and shirkers.

FATHER OF LARGE FAMILY.

"I have 13 children in all," Mr. Charles Shimell explained to the *Daily Sketch*, "but only six recruitable. Otherwise I would gladly see them all go.

"I don't like the word conscription, hate the very sound of it, but at a time like this those young men who can and do not do their bit—well, they are not young men at all! None of my boys—or none of my brother's—wanted the least pushing or urging. My sons were all in more or less good positions. They said to me, 'Dad, we are going to help the Old Country,' and how was I to stop them?"

But for his age—he is 58—he would have been along with them.

DOING HIS BIT.

"Still, I'm not quite useless as it is. I'm doing some local Red Cross work, so that"—with a smile —"none of the lads will be able to say after the great war, 'What did you do in the war, father?'"

A heating and domestic engineer by profession, Mr. Shimmell comes during his work-a-day life in contact with hundreds of men of all classes and ages, old and young, and he tries to "get at" all who ought to be in khaki in his own way.

Mr. William Shimell, his brother, of Balham, who has five lads at the front, is equally enthusiastic. The only son left at home is Walter, just 16. "He is busy at aeroplane work," remarked his mother proudly to the *Daily Sketch*.

CONGRATULATED BY THE KING.

In addition, her son-in-law, a married man with two children, enlisted on the outbreak of war in the Royal Engineers.

Both brothers have received letters from Buckingham Palace on behalf of the King appreciating the efforts of the two fathers. The Royal missives have been framed in each case by the proud recipients, and now occupy a place of honour in the two homes among the photographs of the khaki lads.

Leslie, H.M.S. Cornwallis.

Norman, 2nd East Surreys.

Arthur, Middlesex Regt.   Frank, Army Service Corps.

The boys' mother—Mrs. C. Shimell.

Mr. William Shimell's son-in-law is also with the colours.

Cecil, Army Service Corps.   Harold, Army Service Corps.

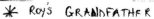

✳ ROY'S GRANDFATHER

15

Blown up text from Daily Sketch

FATHER WHO RECRUITS BY LOOKING AT SLACKERS

Man Who Has No Sympathy With Lamp-post Supports

---

11 SONS AND NEPHEWS IN KHAKI

"When I see them supporting lamp-posts or lolling about with girls, I just look at them! I can do no more, but as long as the war lasts I shall continue to look at them. If I have shamed some of them into proving their manhood – well, then my looks have not all fallen on waste ground."

So said Mr Charles Shimmel of Graveney Road, Tooting to the Daily Sketch yesterday. He and his brother have between them 11 sons in the Army and Navy, and, failing other means of persuading other peoples' sons to join their own, Mr Shimmel employs the gentle art of looking at the slackers and shirkers.

FATHER OF LARGE FAMILY

"I have 13 children in all" Mr Charles Shimmel explained to the Daily Sketch, "but only six recruitable. Otherwise I would gladly see them all go."

"I don't like the word conscription, hate the very sound of it, but at a time like this these young men who can and do not do their bit – well, they're not young men at all. None of my boys – or those of my brother – wanted the least pushing or urging. My sons were all in more or less good positions. They said to me 'Dad, we're going to help the old country', and how was I to stop them."

But for his age – he is 58 – he would have been there with them. DOING HIS BIT.

"Still, I'm not quite useless as it is. I'm doing some local Red Cross work, so that" – with a smile – "none of the lads will be able to say after the Great War 'What did you do in the war father!'"

A heating and domestic engineer by profession Mr Shimmel comes during his work-a-day life in contact with hundreds of men of all classes and ages, old and young, and he tries to "get at" all who ought to be in khaki in his own way.

Mr William Shimmel, his brother, of Balham who has five lads at the front is equally enthusiastic. The only son left at home is Walter, just 16 "he is busy at aeroplane work" remarked his mother proudly to the Daily Sketch.

CONGRATULATED BY THE KING

In addition, her son in law, a married man with no children, enlisted on the outbreak of war in the Royal Engineers.

Both brothers have received letters from Buckingham Palace on behalf of the King appreciating the efforts of the two fathers.

The Royal missives have been framed in each case by the proud recipients, and now occupy a place of honour in the two homes among the photographs of the khaki lads.

EVACUATION AT IPSWICH

My recollections of life in Ipswich during 1939 are of a comfortable home and being well looked after by my uncle and aunt. Uncle Cecil was a printer by trade and he often took me to his works in the centre of town. He was obviously very popular despite the fact that he was always very much the practical joker – it was very difficult to take umbrage at many of his many pranks – and those continued throughout his lifetime. As Mum said, he never really grew up. He had a passion for the cinema organ and over the years he must have had his favourite tune "Moonlight and Roses" played by nearly all the famous organists in the country from Reginald Dixon onwards. On one Saturday morning he took me to the Ritz cinema in town and persuaded the organist to let me play his tune for him. On two occasions I was taken to see his Uncle Willey who lived in a disused chapel in Woodbridge just outside Ipswich. He played trombone in the local brass band but his hobby was collecting all types of organs and pianolas and the place was a veritable museum. Most of these instruments could also be played using music rolls and these were stacked in huge piles against the walls of the chapel. He had built his own organ, the pipes of which were all over the place and you had to try to avoid falling over them when walking around. He even had an organ which came from a cinema in Tooting and he had a panel over the keyboard which lit up to show a waterfall. I had a most enjoyable time there. On our first visit he also had a parrot on a perch alongside a complete suit of armour. On the second occasion the parrot had died and been stuffed and was still on the perch and I was standing immediately in front of it when all the lights went out during a power cut and I felt a chill down the back of my neck.

One overriding memory that I have is how good the weather seemed to be most of the time and we frequently had breakfast outside the French windows. I used to cycle to school and come home for lunch most days. In so doing I met up with John Denny who lived fairly close and who was to become a lifelong friend. He too married a Jean and we still see each other at least twice a year. The only period in my life when I kept a day to day diary was from 1940 until 1944 and these show a strange mixture of going to the cinema – playing cricket and taking five wickets for five runs – I kid you not – the number and duration of air raid warnings for that day, on April 9th 1940 the German invasion of Denmark and Norway, and later the sinking of the Bismarck.

Fairly soon after the war started, Uncle Cecil became an Air Raid Warden attached to a post on a recreation ground nearby and I came to spend many hours with him at the post playing darts and a game called P.M. which I cannot recall for the life of me. For some considerable time there was very little activity and it was not until the summer of 1940 that we experienced any air raids. On the 18trh June during a warning lasting from midnight until 4 a.m. we saw some German planes being shot at in the searchlights and we heard their bombs explode and on the same night some shrapnel hit our roof. The first bombs on London fell on Sunday 25th August. Despite the situation we went to the pictures two or three times a week and saw many of the classic films of all time including The Wizard of Oz – The Hunchback of Notre Dame – The Birth of the Blues – Dangerous Moonlight – and The Great Dictator.

At the end of term, I would return to London for the holiday period where I not only saw more films but many West End shows including Ivor Novello in The Dancing Years.

The whole of London was covered by barrage balloons tethered to heavy cables to deter the enemy planes from diving low over the capital. Going back to Ipswich the raids continued and on 10th September the town received an order for Temporary Voluntary Evacuation to Northampton, Loughborough and Leicester. Shortly after, the Germans were dropping land mines by parachute and by November they had introduced an anti-personnel mine which was dropped in very large numbers. I found these quite fascinating as they were not very large and consisted of a canister possibly 4" long by 2 ½" diameter which had a hinged metal covering mounted upon a shaft rather like meat skewer. As the air got under the vanes they slowly revolved on the shaft until they were wide open and at a pre-determined point, which was, I believe, variable, the thing would explode. On more than one occasion I dived off my bike and went to ground when they were dropped nearby and also on one or two occasions when they were using machine guns nearby. I recorded that on one night over 300 Butterfly Bombs (as they became known) were dropped and some were primed not to explode in the air and became quite deadly on the ground. On that night 7 people were killed and many others injured. Looking back it would appear that the authorities were not expecting Ipswich to be in the firing line. However shortly after these raids I helped to dig a hole for the corrugated iron Anderson Shelter in which we were to spend many nights in the months to come, sometimes in the company of one of the neighbours whose husband was on duty at the post with Uncle Cecil. The war certainly brought with it a very close community spirit which does not exist these days – or at least to the same extent.

As I no longer had piano lessons I started to collect the popular sheet music of the day. Here again I consider myself very fortunate because this included some of today's standards such as "All things you are" and "Over the Rainbow" which I must have played more than a thousand times since then! Over the next year or so I built up a small library of dance music which eventually provided the basis for the band we later formed at school. I also tried my hand at novelty piano pieces such as "Nola" – "Marigold" – "Canadian Capers" and "Rhapsody in Blue". As far as the latter was concerned I reckoned I could make a reasonable showing of around 95% of it but there were one or two pages near the end that were nigh on impossible for me. My hands are very small and it is fortunate that I am very double jointed and this made it possible to increase the overall span slightly. My thumbs bend back 90 degrees naturally and when I was much younger my fingers could bend backwards to reach my wrist although I am sure this is not a really good idea!

I was well received at the Northgate School and looking at my exam results I was generally within the top six overall and sometimes top. In the individual subjects I was best at Maths English and French – worst at Handwriting (32nd) and Handicraft, Physics and Chemistry. Auntie Edie was always proud of a brass biscuit tin and tray that I brought home but truth is that apart from providing a decorative pattern using a hammer and a punch there was very little else in them I could claim as "mine"! Of the teachers, our French Master – The Reverend Yates and History Master Bishop come to mind instantly. Bishop for his habit of throwing chalk at the boys and when really roused had been known to rub the noses of any malingerers in the chalk on the blackboard just to emphasise the point! Yates included me in a small band to take a special French exam – the "Concourse Speciale des Professeurs de Francaise en Angleterre" which proved to be rather wasted on me.

At least when we went through France on holiday shortly

after the war I would approach the hotelier and say "Avez vous deux chambres pour quatre personnes pour ce soir" and without exception they all said "You may speak English Monsieur!"

I played Cricket, Rugby and Hockey for my house and in 1942 I also played cricket for the school's 1st Eleven. We had several tennis courts and generally played doubles most of the time. Came the day when I entered a knockout singles competition and was drawn against the school captain and I thought I was doing fairly well when I discovered for the first time that in singles you cannot use the outside tramlines!

After a while I used to go regularly to John Denny's house to play the piano and we then teamed up with Ken Driver also from our school who also had musical interests. As I recall when we first got together as a trio both John and Ken were playing Ukuleles and then first one purchased a guitar only to be followed closely by another. Finally Ken took to the saxophone and we had the nucleus of a band. We also spent many evenings at Ken's house and both sets of parents were most accommodating. Funnily enough Ken too, married yet another Jean, but I never actually met her and Ken died rather suddenly a couple of years ago. At the end of term there was usually a concert at which we played a few tunes and on one memorable occasion we played a popular tune of the day called "An apple for the teacher" and to our astonishment the English mistress walked out in protest. Apparently she thought we were taking the Mickey! Towards the end of 1940 I was taken by my Uncle and Aunt to The Conservative Club at the top of our road – Fairfield Road – and I played the piano in public for the first time. They put the hat round and came up with collection of 4 shillings and 2 ½ pence (about 21 p today). Fame at last!

Early on in my days at Ipswich there was a sad event when their dog Rex accidentally killed a kitten they had and although I do not remember the departure of Rex, another dog named Guy took his place some time later. So called because Auntie Edie's Birthday was on November 5th and he was a present. He was quite a character and there is a photo of him around wearing my school cap & blazer and looking quite at home in them. Most winters we had snow and we were able to go tobogganing in Holywells Park which was ideal. Although I was at Ipswich to avoid the air raids I still went home for the holidays and on occasion took Ken Driver with me. I was in Balham in 1940 when Grandad Shimell died and during that holiday there was a massive incendiary attack on the City of London which lit up the night sky for miles around. In March 1941 Uncle Cecil received his calling up papers for the RAF and he left for Blackpool on May 26th.

Early in 1941 Ken and I became involved in playing for a concert party (possibly for the Boy's Brigade) and later in the year we played for a dance at Churchman's Social Club. As a result we met up with one of the managers named Chris Orpen who took us under his wing and would take us out in his car to pubs and clubs around Ipswich where I would usually end up at the piano. By autumn we were playing for dances at the Co-Op Hall, St.Lawrence's, and various other halls plus the occasional concert. On occasion we deputised for RAF bands and sometimes played alongside them which was a great way to learn how to do it. Considering most of us were only 15 years old at the time this shows how depleted Civvy Street had become musically! We would often rehearse in the Gas Works Hall where John Denny's father worked and I well recall seeing another group of more mature musicians playing in the same hall on one occasion.

The pianist was Danny Inman, a very competent player

23

who was a personal friend of Freddy Gardner, one of our finest alto players at the time. The drummer was Pip Cornell who was slightly mad but a very fine drummer and there was also an electric guitarist name of Les Green who often won prizes in Melody Maker contests. As we got to know him better we were invited to his home on the outskirts of town where he had a grand piano which was a joy to play. Unfortunately although every hall had a piano the condition varied considerably and I propose to devote a separate chapter to the trials and tribulations of the dance band pianist. Even if they did have a really good instrument they wouldn't let you play it in case you ruined it for them! In my diaries there is occasional reference to lodgers staying for a matter of days and sometimes weeks and I recall a young evacuee, a girl of around seven years old but have made no mention of her in my notes. I believe this would have been for a relatively short period and other friends of hers were billeted in our area and my guess is that they were moved on perhaps to the Midlands when the raids began in earnest.

Most weeks we would go to Whilliers Music Shop in the main shopping street where apart from buying music we would go upstairs to listen to the latest Jazz records. This is where I was introduced to the Benny Goodman small groups and this most certainly influenced my playing at that time. Another Northgate pupil, one Ian McCaughey, who played double bass with a separate group worked here at weekends and would introduce us to the latest issues although I personally did not start collecting records until much later in life. Mind you it did not take much time to hear a complete side as this was long before the advent of the L.P. In 1942, nearing the end of my school days, my diary records an increasing number of engagements and by the time we were taking final exams we were on occasion playing for dances the night before.

My outstanding musical memory was one afternoon when we went to see the Blue Mariners Dance Band rehearsing for a concert that same evening and although it was very competent as they were all professional musicians in uniform, it was not that notable. However at the show in the evening after the band were set up in walked four black trumpet players who were from Lucky Millinders Orchestra who were touring the American Bases. This was probably the first time we had heard The A Train played properly and the difference they made was phenomenal!

In compiling my story with the aid of my early diaries I cannot help being amazed at the freedom I was allowed, thanks to my Aunt and Uncle and there is no way that I would have had such as enjoyable life as a normal evacuee with complete strangers. Jean will confirm this and conditions for her were so bad that she actually tried to run away!

During the many dance band outings I met my first girl friend Edna Richardson who lived almost opposite Ipswich Football Ground but although we kept in touch until I was in the Army in Palestine it became obvious that nothing would come of this relationship. At the end of my final term I returned to London for good in company with John and Ken on the 7th August 1942. That same night we all went with Chris Orpen from Churchman's to the Saville Theatre to see Leslie Hensen, Douglas Bing and Dorothy Dickson in "Fine & Dandy". By the time John and Ken left on Sunday16th we had seen seven West End Shows starring Vera Lynn – Ben Lyon – Beatrice Lillie – Fred Emney – Vic Oliver – Jack Hulbert and Cicely Courtneidge – Robert Newton and Lupino Lane. Oh! What a lovely War! – Sorry that came much later. A few weeks later Ken wrote to tell me that my Matric results gave me Credits in English, History and Chemistry – passes in English Literature and Physics and Distinctions in Maths and French.

When it comes to Shakespeare I have often said if you can purchase his complete works for £2.50 they can't be that good although I feel that perhaps we could have had a better teacher. In one diary there was a page for a book list and alongside "Twelfth Night" I wrote "Not much good" and at a later date in a different hand one word – "Lousy"! Perhaps I should try Kenneth Branagh next! I am absolutely certain that my wartime at Ipswich gave me a lot of confidence towards my future in both work and pleasure.

WARTIME IN LONDON

After the return of John and Ken to Ipswich I teamed up once again with Peter Jones and Ken Lucas and we had a few weeks holiday but at the same time I wrote to Lloyds of London to try to get a job. I was called for an entrance exam during the first week of September 1942 and also had a medical. A week later I was turned down but immediately went for an interview with Bayer Products Ltd in Africa House, Kingsway next door to Holborn Tube station and started in their Agricultural Department on Friday 11th September. I also worked the following morning, as of course Saturday working was an everyday event.

Their products included "Ceresan" a mercurial seed dressing for cereals which was positively lethal. One of my regular jobs was to keep sample jars of individual batches which were housed in a special cabinet with shelves which slid out each housing a large quantity of jars. If you held a jar down firmly on a bench and removed the lid carefully without causing any movement of the jar inevitably some of the material would float out – it was that volatile! Needless to say it has long since ceased to be used although at the time it was regarded as absolutely essential.

Apart from this they sold a product for Club Root Control in Brassicas called C.R.C. and one or two lesser items. Inevitably this was the office boy's job but there was a reasonable office staff there, the one drawback being the typist with whom I had to share an office. On one occasion the bosses' secretary who was in the next office came in to show her a present that her boyfriend had given her for her birthday. I had my back to them looking for a file and she screamed out at full volume "Knickers"!! – not that I heard a thing of course!

At the time I did not realise it but of course they had strong connections with I.G.Farbenindustrie who were said to have provided many of the chemicals used in the gas chambers. As time passed I began to be fairly well appreciated and could have progressed well here but the boss and Chief Chemist spent a lot of time trying to persuade me to study for a B.Sc. Frankly I was just not interested as by this time I had managed to make some headway in music. In fact prior to starting work I had been to the Regent Ballroom in Tooting where I won a wallet in a talent competition against six crooners. This was where I used to go regularly and on Sunday afternoon's they had a very fine outfit led by Derek Hawkins, a wonderful musician who played the alto saxophone just like Benny Carter and the clarinet like Artie Shaw. Also included in the band was Billy Riddick who became a good friend and eventually joined the Vic Lewis/Jack Parnell group before Jack joined Ted Heath and later formed his own band. I usually played during the interval with some other musicians and this was where I first met Norman George and a drummer called Ian McMeikan mostly known as Billy Mac and these two were to prove of considerable help to me over the next 18 months or so. Incidentally Billy Riddick had a brother called Charlie and the contrast between the two was quite amazing. They both played trumpet but whereas Billy had a really easy swinging style on the trumpet Charlie actually played with a circus band and if you can bring to mind the worst you've ever heard that was Charlie! In addition Billie was the quietest chap you could hope to meet whereas Charlie had been injected with a gramophone needle and when he had had a few drinks he talked so loudly and so fast it was nigh on impossible to understand what he was saying.

Billy once sent his brother to deputise for him at a gig I was on and that was one of the longest evenings of my life.

Many, many years later when I had become a director for Barrow Hepburn, the company I joined after completing Army service, after a board meeting, we used to go to the Windmill Pub on Clapham Common. Imagine my horror when I realised I was being addressed by an older and even more incoherent Charlie as this had been a regular haunt of his from time immemorial and I was right in the midst of the Chairman and all my fellow directors. That took some explaining I must say!

Norman George was 12 years older than me and when I first knew him he played the Alto Saxophone but later on he turned to the Tenor Sax. He was very highly rated as a jazz musician and Harry Hayes, one of this country's finest sax players, once said that if Norman could only read music he would have been equal to the best players in this country. Unfortunately he could not and he also suffered from being slightly deaf in one ear although this did not cause any problems during playing. Years later he became the father of the actress Susan George, who at one time became a close friend of Prince Charles, and she accompanied us to several gigs when in her early teens. Later there was a long period when meetings with Norman were few and far between. I saw little of either of them as they both went their separate ways. Norman had a ladies' hairdressers in Northcote Road Battersea and I often used to meet him there after work. We generally ended up in the pub further along the road, sometimes in the company of one of his oldest friends Charlie Osborne who was a fine guitarist. At that time Norman was still with his first wife Eileen but Norman was a man who was very attractive to women. Indeed my own mother thought the world of him and when he visited Laitwood Road he would get down on his knees to greet her – he was after all considerably taller than her. When he was playing in the band he had quite an elegant look about him – slightly reminiscent of Harry James and he was particularly involved with a very attractive redhead called Mary who featured in his life for some considerable time. She was great fun and we spent quite a lot of time together. Being wartime there were plenty of opportunities to play jazz and provided you had some reasonable standard you could sit in almost anywhere and this we did. As a result it was not too difficult to get the odd gig and eventually I remember playing with Norman at a Melody Maker Dance Band Competition. I believe it was at Battersea Town Hall, where I won the piano prize which was a record of Johnny Hodges playing "Daydream". This was my very first Jazz Record and my mother's all time favourite. It took me sometime before I found any one who knew "Daydream" but after the war I met a wonderful Alto player called Jimmy Collins and every time we got together we would perform this truly beautiful ballad. We had a lot of musical parties in those days which I always endeavoured to record and I particularly asked Jimmy to help me get a good version on tape which we did. The only problem was that Charlie Riddick was at the party – well away from the mike – and you've guessed it, when we played it back the following day his voice was completely dominant!

Billy Mac was about the same age as Norman and was always extremely well dressed and I believe he was the manager of an Ice-cream factory. He was a very fine drummer and in those days it was not always considered necessary to have a bass player and those that were around were not in the same class as today's players. Thus my first private recording was made at Levy's Sound Studios with just three of us playing "If I had you" on one disc and "Sweet Georgia Brown" on the other. The base of the record was solid metal and was extremely heavy. I still have them but they are now unplayable and would probably stop the turntable because of the weight. It is important to remember that the playing time was very short indeed and the first take was "it" as this was well before the introduction of tape recorders.

At the weekend I used to frequent the Feldman Club (now the 100 club) at 100 Oxford Street which was open on Saturday and Sunday and which had a regular group comprising Kenny Baker, Harry Hayes, Aubrey Franks, George Shearing, Tommy Bromley, and Carlo Krahmer and this was sometimes varied with other well known musicians. This group had a wonderful rapport not least because of the infectious way that Kenny Baker made things happen and the phrase – "The joint is jumping" came to life every weekend. I know that as I walked down to the Embankment to catch the all night tram I was generally on a high with the engine running flat out - so to speak. Being genuinely scared of injections and drugs there was no way that I could ever have succumbed but I guarantee that I got my fix this way every week.

I do not remember exactly how it started but I imagine Norman or Mac somehow engineered it for me to play solo boogie-woogie in the interval taking over the piano from the great George Shearing. This became a regular feature and ultimately I was allowed to play with whoever wanted a blow and as a result I got to play with the young Victor Feldman whose father ran the club and at that time Victor would have been 9 years old. The following year he played with the Glenn Miller Band at a concert in London and was an amazing drummer for whom it was not necessary to add "for his age". He became an accomplished pianist and vibraphonist in later years playing with Miles Davis and as accompanist to Peggy Lee.

Amongst others I played with Jack Parnell, Derek Neville,

Frank and Joe Deniz, Jimmy Skidmore and many more and I consider I was very fortunate to get such a good grounding in Jazz at such a splendid venue. On one occasion after I had just come off the stand I passed by Stephane Grappelly on the stairs and he was quite complimentary regarding my playing and as I moved on he patted me on the bottom (and I was completely green about such matters in those days). I was somewhat surprised at this and to this day I can never be sure it was my playing that he liked!

In those days the band played at the narrow end of the rectangular room with a small dance floor immediately in front of the band on which a regular group of Jivers performed with great gusto. I seem to remember fairly long skirts swinging out high over the tables (how can I forget!) and this coupled with the music created a wonderful atmosphere. Many years later long after I was a regular at the club I went to a benefit being held for Pat Smythe. I was horrified to find that the bands were playing halfway down the long side of the rectangle and that somehow it had lost the cosy effect it held previously. It was just like playing in a barn! I have not returned since and prefer to remember it in its heyday.

One thing always stays in my memory is that although George Shearing was to my mind the star of the show it was usually the drummer who got the most applause and thankfully the balance has been restored in recent times. Conversely I can recall being back stage at a number of Swing Shop Concerts run by Sid Gross at the Adelphi and when George was taking a solo, and only then, most of the musicians were in the wings watching intently.

At some time towards the middle of 1943 I was approached by old man Feldman on the subject of performing solo at a concert he was arranging to feature young Victor at the London Coliseum on Sunday October 3rd in the afternoon. Fortunately by now I had enough confidence to accept without hesitation. He called it a "Tribute to Swing" concert. Apart from the regular club group including Kenny Baker, George Shearing and the rest he also had the newly formed Carl Barriteau Orchestra, Bertie King and his West Indian Sextet, Buddy Featherstonhaugh and his Radio Rhythm Club Group, Victor and the Feldman Trio, and Max Bacon and the pioneers of swing and myself. In addition there was a symphony orchestra made up of Jazz musicians playing classics conducted by Albert Goossens and Eric Henderson, a classical pianist trying to play Jazz. This was to be my one and only appearance on the London stage and I had first to join the union and then to borrow Gwynn, my neighbour's dress suit as mentioned earlier. On the big day I was well supported by friends and neighbours and a fair sized contingent from Ipswich including Edna and I was to be the second act in the program. The compere for the show was a very well known Canadian – David Miller – and Bertie King was on first. As he came off the stage he asked me to ask David to bring him the mouthpiece cover from his saxophone which he had left on the piano. In my rather nervous condition I said something like "Bertie asked me to ask you to bring his top off the piano". David turned to the audience and said "I think Roy must be feeling a little nervous as he has just asked me to take the top off the piano" and of course there was no lid to the piano!

However once I started playing I felt no nerves and quite enjoyed it. I started with a version of "If I had you" with a boogie bass in part and my second and final number was a combination of every type of boogie-woogie bass in the 12 bar format which I called "Counting the Basies". How's that for original thought. Anyway it went down pretty well and I really enjoyed the experience. In the evening I went to the club with Edna and bearing in mind that I had not received a penny piece for my efforts, I was astonished to be asked to pay my entrance fee as well as for Edna. This was to have a profound effect on me for years to come and because I frequently ended up on the piano I did not expect to have to pay as well as perform and there is a rather nice story to come a bit later.

Around this time I started to attend a Jewish Boy's Club in the East End of London and this is where I met Ronnie Scott and many other musicians including Harry Pitch. At that time Harry played trumpet but he later changed to the Harmonica and became famous as the player and composer of the theme tune for the "Last of the Summer Wine". He developed a very fine Jazz style on the instrument – not one very often heard in this context. I have a very old and worn photo of Ronnie taken at this club alongside a trumpet player called Derry Gascoigne and on the extreme edge there is just the face of Denis Rose who played both trumpet and piano. He was later credited with being the musician most instrumental in analysing the Be Bop style of playing jazz and passing his findings on to the English musicians. After Ronnie died I met Roy Babbington – bassist with Stan Tracey and the Radio Big Band who had just learned that I had played with Ronnie in the early days. He suggested I should get in touch with Benny Green who was writing a book about Ronnie and he also said I should have the photo blown up and enhanced – which I did – but they cut out Denis Rose from the frame as it was slightly distorted. Even more unfortunate was the fact that Benny died before he could make much headway. However later on I contacted Mary Scott – Ronnie's partner who with their daughter Rebecca eventually produced her story entitled "A Fine Kind of Madness" – The story of Ronnie Scott and the photo is reproduced inside plus a few comments from myself.

We also frequented any club that would allow us to sit in and in those days, because of the continued absence of so many musicians in the forces we were in a very strong position. Somehow the regular groups in these establishments did not mind being displaced from time to time. It could never happen today. Amongst these clubs was the Nut House in Regent Street where I met another stalwart of the early Jazz scene – Gerry Moore – not to be confused with his classical namesake Gerald Moore and he was more than generous in letting me play his piano for quite long periods. The Mazurka Club situated just off Piccadilly was another rather less salubrious place we visited from time to time and the bandleader was trumpeter Ronnie Fenner. On one or two occasions I was appalled at the way the "ladies" of the establishment were treating some American Servicemen after having taken them for almost every last penny they had but this was no place to start standing up for principles - the doormen were well chosen!

In early November I received a call from John Denny to say that the band from Ipswich had an audition for E.N.S.A. at Drury Lane Theatre but my replacement on piano could not get time off – could I possibly help out? This I did and after the audition was over we walked out into Aldwych in a very heavy fog which was a fairly regular feature of life in those days. As we turned into the Strand someone suggested we ought to get a bite to eat and someone else said let's go in here – which we did. John Denny reminds me that at the time there was a limit of two shillings and three pence that could be charged for lunch at any restaurant. Now the Savoy Hotel is not the place that many would choose and this was to be the day when I ate my first and last curry! You must also bear in mind that in those days there were only a very few Indian restaurants around but nevertheless I felt that if I could not stomach it at the Savoy then it was not for me.

Bearing in mind the fact that we were drinking pints of beer, this meant that despite the restrictions we ran up a relatively expensive bill and as I recall we skipped the sweet and still had great difficulty paying our dues. Perhaps it will put it into perspective if I point out that my total weekly wage packet in those days was £2. Fortunately I have better memories of the Savoy when I was working for Barrow Hepburn many years later on special occasions. Whilst on the subject of wartime regulations I read recently that there was an annual allowance of 66 coupons for clothing and a 3 piece suit took 26, a woollen dress 11 and a tie just 1. We had a hanger-on known as Johnny the spiv who was always doing deals on street corners with illicitly acquired coupons.

Towards the end of 1943 there was a period when I went to Brighton with Norman at the weekends, sometimes for Saturday and Sunday and occasionally just for Sunday. We would be in the company of Johnny Murray who played the drums but who was also an ice hockey player who was then the captain of the Wembley Lions Ice Hockey Team and also the Great Britain Team. Into the bargain his uncle was the famous alto sax player Harry Hayes mentioned earlier in the book. With him would be another ice hockey player Johnny Oxley who was very well known in those days.

We had a fixed routine starting at Maxims, a drinking club on the front, from around noon until half past two. From there we would go to Sherry's Ballroom where there was an afternoon tea-dance and have a bite to eat. Then if there was a game on we would go to the Ice-Rink at around 5.30 and watch the two Johnnies in action. Finally we would return to Maxims for another session of jazz and either catch the last train back or on Saturday night put up in a hotel.

During January 1944 it was Johnny Murray's 21st birthday and Norman and several of the gang went along and who should be there but Uncle Harry Hayes who deigned to sit in with us. I use the word deigned deliberately as when someone asked him what we should play he suggested "After you've gone" ------- in the key of B. Now the recognised key for this was – and still is- B flat which involves just two flats whereas B is a key which in all my experience never occurs in the jazz repertoire (and I claim to know quite a few tunes) and requires finding your way around 5 sharps! Needless to say we had been put in our places quite deliberately and to this day I cannot understand why it was necessary to spoil his nephew's big day. However in the early part of 1944 we visited several clubs with Harry just to sit in and I suppose we must have passed the test after a fashion.

Around this time I played occasionally for the "Loafers Dance Band" which was composed of members of the Fire Brigade although why I became involved I shall never know – possibly another indication of the dearth of musicians at that time. Mind you in retrospect it is hard to visualise how they could spare the time during a war for such activities.

Early in 1944 I applied for vacancies in the offices of both Ambrose and the Harry Parry Orchestras and fortunately I was turned down in each case as being "too old" – at 16! Occasionally we would attend broadcasts at the Paris Cinema in Lower Regent Street where I first saw Leslie "Jiver" Hutchinson playing with the Geraldo Orchestra little realising that I would some years later be playing with him at Kingston on Thames. At another occasion at the same studio I was very impressed when there was a two band broadcast involving the Geraldo Orchestra opposite a small Latin American outfit. Kenny Baker was playing with Geraldo but the trumpeter with the small group did not turn up and Kenny just crossed the floor and played everything from sight as though he was the regular guy. He would have been just 22 at the time and when he died recently I had seen him playing just a couple of months previously and he was still top of the class - at the age of 78! I did hear that someone once asked him if he ever played a wrong note and his reply was "Why should I?"

In case the reader should think the war was over at this time I should mention that from time to time we had raids and on occasions some of our gigs were cancelled as a result. On the March 2nd 1944 around 70 incendiaries were dropped on Laitwood Road in the middle of the night and 12 houses were damaged 3 seriously and dad was out all night and I spent an hour and a half trying to help.

A week later Norman took me to the Orchard Club in Wigmore Street just behind Selfridges where he was depping for the band run by a drummer/vocalist called Cab Kaye whose father had been born in Africa and died in this country a year after Cab was born. The club was open 6 nights a week from 8.0 pm until midnight and I was allowed to sit in and Cab gave me a lift home. That was a most enjoyable evening and this was a far superior club to most of the places I had been to previously.

In the weeks that followed I had to attend a medical for the R.A.F. and was provisionally accepted for Air Crew Grade 1. Later on I had to attend for further tests and was informed that I did not reach the required standard. One of the tasks I had to perform involved blowing into a tube and I had great difficulty in getting the pressure required. Nevertheless I was told I would do well in whatever position I was placed. This turned out to be the P.B.I. – poor bloody infantry to you!

Shortly after this I had a week's holiday which I spent at Ipswich and went to the Navydrome where I had previously seen the trumpet section of Lucky Millinders Band. There was to be the final session here which had been run especially for merchant navy men and had been run by Barry Wicks. I took part in a jam session with Nelson Bryant the lead trumpet who was a very large gentleman indeed and a fine musician. After the show we had quite a celebration.

We had several wonderful sessions at the Wedgwood Services Club at Aldgate East with Ronnie, Jimmy Skidmore and another of the eventual Club Eleven group drummer, pianist, M.C. and comic Cecil "Flash" Winston. He had worked at several establishments run by London gangsters including Jack Spot and on one occasion accompanied Benny Goodman at the London Palladium. I also went for an audition at the famous Rainbow Room in Piccadilly but nothing came of this.

Towards the end of April I went to the Orchard Club again and this time Cab offered me a job on a regular basis and at that time I refused. Then on May 1st I went to Wimbledon Town Hall to see a charity event run by Bill Waller and Bill Foreman who ran the Regent Ballroom at Tooting. The line up comprised Woody Franks, Johnny Claes, Jimmy Skidmore, Teddy Wadmore and Dave Fullerton and a piano player called Franz Conn (or Francisco Conde when playing Latin music). At the door Bill Waller was adamant that as it was a charity event I would have to pay but, as explained previously, I was very reluctant to do so. Very soon events were taken out of my hands with the arrival of Jimmy Skidmore whom I had got to know quite well by then, who put his hand on my arm and ushered me inside with a typical comment of "Come on me old nut!" and I don't think he was fully aware of what had happened previously. Anyway the upshot was that Franz Conn did not turn up and I ended up doing the gig! A further example of lady luck being on my side.

Two weeks later I received a phone call from Cab again offering me the piano chair at the Orchard Club – 6 nights a week excluding Saturdays for £8.50 per week and this time I accepted. I started that very day Sunday 14th May and remained there until I was called up at the end of August. Ronnie Scott was the regular tenor player and the bass player was a Charlie Scott (no relation). Cab played drums and sang a few vocals in a very pleasing style and on occasion we had to join in behind him. Some of the regular numbers we played included "Doggin Around" – "Knock me a kiss" – "Blue Lou" – "My blue heaven" etc. Sitting in was the done thing in those days and Aubrey Franks who had won the Melody Maker Poll for tenor sax on more than one occasion was a fairly frequent visitor. In my opinion Ronnie even at this early stage was a far more exciting driving player and he literally blew Aubrey off the stand! At the time Kenny Baker was in the R.A.F. stationed not far away and he came in quite often and I cannot describe what a lift he provided. There were one or two tunes with which I was not familiar and he would quickly sit at the piano and show me the ropes and in no time at all we were away. In addition Eric Winstone also came to watch and occasionally sit in with us as did Frank Deniz – a very fine guitarist from a family of Jazz musicians – and Joe Crossman a veteran sax player (all of 39 years old). Then there was Jimmy Henney from Australia who buzzed whilst playing the piano. Jimmy Skidmore and an alto sax player from the Midlands who was in the Army called Geoff Gough sometimes depped for Ronnie. At one time we had a girl bass player called Eve Cliff who was extremely good but we all wondered how she was able to play at all as her fingernails extended nearly an inch past her fingertips. Two tears later when I was in Palestine I came across her working for C.S.E. – Combined Service

Entertainment – touring the forces in the Middle East with Billy Penrose a well known pianist.

One very regular customer was Johnny Claes, a Belgian trumpet player who led his own group called the "Clae-Pigeons" and Ronnie was to join him shortly after I left in October 1944 when the engagement finished. Obviously Johnny had been scouting for Ronnie all the time. Later on Johnny Claes became famous as a racing driver and competed at Goodwood and Silverstone and I understand he was second in the early 50's in the Le Mans 24 hour race.

One evening before we started playing we were in the club listening to the radio and for the first time we heard the American Band of the A.E.F. playing Holiday for Strings. I remember Ronnie and I were most impressed as it seemed to offer a new dimension to our ideas of music. Shortly afterward I used to feature a slow locked hands version of the same tune which went down well with the customers. Until I recalled this incident I had not realised how early I used this style which I often use even today – well George seems to be finished with it! The journey home from the club was in effect quite hazardous as of course this entailed walking along Oxford Street and Regent Street on the way to pick up the all-night tram at the Embankment – passing all the very large windows en route. Fortunately nothing came our way whilst I was working there.

This reminds me if my all-time favourite George Shearing story. The blackout and all it entailed was no problem to George and indeed another fine blind pianist Eddie Thomson. Rumour has it that one night George crept up behind Eddie – put both his hands over his ears and said "Guess who"! There was also an occasion much later after the war when I saw Eddie playing at the B.B.C.'s internal

Jazz Club. A member of the audience requested "I've got a crush on you" and Eddie started off the verse when the chap who asked for it started singing along with the piano. Eddie called out! "It's alright sir I know how it goes".

Before I took the job at the Orchard I had booked a holiday for just one week. As my likely call up date was not far away I wanted a last period of relaxation and I needed a capable replacement. The only available dep was certainly very capable being Dick Katz one of the country's finest pianists. The only problem was that I had to pay him more than twice the rate I was getting. Into the bargain Cab decided to have the band's photograph taken during that week and it appeared in the Melody Maker the following week. I have only recently obtained a copy of this and I had not previously realised that I was actually given credit for being the regular pianist in the caption. This incidentally was the very first photo of Ronnie Scott to appear in the Melody Maker.

After I joined the Army, before going overseas, I used to call on Dick when he was working at the Caribbean Club in the West End with the famous Lauderic Caton Trio, Lauderic being a wonderful guitarist and the equally famous bass player was Coleridge Goode. This was a very small select club and all I ever did was to sit and listen enthralled at the rapport they enjoyed. Sometimes Kenny Baker would sit in and with or without him this was jazz of the highest order and I would sit within a few feet of the band – if only we had tape recorders in those days!

Lauderic died early last year and in his obituary it gave the following description of the club and I quote "But it was with the trio at Soho's Caribbean Club that he made a solid reputation. There Caribbean and African-American officers rubbed shoulders with Whitehall mandarins and aristocracy as they listened to Caton, pianist Dick Katz and bassist Coleridge Goode; and Soho's raffish element drank alongside Picasso, Michael Redgrave and Lena Horne". Perhaps I should add that I do not remember seeing anyone famous but then I wasn't looking at them!

On one occasion on leave I called at the club and asked for Dick and when he appeared he apologised for the fact that there was a private function taking place and I could not go in. I asked if he had any idea where I could go and he suggested the Pluto Club where the band was run by Claude Bampton and said he would almost certainly let me sit in. Claude was the coach during the mid-1930's for the National Institute for the Blind Dance Band which included George Shearing – Bampton himself had normal eyesight. To my amazement he let me play the piano for over 3 hours and the alto sax player was none other than Johnny Dankworth who would have been 17 at the time.

The trend in those days was for musicians to wear rather large suits with very padded shoulders and Norman George was a very dapper dresser and he persuaded me to get with it. As Mary was working at a tailor's in Tooting called John Barnes I obtained a couple of suits from there. This was when bird's eye maple was all the rage. I don't think my parents were too enamoured with this but they didn't complain. However the piece-de-resistance came when I decided it was time to buy my own dress-suit. Norman persuaded me to have it made with forward cut arms so that when playing it was immaculate. However when walking down the street with arms at your sides it became rather peculiar looking!

Finally on Friday 25th August I received my call-up papers to report the following Thursday to Redford Barracks in Edinburgh and I immediately left Bayer's and the following day was my last at the Orchard Club. Unfortunately Cab was very annoyed with me for not trying to get out of army service and I was not prepared to try to swing the lead. For this reason it took quite a lot of effort to persuade him to cough up my last week's wages – but ultimately he paid up.

Cab had been in the Merchant Navy and I recall how bitter he was at having been elbowed off the streets in South Africa because of his colour. He was a great inspiration to work with and in the three months I spent at the Orchard I was given a splendid insight into the Jazz world. After the war he took up a post in Ghana as a Government Entertainments Director. Afterwards he returned to playing and worked both in America and – mostly – on the continent, finally settling in Amsterdam where he opened a Piano Jazz Bar. His death was reported at some length in the Guardian, the Telegraph and of all things the Times – I wonder what he would have made of that!

I would like to be able to say that Ronnie and I had deedy discussions about jazz in those days but this would be far from the truth. At that time your only way of learning was by "doing" and although I can admire the wonderful techniques of today's young musicians so often it all sounds very similar as they often seem to reflect one person's style of teaching. Fortunately those better equipped eventually emerge with their own individual style and the best of these are quite tremendous. In fact much later when I visited the club we sometimes got on the subject and my understanding was that he was generally in agreement with me on this.

This seems a suitable time to move on to the next part of my life when I eventually became Acting Local Unpaid Lance Corporal Cook – I.C. Dance Band – it's true!!

Roy Cook aged 17 at the London Coliseum

Victor Feldman aged 9

Surrey Starlites

ARMY SERVICE

On Thursday 31st August 1944, I said goodbye to Mum and Dad and made my way to King's Cross Station on my way to Redford Barracks, Edinburgh to become 14838858 Private Cook. We were kitted out and allocated to various platoons and I well remember on that first night the barrack room windows were left wide open all night and although it was August it gets much colder earlier in the north as I soon discovered. Next morning breakfast was served on tables spread around the room between the bunks and it had obviously been too much for one member of our intake who upended his table and everything on it hit the deck! What the outcome was I never found out but I doubt if they sent him home. During the same day we went through all sorts of formalities before ending up in a huge gymnasium lined up for various injections. I can't tell you how many rows were spread across the room but there must have been at least fifteen. There were some four or five rows from us when I went down in a heap on the floor. There's no doubt the mind can do wondrous things.

There followed a six week inaugural course to make you fit and this was no easy ride. As I recall my weight at the time was 9 stone 7 ½ lbs – possibly the last time it was ever this low. From here we were sent to the barracks at Canterbury where I became a member of the Buffs Regiment and here we underwent further training which included a 42 mile route march from Canterbury to Reculver and back in full pack which took 2 days. The outward journey was very frustrating because we were on an extremely winding road and after a short time the towers of Reculver came into view but one minute they were on your left, next on your extreme right and this continued until we finally arrived at our destination. I believe this was one of our earliest experiences of shaving in cold water in the open air at 6 o'clock in the morning – not to be recommended! When I arrived back in Canterbury I remember some dear old lady commenting to her friend "You wait till they do the long route march". Canterbury at the time seemed to be a place where every other building was a pub and needless to say we spent quite some time in them.

Our next move was to Shorncliffe Barracks near Folkestone and it was here that I was transferred to the East Surrey Regiment. The original 2nd Battalion had been virtually wiped out in Singapore and we were required to restore the name. This was not a long posting but I remember attending, and on one occasion taking part, in concerts at the Leas Cliff Hall. I also remember a certain Sergeant Major who was obviously proud of his notorious reputation who once screamed on the parade ground "I know some of you think my mother had rusty tits" an expression I have never heard before or since. After a while, the exact date I cannot pinpoint, we were transferred to a camp just outside Helmsley in Yorkshire. Of course at any opportunity I would end up in the NAAFI on the piano and shortly after our arrival it was decided we would form a concert party and this meant I was excused quite a lot of duties. However, every now and then we were made to take part in lesson one on the rifle and one day the sergeant major was going through the usual drill "Up two three – over two three and away – Waltz time Cook!" He had a sense of humour sometimes.

When we got organised we had to produce a new show every week, which is quite a tall order, but somehow we managed. I was persuaded to take the part of one of the Western Brothers complete with monocle for one of these concerts and bearing in mind that I find it almost impossible to say anything whilst playing this was quite an achievement. On one or two occasions we managed to combine with girls from a nearby army unit which did help considerably – from a show point of view of course! We were able to visit both Bridlington and Scarborough fairly regularly when off duty and this was one of our better camps in the U.K. This is where I first met Colin Rowe who was in our Sniper section and he is the only member of the battalion with whom I have remained in constant touch ever since. I have been grateful for his assistance with some of the memory losses I have suffered in compiling this part of the book. I am not sure exactly how long we were here but ultimately we had to move south and we had an extremely long journey on a train which took us right round London back to Kent under canvas at Charlton Park not far from Canterbury.

The war in Europe ended on May 7th 1945 and sometime after this the C.O. did a Montgomery on us by driving a jeep to a point where we had been assembled in a semi-circle, jumping on the bonnet, and announcing that "We are going to knock the shit out of the Japs". Apparently the intention was that we were to form part of 184 Brigade in 61 Division which was to fly via America and land in Japan by glider. It was to be formed as a Light Division which would not be equipped with mechanical transport and would rely on mules for heavy load carrying. In August 1945, the two atomic bombs were dropped on Japan who quickly surrendered. On V.J. day our battalion was taking part in a three day Divisional exercise in Kent using the Romney Marshes to represent the paddy fields of Japan. The last two paragraphs come from an excellent book on the East Surrey Regiment published in 1996 as, needless to say, none of us had a clue as to what was going on at the time. I was not part of the Romney Marsh exercise but I believe that around the same time I was on night manoeuvres on Sandwich golf course trying

49

to dig a trench in torrential rain. I swear the ground was so sticky that all I was doing most of the time was lifting the same sod in and out. At least I think I said something to this effect at the time! A little later, as autumn approached, I was very upset at being required to pick up the leaves from under the trees in order to keep the place tidy. I know it must be difficult finding things for inactive soldiers to do but this was O.T.T. especially as we were in the woods!

Shortly after V.E. Day the battalion attended a celebratory service in Canterbury Cathedral after which there were sports and other activities which carried on the following day. At the end of August we moved to West Chiltington near Pulborough and by the end of September we were ordered to prepare for overseas service.

Then in November several officers and N.C.O. s went to Liverpool to meet members of the original battalion returning from Japanese Prisoner of War Camps and to collect from them the Colours and Regimental Silver which had been in a bank vault in Singapore. This then led to a Trooping of The Colour ceremony on the 30th November to retire the old colours dating from 1867 and install the new ones which had been prepared in the early 30's but had not been presented when the war intervened. The amount of effort required for the ceremony to take place was quite staggering even involving clearing trees and bulldozing the ground to create a parade ground. Fortunately, the band was excused this parade – a wise decision as we were not too skilled in this department. This was followed by 48 hours leave after which on the 5th December we went to Liverpool to board the Cunard liner the S.S. Samaria in company with a battalion of Black Watch and 350 W.A.A.F. s and a number of E.N.S.A. entertainers. Sleeping arrangements excepted I reckon this would take a lot to beat and cost a small fortune into the bargain today. I was introduced to the ship's piano and it barely left my fingertips during the whole of the 9 day journey to Port Said. We accompanied our concert party, that of the W.A.A.F.'s, played for dances on the deck, for a pantomime, and special functions for the officers and it was sheer delight throughout. I shall never forget watching schools of dolphins diving in and out of the water whilst I was playing piano on deck using a ship's piano which has a fold up keyboard for protection in inclement weather. (I intend to devote a separate chapter to "Pianos I have met" and will expound more on this in that). We also played alongside the E.N.S.A. contingent and one act I remember was the Gibson Sisters and Buddy with whom we got on famously well. There were a number of civilian families on board and we also entertained them and at the end of the voyage they presented each member of the band with a leather wallet together with a note of appreciation signed by the parents. A few months ago I met up with Geoff Banks, our sax player, for the first time since the immediate post war period, and he still has both items intact. Apart from our efforts there were film shows, boxing tournaments and tombola which overall provided a welcome relief from life in Amy Camps for most of the troops though speaking for myself I really cannot complain as my luck was continuing to hold. It has been suggested that had at any stage of the journey the order to man lifeboats been given, a large percentage would have had occupants already. I was on the piano so "I couldn't possibly comment" as the saying goes.

We arrived in Port Said on December 16th and were taken by train to Qassassin in the desert not far from Ismailia by Lake Timsah on the Suez Canal under canvas and this was primitive to say the least. Our transport consisted of a water cart and one 15cwt truck. I managed to get to Cairo just once on a day trip but did not really see very much of it. For Christmas dinner we had fat pork and baked beans and believe it or not this resulted in the C.O. resolving to use the dance band to obtain funds so that in future we could have a decent meal on occasion. Apparently, they had been unable to bring any accumulated funds abroad and he decided that the band would be offered out for gigs at the rate of £1 per man. Of this ten shillings would go to the fund, two shillings and sixpence towards a memorial for those lost in Singapore, and the remainder was ours to keep. Quite a nice arrangement you might say! The following Christmas our efforts were able to provide a full Turkey dinner for between 5 and 600 men and the complete day's menu is set out in full in the story of the regiment mentioned previously.

After Christmas we were sent by train to Palestine and on board were a number of the W.A.A.F. s we had met on the boat. The train was of the American style with open platforms at each end and there were one or two romances under way helped by the starlit night skies under which we were passing.

When we reached Gaza a cloudburst had swept the line away and we were brought to an abrupt halt. It was to take 2 days to repair and the first thing I remembered was the crate of oranges that miraculously appeared in our carriage. The C.O. decided that we needed some exercise so he took us off on a route march on the second day and in the meantime they managed to open up the line once again. By this time we had lost our bearings and in the end they sent the engine down the line to find us! Not a very good start. We finally arrived in Haifa on December 31st 1945 and set up in tented camp on the opposite side of the bay to Mount Carmel overlooking the town. Here we were to remain until 1947. That evening and next morning and for the whole of the remainder of our stay we were treated to some of the most wonderful sunsets and sunrises I have ever seen anywhere. Haifa itself was divided into Jewish and Arab Quarters and as you crossed from one side to the other it was immediately noticeable. The Jewish side was ultra modern for those days with Cadillacs everywhere, the main cinema had a retractable roof, and there was a profusion of clubs and restaurants. One club high up on Mount Carmel was the Eldorado Club and what amazed me was that our officers had no objections to other ranks using it. I was particularly pleased to be able to go there as there was a fine piano manned by an equally fine pianist called Gary who used to let me sit in. This was indeed a very high class establishment and I have often likened it to the Astor in London where much later in life I once played when I was working with Eric Delaney. I cannot believe that we endeared ourselves to the locals very much as the Adjutant used to stand at the door and snip off their ties as they came in and displayed them as trophies in the Officer's Mess. The C.O., Lt.Col. T.A. Buchanan was extremely keen on running the band and before long we were playing regularly at the Sergeant's Club in Haifa and many other odd gigs including a camp for Polish soldiers further up the coast. All went well here until they insisted that I should play the Polonaise which I did most reluctantly and with good reason – it was not one of my better performances! The band originally comprised Laurie Keary on drums, later on to take on the double bass when a drummer called Denis joined the unit, Geoff Banks on the tenor sax and myself. We had left behind in England another sax player who was deemed unfit for overseas duties and we really needed someone else in the front line. One evening at the Sergeant's Club we were approached by a civilian with a trumpet who asked to sit in and he was very good indeed. He was attached to the Royal Naval Torpedo Depot in Haifa and when I related this incident to the C.O. next day his reaction was "Give him a uniform – give him a paybook – he's in the band!" Now I often wondered what on earth would happen if anything untoward befell our new recruit whilst he was with us – it doesn't bear thinking about. Incidentally his name was Rev – his father was a vicar!

This incident was not untypical of the C.O. and a little later Laurie who was attached to the transport section took a jeep into Haifa without permission and managed to overturn it. He was of course put on C.O.'s orders and given 30 days for this transgression. However, when he came out the C.O. appointed him as his driver! I gather that the C.O. and the officers knew how to let their hair down when off-duty and perhaps I should draw a veil over further revelations. Mind you the C.O. had an outstanding record having the D.S.O. and the M.C. and had been wounded 5 times – he was a very fine soldier and knew how to get the best out of his men. After leaving the army I discovered that he married Kay Kendall, the actress of "Genevieve" fame. Laurie was certainly the right man for the job and I have in mind a completely separate chapter to deal with his exploits after the war which were many and varied and fascinating – but he was not easy to deal with!

Our camp was adjoining a large Jewish settlement comprised entirely of single storey flat roofed buildings. On one occasion we were taken to see a Kibbutz to show us how they operated. When we were in the children's classroom one of our bright sparks said to our guide "I see you learn English. Is that because you are a British Colony?!!" The temperature dropped rather suddenly after this remark. We played rugby and also hockey on a six-a-side pitch built on a sort of roofing felt over the sand surrounded by petrol tanks full of sand half embedded in the ground to denote boundaries. We also went swimming off the coast but this required extreme care as the undertow was very strong in places and one or two of us experienced some very hairy moments out there.

There were leave camps both at Beirut and Nathanya and we had some very enjoyable times in these. Geoff Banks reminds me that on one occasion we played on the ground floor of an establishment known as Sans Rival, a house of ill repute, but he assures me that we were not rewarded in any way shape or form! In those days, Beirut was a very attractive place and I always found it hard to equate the troubles that have taken place over more recent years with the place I visited.

During the course of our stay in Palestine we visited Bethlehem, Nazareth, Lake Tiberius, and Jerusalem, and impressive as these places are I fear I saw nothing that would make me embrace religion. When you consider that here we are nearly 60 years later and they are still at loggerheads and balance that against the Irish problems it seem to me that religion per se has a lot to answer for. We also visited Tel Aviv which was far removed in style from any of the above mentioned places and was probably at that time one of the most modern cities we had ever encountered.

After the war I joined Barrow Hepburn and Gale and ended up running a department which amongst other things produced special leather for ginning cotton in Egypt and Sudan. I intend dealing with this separately but at one stage we were investigating other possible markets and learned that Israel was producing cotton. A map came into my possession showing how they had developed a countrywide network of water supplies since I was there to help facilitate their cotton industry and of course the country as a whole. When you consider how much hotter it is out there it rather puts us into the shade when we have our periodic water shortages and you realise that not much has changed since the previous crisis.

The band was attached to the Corps of Drums in Headquarters section and the Drum Major came from Cornwall. We were all rather amused when he had a sign put up outside their stores tent reading COR OF DRUMS. The dance band was used to from a unit to combat malaria and we were sent on a course to learn all about the anopheles mosquito. I believe quinine is quite useful in this respect and maybe this accounts for my fondness for a gin and tonic! Geoff Banks reminds me that we were told to disperse puddles by throwing large stones into them – isn't technology wonderful!

We had a dance to play for once at a place just south of Nathanya and we loaded up in a 15cwt and set off complete with a brand new double bass we had just been given. Not very far south of Haifa we crossed a railway line (there was no marked crossing – just the lines). Unfortunately for us, our brand new instrument broke into two pieces as there was a drop of nearly 12" on the other side leaving us with a real dilemma. After some thought, we obtained a piece of stout rope and a metal bar and attached the rope to the top and bottom of the bass at the back and loosely fitted the strings to the front. Then using the metal bar to create a windlass we gradually tightened back and front until we had an instrument to play. Mind you if anything had given way there could have been a nasty accident! Next day we smuggled it into the carpenter's store and had it properly glued together.

Our main function as a unit was to combat the two main terrorist organisations – the Stern Gang and the Irgun Zvai

Leumi who were particularly active in the Haifa area.

The Consolidated Refinery was considered to be the most important oil installation in Palestine and we were also manning another oil installation in the dock area and the airfield, apart from manning road blocks, and dealing with shiploads of illegal immigrants from Europe. These unfortunate people generally arrived on overcrowded vessels which were in the main quite unsuited to the loads they were carrying. I was once on leave in the dock area of Haifa at an army club when one of these vessels arrived. It was so overcrowded and listing so badly that one of our naval vessels had gone alongside to support it into port. The angle was so great that I am sure it would have gone over without this help.

Unfortunately our chaps had the unpleasant task of sending the majority of these refugees back to Cyprus where they had to wait until they could be included in the numbers allowed in on a strict rota basis. On one occasion the radio station on Mount Carmel was blown up and several bridges around Haifa damaged. Because of this type of activity another of our duties in Palestine was to search Jewish settlements and in July a large quantity of arms was found at Mesheg Yagur.

Whilst the band did not get involved in these major activities we had to do a certain amount of guard duty and on one such night I collapsed outside the unit I was guarding and ended up in the sick bay with Sand Fly Fever! I was also troubled with infections, mainly on the back of the neck, but one day I developed a whitlow on my left index finger and I remember playing for a dance at the time using my right hand only as the left one was in a sling. To this day this finger is tapered at the point from the effects of the infection.

In June 1946 the terrorists blew up the railway workshops which were being guarded by Arab Militia and members of our battalion immediately set up roadblocks on roads leading from the workshops. A very heavy lorry with 30 terrorists on board met up with one of these roadblocks and charged with guns blazing. Our men returned fire and stood firm and the firing continued until one of our chaps got underneath and fired upwards whereupon they came out firing as they did so. Our unit killed seven instantly, two more died in hospital, eleven were wounded and the remainder captured. They found out afterwards that the sides of the lorry were protected with metal shields. Furthermore some of the occupants of the lorry were pregnant women bearing and using machine guns. Fortunately we suffered no casualties and one man was awarded the British Empire Medal for holding steadfast in his carrier. The terrorists used this incident to label us as "butchers". Shortly afterwards we took over the guarding of the Railway Workshops.

Towards the end of the year we were playing at the Sergeant's Club in Haifa when we received a visit from Chick Mayes, a well known trumpet player from the U.K. who was in charge of C.S.E. – Combined Service Entertainments in the Middle East at that time. He sat in with us for the rest of his stay in the area and we used to go into Haifa and take over from the local bands quite often. Unfortunately we always had to take our rifles with us but generally we were well received at these clubs and restaurants.

One day a dog attached to the Sergeant's Mess was found to have rabies and anyone that had any contact with the Mess had to have an injection a day for nearly two weeks. I understand it was a very painful process indeed using a very large needle. All those involved were permitted to remove their jackets as wearing them was too painful and to see the Sergeant Major walking about with his tunic over his shoulder was surely one of the rarest sights in the British Army. Needless to say this was a lucky escape for me. As a result all the remaining pets in the camp had to be destroyed.

On New Year's Eve 1946 we were booked to play for a fancy dress ball in Haifa at a club for English civilians and we had a whale of a time, arriving back at camp at 4 o'clock in the morning. On Friday 2nd January our camp was attacked by terrorists using flamethrowers targeting our transport section. They made off into the nearby Jewish settlement and we sent a carrier to chase them which ran into a landmine which killed one of our officers – Lt. Elliot and injured six other ranks, one of whom lost an eye. After demob I frequently saw this man in Balham. The last and most devastating action in which the East Surreys were involved in Palestine was an attack on the C.R.L. when the terrorists succeeded in blowing up part of the refinery which was nearer to Haifa further round the bay. This created a massive smoke screen between us and Mount Carmel which blotted out the view for over a week. Some of our men were sent to help contain the blaze.

Before we left Palestine we were presented with a cartoon of the dance band which had been produced by one of the chaps in our unit. This is very lifelike and representative – but the beauty of it is that it was painted by a cousin of George Shearing also named Shearing!

We played for a concert run by a chap called Ossi Race which comprised acts from all parts of the unit and had rehearsals with all of them with the exception of the boys from the cookhouse who could not be spared at any reasonable time and were excused. When the day came they produced one of the diesel burners from the cookhouse and proceeded to light it on stage. The band were in front of the stage at ground level, my eyes being slightly above the stage, when gradually fumes percolated across us and we were taking the full blast. In the end the performance had to be abandoned for safety. As if we did not have enough problems with terrorists!

Finally on 27th April 1947 we left Palestine en route for Egypt where we were stationed at Fayid where camp facilities were excellent. After a month we again moved, this time to El Ballah which was 15 miles south of Port Said very close to the canal. Most afternoons we would go swimming in the canal where it was necessary to keep watch for the ships which passed through fairly frequently and this was a very pleasant life. Here again we produced concerts and for one of these I wrote two songs – the only time in my life I attempted this. One of them was a ballad called "If you are at all in doubt" which was sung by Paddy Dunne and if I were to play it you would probably say I got the idea from Anthony Newley's "What kind of fool am I". The fact of the matter is that his song did not see the light of day until 1961! The other tune was entitled "Eros is back in Piccadilly" a more up tempo number which had the immortal line – "Who could make love with posters everywhere saying – save all your money with your backs to the wall". I was never keen on the effort required to put music on paper and as everyone who knows will tell you my handwriting is atrocious. Without a computer I would not be trying to write this book. Today there are wonderful programs for budding composers which do so much for the tedious part of the job. Included in the cast of the show was a chap called Len Buckle who wore a large pair of wings to denote Eros and he was undoubtedly a predecessor of Boy George and really looked the part and loved every minute of it.

We spent some time on leave in Port Said which was most enjoyable. Long after the war I was invited to go on a Jazz Night Cruise on the Thames by Sid Clements a good friend and drummer who said I would meet someone called Lennie Best, a vibraphone player who said he knew me well. I said at the time that although I knew the name I had no idea what he looked like. Anyway, I was invited to sit in after the interval and after the first number Lennie turned round and said "I remember you playing the piano in a leave camp in Port Said in 1947". It transpired that in those days he was not a musician and had spent several hours getting me to play requests and of course I did not recall this at all. Lots of people asked for requests.

Back in the camp the toilet facilities were ultra modern. There was a large circular hole in the ground with seats all round facing outwards and if I were to tell you that periodically one of the natives would go down into the pit and empty it bucket by bucket you probably wouldn't believe me – so I won't!

About the middle of the year we were granted a month's home leave – known as L.I.A.P. – leave in anticipation of Python (a term for home posting) and we left Port Said on the S.S. Windsor Castle returning on the Donata Castle. We were very upset to learn that in our absence a chap with whom we had shared an underground bunker set in the sand had died of typhoid – not a nice welcome back. Geoff Banks reminded me that on our return we sometimes had to guard some of the Italian and German P.O.W.'s on our own each with a rifle and five rounds of ammunition. Apparently they often complained that the locals sometimes threw stones at them.

In December our time was up and we were returned to Blighty on the S.S. Otranto which if my memory serves me rightly called in at Pyraeus and Malta on the way home.

We were given one of those wonderful demob suits which were rather akin to being another uniform which was replaced at the earliest moment. All in all I would not have missed this experience for anything although I have to concede that I had a privileged viewpoint but that's where luck comes into it!

Return to Civvy Street

I had a really good holiday particularly as it covered the Christmas period and in January we held a belated 21st birthday party as I was in Palestine on the actual day the previous year. This of course was musical and I remember that amongst others Derek Neville the alto player was there and Norman George as well. I soon got back into the swing and was doing gigs and playing as much as possible but it was equally important to get a permanent regular job as I never felt cut out to be a full-time musician – a very wise decision as it transpired. On balance I feel I obtained more satisfaction the way things turned out as I was lucky enough to play with some of the finest musicians a lot of whom were full time pro's. At the end of January I went to Tooting Labour Exchange who sent me for an interview with Barrow Hepburn & Gale Ltd in Church Road, Mitcham where I landed a job as a costing clerk starting on February 10th 1948 at 4 pounds 5 shillings a week. As I was starting "late" in the year I was only entitled to August Bank Holiday week (including the Monday) for my annual holiday – that's how it was in those days – all Saturdays included! The company was divided into two main sections the larger of which manufactured rubber and plastic conveyor belting. There was also a sub section producing rubber flooring, sponge rubber sheeting and similar items. The other main section was entirely based on made up items produced from leather. This include flat and round transmission belting - textile leathers such as picking bands and tuggers – a wide range of hydraulic and pneumatic leather seals and packings and leather for ginning cotton produced in those days from the heavy parts of bull shoulders. I was involved in costings for all sides of the business and as I like figures (it is acknowledged that maths and music go well together) I was quite happy with my job. Fairly early on a vacancy became available for a representative to take over one of the northern areas and this was offered to me. In those days there seemed to be a general feeling that this really was a prime position but I could never have taken this up. Put simply I have always seen myself as a "do-er" rather than a talker. Over the years I was to find that many people with the gift of the gab nearly always created a better initial impact but in a high percentage of cases talk was all they had to offer. I have to be honest and admit that from my point of view it would have been more difficult to maintain an interest in music and it is my contention that this is what kept me sane as things do not always run smoothly in factories.

Whilst the leather section at Mitcham was the smaller of the two in fact the main interests of the Barrow Hepburn Group were in leather in its many forms. It covered the tanning process, currying or dressing for a particular application and indeed all stages up to and including the production of high-class luggage and equipment. Until very recently they even produced the budget type cases which were fitted with special locks by visiting inspectors. They also had companies in South Africa which produced various tanning extracts and in the years that followed these were added to on a very large scale until we as a group were one of the largest in Europe – if not in the world! The Group Chairman was George Odey who took over this position in 1937 when he himself was only 37 years old. He had a particular interest in the Gin leather side of the business having had a large part to play in obtaining the original business soon after he joined the company. After six weeks or so it was proposed that Bob Banfield, who was running the leather department, should go round all the London shipping houses looking for business. As a result, someone was needed to hold the fort while he was out and I was offered the job of Assistant

Manager "A" Department (i.e. the leather section) – which I accepted.

When I first joined the company I was interviewed by Douglas Dew whose father Albert Dew was at that time in charge of the factory as a whole. Not long after Albert retired and Douglas took over from him and remained my direct boss until his retirement in the late seventies. Whereas Douglas was quite tall, Albert was much smaller and had a habit of walking through offices wearing a Homburg hat. On more that one occasion on a Saturday Albert came up to my desk and said "Come on young Cook – follow me" – whereupon he would take me to the canteen to give him a game of table-tennis. During the week I used to play this regularly after having lunch and I was fairly good at it but – like cricket – I had an unorthodox method of playing in that every stroke was played from the inside of the bat. This meant that to play a backhand shot my hand had to cross over the body with the back of the hand facing over the left shoulder. Despite the apparent awkwardness of this I was able to deliver a very fast return taking the ball on the rise. As a result, I very nearly won the company knockout tournament singles only losing after my opponent fluked a return from the net support outside the table. Bob Banfield and I did win the pairs once. In fact table tennis was the best part of the lunch hour as I was not at all happy with canteen food. This was too soon after the war and rationing was still in operation and the cooks did not have much choice to offer. We had a team in the London Business House League in which I used to take part and I remember having some tremendous battles. Unfortunately, some time later they introduced many different surfaces on the bats which made it easy to create an enormous amount of spin and that started my decline as an effective player.

Everything we produced in the leather department was functional – from the smallest cup leather to the widest transmission belt. This made it an absorbing material to work with, as of course no two pieces are alike and a good cutter can make or break the company. For this reason most of the employees when I first joined were of fairly long service with the department and had great pride in their work. We had an enormous range of rings and moulds from which to produce seals which enabled us to supply packings ranging in size from ½" diameter to around 36" and many even larger than this. On occasion we had to cement two pieces of leather together with joints in order to produce the very large sizes although this was not considered desirable. We once produced a Ram Leather 72" diameter x 1 ¾" deep which would have required a piece of leather about 83" diameter. The finished article would have a "U" section measuring 72" outside diameter and around 69" inside diameter – rather like a very large posy bowl.

Of course, leather was the first material used for sealing purposes and although it has been superseded by modern synthetic packings, some reinforced with fabric, it remains a fact that a leather seal will give a warning before failing completely. This is not the case with synthetics which also require their housing to be finished to much tighter tolerances. One of our regular customers regularly employed rough drawn tubing on his equipment which would have ruined a synthetic instantly.

When I first began in the department the major customer was The Westinghouse Brake & Signal Co. from Chippenham who probably accounted for almost 2/3 rds of the seal business. This was because Barrow's had been instrumental in helping with the introduction of their equipment back in 1880 or thereabouts. To this day, there is still a call for replacements on certain applications.

There was an amusing incident when the railways were deciding whether to opt for the Airbrake or the Vacuum Brake for the future supplies and this would have meant a tremendous increase in production. At the eleventh hour, I received a phone call asking "Tell me Mr. Cook, are there enough cows in the country to do this job?". In fact because of the stresses involved in calving, cowhide would have been quite unsuitable, being too thin and very uneven. The grandfather of Joe Weight – the foreman when I arrived – had been working for the company from the start of the Westinghouse account. When I joined the company no real attempt appeared to have been made to diversify into other areas. This was because at that time the emphasis was still on supplying Leather Transmission Belting – both flat and round and of course Gin leather which I will deal with separately. In the ensuing years the competition from overseas and in particular India made a change of direction absolutely imperative.

Joe Weight was an amazing character. He originally worked for the previous Foreman – one Peter Middleton who, during the war, was Mayor of Southwark (this was when the factory was still in Grange Road, Bermondsey). I gather he was almost a legend in his own lifetime. Apparently Joe used to act as chauffeur to Peter who had access to nearly every pub in the area during or after hours. Joe himself was a true Christian, without being a churchgoer. For example, when one of his under-foreman was called up he looked after one of his children until he returned to civvy street years later! Many years after when I was married and living at Clapham Park, he volunteered to pick me up on the way from Bermondsey, where he lived so that I could use his car to learn to drive – and he would often give a helping hand to anyone in need. I suppose you would describe him as a cockney and he was for ever enthusiastic about anything to do with leather. On reaching retirement, we managed to use him to good effect visiting customers and sorting out problems. His brother was Managing Director of Gamages in Torquay – a very important position. The very first visit I made to a customer was to Westinghouse with Bob Banfield. We arrived shortly after 10.15 a.m. and by 11.00 a.m. we were in a local pub playing bowls on an indoor rink. After lunch, we eventually returned to the factory around 3.00 p.m. This was quite an eye-opener to me and I gathered that for their buyer with his numerous suppliers this had become a way of life, almost every day of every week! Mind you, when we visited one of our suppliers – Wiggins, Thomas & Rudd Ltd in Stepney the same thing happened in reverse – i.e. they paid!

Originally, leather packings were wet-blocked, dried under controlled conditions, then impregnated with hard or soft waxes or greases and then re-blocked to the final shape. Later, some leathers were supplied ready waxed and heated rings or moulds employed. However, eventually, in the late 1950's, Dr. Norman Holmes, who operated from Thomas Holmes and Sons in Hull (part of our group), came up with the idea of using Dielectric Heaters with chrome waxed leather for moulding. After some experimentation, the idea was adopted, in particular for long runs of leather seals for the N.C.B. and many of their suppliers of hydraulic powered equipment. The principle was that the heaters used the natural water content to soften the leather. A pile of 8 circles would be heated for a very short period and then placed in a row of presses in cold moulds and by the time the first pack had been removed another pile was ready for moulding. This was of course the forerunner of the microwave oven and enabled us to produce at a much faster rate than previously.

The presses I mention in the last paragraph were

themselves powered by cup leathers of our own manufacture. Many years later when Dick Rooke, one of our Directors on the Conveyor side of the business was due to visit China, I was asked to produce a write-up on the leather side of the business. I'm afraid I could not resist starting off with "In our country we have a saying 'Which comes first – the chicken or the egg'!"

After a time, I was appointed Manager of the Leather Department and I directed my energies to trying to discover new outlets for leather seals whilst still keeping the existing business going for as long as possible. At the same time the opportunity to expand by acquisition arose when J.H. Fenner & Co. of Hull decided to give up producing leather packings and in exchange we gave up the manufacture of flat leather belting. This was by far the largest business we were to acquire – and there were many more to come in later years. To have any chance of succeeding we had to take on one of their key workers and this entailed buying him a house in Streatham for something like £2250 – a sizeable investment in those days. One of their best accounts was Lockheed of Leamington Spa, for whom they produced Servo Leathers for their brakes. What really amazed us when visiting the factory was the fact that they had a special machine to re-process the rejects of which there were a large number of boxes. By the time we were under way with production we had found the answer to the problem and rejects dropped dramatically. Unfortunately, the damage had been done and it was not long before they turned to synthetic packings and whilst this could have happened anyway I am sure we could have enjoyed several years more without this ridiculous state of affairs.

I have always had a thing about plastics as, apart from the problem we all encounter in trying to open a packet of biscuits, I feel they gained an unfair advantage through their power to advertise on a grand scale. One particular instance concerns a Heat Resistant Conveyor Belt which we manufactured at one time. I.C.I. supplied us with one ingredient used in this belt and took out whole page colour adverts in nearly all the appropriate technical magazines at fantastic cost and yet the proportion of the material used amounted to 1/10th of 1% of the belt as a whole. In addition, in the immediate post war years, a lot of younger engineers thought of leather as old fashioned and would not even contemplate using it despite the many applications we were supplying where synthetics could not be employed.

At a later date, we obtained orders for Servo Leathers for Girling in Cwmbran which were quite substantial. After a time, they requested us to find a way of producing them with a joint to save using a complete circle of material. Whilst we achieved the objective, it was not possible to eliminate a hard spot at the cemented portion and after several months they were unhappy with the result and reverted to the original design. I have to confess to having no qualifications as an engineer but from experience I was able to build up complete confidence in leather as a sealing product. Equally, I found that many engineers I came across had no idea of basic principles. The worst example of this came when one of our reps came in with a complaint from the gasworks overlooking the Thames at Battersea where they were using hydraulic grabs to unload coke from barges in the river and the seals were only lasting 48 hours! I visited the site with the rep and after discussion was shown the cylinder in which the cup leathers were operating. The packings were about 3" diameter and made from 1/8" thick leather and the cylinders had dozens of holes bored through the walls. I immediately pointed out that all they were doing was shaving off the outside wall with every stroke.

When I asked why the cylinders were so constructed I was informed that their engineer made the modification to stop the two parts of the grab coming together violently as had been the case before. All I could recommend was that they should use thicker leather unless they were prepared to get rid of the offending cylinders.

The variation in applications was tremendous and I have never forgotten the time when during my lunch hour I was asked to attend to a customer who had turned up out of the blue with a very small pump requiring a new seal. I examined this carefully whilst still digesting the remains of my lunch and asked what the pump was used for. On hearing it was for embalming my appetite waned dramatically!

On another occasion Bob Hall, who became our company secretary when we moved to Bermondsey in 1966, came into my office with a small cup leather which one of his neighbours was having difficulty replacing. As it happens, we had one in our stock of oddments which I was able to give him free of charge. This was a great mistake as he wrote a glowing testimonial to the service he had received to the "Country Gentlemen's Association" of which he was a member. This packing was for a pump on a vintage car he was renovating and because of the publicity we were inundated with requests for all manner of small items and I had to concoct a letter of regret to cover the problem.

When the Dartford tunnel was under construction we had orders for tens of thousands of cup leathers which were used for obtaining core samples of the various layers of sub soil involved. They were used once only in this operation and this was very good business. We supplied British Rail with Axlebox Leathers and much later supplied soft cup leathers to Racal Acoustics for use on throat microphones – the leather was ideal for transmitting the vibrations of the voice with minimal distortion. We also supplied Racal Antennae with thousands of sets of cup leathers comprising seven cups of gradually increasing size used on their telescopic aerials. In later years, we gradually obtained orders for most of the makers of hydraulic equipment for the N.C.B. including Gullick-Dobson, Dowty (who made seals in synthetics), and Fletcher Sutcliffe Wild. Ultimately, we secured the contract for Leather spares for the N.C.B. direct, although the equipment manufacturers were able to restrict our attempts to supply the roof support packings direct on safety grounds. In several instances, we were able to supply other seal makers with leathers which they then supplied to the N.C.B. However, we were somewhat at a disadvantage being in the south of the country when most of the pits and equipment makers were mainly in the Midlands and the north of England. There was undoubtedly a North/South divide which probably still exists and it was only when some of our competitors fell by the wayside that we were able to realise our full potential.

Certainly, there was one occasion when one of our competitors had serious problems and the N.C.B. called a conference at Egham of the relevant members of the Industrial Leather Federation which I attended. After the meeting, I made one phone call and pointed out to the equipment makers that they were already in possession of tests on our seals which could overcome the problem and we were given orders within a matter of days and these continued for a considerable period. Mind you it was extremely difficult business to handle at times as they would ask for substantial weekly supplies which entailed overtime working and this could last for as much as 12 or 13 weeks whereupon they would suddenly halt supplies for several weeks.

Another section of the Leather Department was still producing Round Leather Belting for sewing machines both domestic and commercial when I joined the company although it was described as a dying trade even then. Despite this we continued with manufacture for another 25 years at least. This was a highly skilled operation involving sizes ranging from 3/16" – 3/8" diameters which were first cut in square section round and round the butt measuring approximately 54" x 48" and then pulled through a circular cutter to size. The skill came in having a cutter who knew just when to change size, as of course, a piece of leather varies considerably in thickness and no two pieces are alike. A bad cutter could be the ruination of the business. When I started the cutter was a chap called Bert Hafner who had been severely gassed during the First World War and you could hear him cough from one end of the factory to the other. He also cut Leather Laces by hand 60" long just by the naked eye and was a true craftsman and woe betide anyone that tried to use his tools. He could let fly with his tongue if ever he was upset and despite having a colourful vocabulary it always amazes me that I never once heard him or any of our men use bad language in front of women visitors or staff. The contrast with today I find quite appalling and though I appreciate this is a typical "older generation" reaction I cannot see any merit in it!

Towards the middle of 1948 I was approached by Ken Lucas who asked me to be his best man when he married Pearl Roue. I of course, accepted and this turned out to be the most important day of my life. Her chief bridesmaid, one Jean Bateman, was later to become my wife and but for this we might never have met. We very soon got together and spent what time we could in each other's company but this was not easy. At the time, Jean was working for the Motor Agent's Association in Great Portland Street throughout the week and at the age of 25 she organised an outing to the coast for the whole office. In addition, on Sundays, she worked at the Cavendish Hotel in Jermyn Street. I was at B.H. &G. and still doing gigs at various places of an evening and there were times when meeting was impossible for many days.

For the benefit of those who did not see the series I should explain the Cavendish was run by the famous Rosa Lewis, about whom Daphne Fielding wrote a book called "The Duchess of Jermyn Street". The television series "The Duchess of Duke Street" was based on her life and perhaps now is the time for a separate chapter dealing with Jean's involvement here.

ROSA LEWIS & THE CAVENDISH HOTEL

Jean's father had a very successful gentlemen's hairdressers business in the City of London – not far from the Monument and many of his clients were from landed gentry including the Governor of the Bank of England. One day one of his customers Lord Ebbisham happened to mention that he was in need of a young girl for his office and as Jean was available at the time her father offered her services and these were accepted at once. On his way home Lord Ebbisham called on Rosa Lewis at the Hotel and by coincidence Rosa told him that she was on the lookout for "a little gal", as she was wont to say, and being of a generous nature Lord Ebbisham parted with Jean even before she started work for him. Her primary task was to become a book-keeper for Rosa but in essence she became much more of a companion and accompanied her on walks and to church and also read to her from time to time.

For the benefit of those not familiar with the story I must mention that early in the century Rosa became a famous cook who for a short period became the mistress of Edward the Seventh when he was Prince of Wales. Her fame was such that when asked to cater for a function she would organise everything and then make her entrance through the front door wearing her furs and it is generally believed that the Prince of Wales actually gave her the Hotel. Daphne Fielding wrote a book about her entitled "The Duchess of Jermyn Street".

Of course Jean only knew Rosa during the last years of her life as she died in 1953. The hotel was famous for serving champagne, most of the time from double magnums, and apparently Rosa had a theory that people did not get drunk on it. They had a succession of Yorkshire Terriers all called Kippy which Jean used to take for walks and they were trained to run after champagne corks. Rosa had a reputation of being a sort of Robin Hood in that she would ensure that her guests were well mixed in every way and those that could afford it ended up paying for the less fortunate. Jean was included as part of the family and would sit at table with many of the honoured guests. The Hotel backed onto the Foreign Office and part of their war effort was to take in members of the resistance who had been behind lines in France following the de-briefing and to build them up for a return visit.

Among the guests at table was Commander Crabbe who disappeared in the vicinity of a Russian vessel in Portsmouth Harbour in very suspicious circumstances in May 1956. His headless body was found in the same area in June 1957. The Russians were convinced he had been carrying out underwater espionage. Lord Lambton, who achieved considerable notoriety in 1973 as a junior government minister, and resigned when photographs of him in bed with two women of ill repute were published in a National newspaper, was another of her guests. He had previously used Jean to rehearse his maiden speech in Parliament, and I'm glad that's all he did!

Rosa would not just accept anyone as a guest and apparently Tennessee Williams, who she disliked, succeeded in getting in with the aid of a friend and dark glasses. Once installed he used Jean to rehearse some Brer Rabbit stories he was working on at the time.

In the T.V. series based on her life, "The Duchess of Duke Street", the hall porter was called Starr whereas in real life his name was Moon and in Jean's time there he was so old he used to dribble over the leather visitor's book.

Edith Jeffrey was Rosa's lifelong companion and was

portrayed in the series as Mary. One of Rosa's famous sayings was "You are treating my house as a Hotel". She was nevertheless a shrewd business woman and all her rooms were made out in different styles and quite often the guests would express a desire to own either the furniture or perhaps a series of related paintings or drawings. After careful discussion she would reluctantly agree to part with them – for a price! No sooner would the customer leave then replacements would be brought up from the basement.

Jean's mother fortunately retained a number of Xmas cards sent to them from the Cavendish one of which shows a portrait of Rosa by Whistler and others show her favourite sitting room known as the Elinor Glyn Room and also the Hotel and the main entrance. In addition there is a telegram from Edith Jeffrey which reads "Hoping to see you on Sunday Miss Blunt ill all alone". Anthony Eden stayed at the hotel and had been known to have quite a bad temper which he sometimes took out on the electric fire with his foot.

On one occasion they were awaiting the arrival of a courier from the Norwegian Embassy to collect some important documents and he was extremely late. In the end Rosa got hold of Jean and put her overcoat on and stuffed these papers inside and buttoned her up. They then hailed a cab but fortunately, just as she was about to depart, the courier arrived and Jean heaved a huge sigh of relief!

All this happened before I met Jean and when she was working full time at the Hotel. When I first met her in 1948 she was working full-time at the M.A.A., the Motor Agents Association, but by then she only worked every Sunday at the Hotel. I used to meet her in the evening and was introduced to Rosa on a couple of occasions.

Sometime later an American staying at the Hotel wanted to have a party for his birthday and Rosa said to Jean "You know a fiddle player don't you?" and the net result was that I supplied a quartet for the occasion. Now on this particular day Jean had sprained her ankle and was in some pain and of course we had to use public transport. The bass player was a confirmed beer drinker and very sceptical about having to put up with champagne. He did not object to the York Ham and fresh strawberries and this was the height of luxury when you consider how soon after the war it was. Anyway a good time was had by all of us and the bass player became a changed man and into the bargain Jean positively skipped down to the Embankment to get the tram home.

When we eventually married in 1952 we had a telegram from Rosa and Edith and they presented us with a pair of sheets and frankly I have never seen anything larger. They were far too big for ordinary use and when our daughter Linda moved into a flat in Frome when she had become a teacher she used them as curtains – and later to hide some shelving modules she had bought.

After Rosa's death in 1953 Edith Jeffrey continued running the Hotel until it finally closed in 1962 and Jean wrote to Edith and we still have her reply in an album of memorabilia that we put together when the T.V. series came out.

Eventually the New Cavendish Hotel was built and in 1980 there was a request put out on a commercial radio program for anyone who had any items connected with the Hotel to get in touch – which we did. The Manager at the time wanted to organise a theme night in particular for the Americans and after some discussions it was agreed that Jean would act as receptionist when the event took place. We left the album with them and there followed a very long interval and I finally got in touch only to find that the management had changed and they would not be pursuing the matter. They were full of apologies and hoped we would call in some time later.

Now one of my leather suppliers used to take us out for dinner once a year and when he asked me for suggestions as to where to go I mentioned the Cavendish. We went, introduced ourselves, and had a very enjoyable evening culminating with my playing the grand piano. As we left we noticed a showcase on one of the walls near the staircase with one or two items from the old hotel and were delighted to see two handwritten bills in Jean's writing.

Over the years Jean has felt that Rosa, who was very tall, like Jean, had always regarded her as the daughter she never had and it was for this reason that she was always included at table with her guests and never treated as an employee. Coming from a woman once described as "the finest cook in the world" this was quite a compliment.

Jean of course went on to become a "Cook" in her own right – but that's a different story!

TELEPHONE: WHITEHALL 4503.
TELEGRAMS: EXCELLETH, PICCY, LONDON.

CAVENDISH HOTEL,
81, JERMYN STREET,
ST. JAMES'S, S.W.1

5th June, 1962.

Mrs. Jean Cook,
8, Queensville Road,
LONDON, S.W.12.

Dear Jean,

　　Thank you so much for your very sweet letter, it was so nice hearing from you.

　　As you can imagine, we are all very sad that the hotel has to close, but as you know, it was inevitable. We have now got the gigantic task of winding up the Cavendish, and my sister is here with me to help, also Charles, and they both send you very kind remembrances.

　　Thank you for your kind invitation to come and see you which I certainly would like to do when — as you say— the bustle is over.

　　With much love to you and the family,

　　　　Sincerely

　　　　Edith.

TO CONTINUE

Now where was I? Oh yes, during the next 18 months or so I continued to take on a wide range of gigs and it was about this time that I met up with Allan Ganley who was to become our best man. I believe my first contact with him would have been at a dance hall above Burton's the tailors in Kingston – on – Thames. The venue was run by the Kendrews, a husband and wife team who were, I believe, formerly professional dancers. Their son Jock was the drummer in the band and very occasionally he would let Allan sit in for a waltz which was not very encouraging for a budding jazz musician. Shortly after I met him he was discharged from the R.A.F. and I remember only too well that when he told me he intended becoming a professional musician I advised him strongly not to.

Now within a very short space of time he was to become Johnny Dankworth's drummer with his big band, although his very first big band engagement was for a broadcast with Geraldo, depping for Eric Delaney (the regular drummer at that time) who had a serious accident, catching his fingers in the fan belt on his car. Since then Allan has become a highly respected composer, arranger, and conductor and has frequently fronted the B.B.C. Radio Big Band and strings and to this day is still with John Dankworth accompanying Cleo Lane in their many concerts both here and on the continent. You would be quite right in assuming that my advice was pretty inadequate!

However I am getting a little ahead of myself so let's go back to where I first met Jean at the wedding. In my first full year after leaving the army I reverted to playing with Norman George and also worked with the band at the Kingston Palais. At the same time I met up with a guitarist called Gordon Soppitt who, with a bass player called Geoff Parsons, had been in the R.A.F. in Italy with Keith Bird, a very fine instrumentalist who played tenor sax, clarinet and flute and was by now working with Geraldo. It was during this period that a musician's jazz club was formed meeting around once a month in a private room at the Greyhound Public House in Bromley. The organisers were a husband and wife couple Jon and Penny Ledigo who played bass and piano respectively. As I recall the charge for the room was £3.00 and this cost was divided between the members present and there were no spectators other than wives or girl friends. The regulars included Ronnie Ross, Keith Bird, Ken Sykora, Allan Ganley, Ray Dempsey, Jimmy Collins, Ted Taylor, plus Gordon, and Geoff, the Ledigos and myself. There were one or two others but I'm afraid their names escape me. Nevertheless all of the first five names listed above made quite an impact on jazz in this country but unfortunately Ronnie and Keith are no longer with us. It is an interesting fact that you could not possibly have such a club these days as, most establishments now make maximum use of space – alternatively the cost would be prohibitive.

At some time I cannot quite pinpoint the policy at Kingston altered and we had jazz nights I believe on Friday, Saturday and Sunday and I can remember the very young Tubby Hayes coming in quite frequently for a blow and later on we had the Kenny Graham's Afro-Cubists as the main attraction and I was in a relief piano trio working opposite. After a while the band was changed and in came Leslie "Jiver" Hutchinson with a group which included Kenny Graham on tenor, Rupert Nurse on bass, another West Indian tenor player whose name escaped me, Jock Kendrew the proprietor's son on drums, and myself on piano. "Jiver" who was father to singer Elaine Delmar, tried to show me how to play a calypso properly. I'm still uncertain as to whether he actually succeeded. He was very easy to get on with and I believe this was a very important stage in my development as a jazz pianist.

Now at the same time at the weekend there was another jazz club operating just around the corner in the Dolphin Public House which has since been demolished to make way for the new Bentall Centre. We used to call in for a drink before we started playing and on occasion we would dash across during our interval to sit in with them. This was the first time I came across Pete Towndrow – a wonderful flugelhorn and trumpet player and we have been firm friends ever since and play together on the odd occasion. The pub was run by Don and Gwen Kingswell and it was at the bar that I first met Ralph Sharon who at the time was making a name with his own sextet in this country. Later on of course he was to make a very fine reputation in America and ultimately became accompanist to Tony Bennett, a position he still holds to this day after many years.

He once told a story that had quite an impact on me, particularly as it was effectively against himself. Apparently he once received a phone call from Bob Farnon the Canadian composer and conductor offering him a job in a studio for a recording, which he accepted. When he arrived he found a studio containing a very large orchestra with masses of strings and in the centre of this was a large grand piano. When he looked at the parts he realised that he was expected to read the most complicated score and was not at all happy. Anyway they started and after just a few minutes Bob Farnon called for a 5 minute break. He then approached Ralph and said "Before you take a job on you should always ask what is required of you!" He then sat at the piano and showed him how to approach this very difficult opening part and after a few moments Ralph managed to get through safely. Having told me this story Ralph suggested that I too should be a little more curious when offered any gigs. The outcome was of course that anyone offering me engagements after this had to endure the Spanish inquisition – quite needlessly in most instances.

During the same period I was gradually seeing as much of Jean as could be arranged and because one of her colleagues was a balletomane who used to queue for tickets for the Amphitheatre at Covent Garden, at one stage we were going sometimes 2 or 3 times a week. I believe at the time the tickets cost three shillings and sixpence. Now personally I do not appreciate the very old ballets such as Swan Lake and Giselle etc. but around this time Margot Fonteyn, Michael Somes, and Alexander Grant were the stars and there were quite a number of more modern ballets to be seen. Amongst my favourites were "Daphnis & Chloe" to the music of Ravel, "Enigma Variations" by Elgar, "The Rakes Progress", "Serenade for Strings" by Tschaikovsky, and at a later date we saw "The Concert" which was quite hilarious and had Wayne Sleep in the lead. Of course from my point of view it was the music that counted most and I later learned that Ronnie Scott was very fond of Ravel and Debussy obviously because of the very full rich chords involved. Personally I feel this is a more interesting way of enjoying classical music as when you hear it repeated elsewhere it immediately brings to mind the action on the stage. A few years back they had a revival of "Daphnis and Chloe" and we took a close friend to see it and were most disappointed. In the original there were separate dancers for the brigands but in the revival the same people were used for two separate bands of people but in the finale there was no one wearing brigand apparel. Considering how much more expensive the modern production was we all felt cheated, and of course it no longer had Margot Fonteyn in the lead. On another visit we saw a ballet performed to the music of Tchaikovsky's 2nd Piano

Concerto in G and on this occasion our seats were on the side overlooking the orchestra pit. I was able to read the piano part through my opera glasses and when the performance ended I realised that I had seen absolutely nothing of the dancing. Following this I bought the music and spent quite a time trying to make a fist of it. I think "fist" is what any decent classical pianist would call it! Well – it wasn't quite that bad. Much later on we went to Covent Garden to see a ballet called "Jazz Calendar" written by Richard Rodney Bennett and it was quite gratifying to see a special jazz ensemble in the pit which included Ronnie Ross – it gave the feeling that perhaps jazz had arrived after all.

At the Kingston Palais we had a singer called Freddy Harfield who wanted to make a demo record and we ended up at Star Sound Studios with Gordon Soppitt and Geoff Parsons, Allan Ganley and myself but Allan had persuaded Johnny Dankworth and Leon Calvert, a modern trumpet player to come along. After playing "Small Hotel" for Freddy we then launched into "Out of Nowhere" and a 12-bar blues called "Sipping at Bells" and you have to bear in mind that this was at the onset of be-bop. Frankly the first tune was bearable but the blues became quite excruciating particularly on the trumpet solos – but we all have to learn!

On another occasion Keith Bird organised a recording session at Carlo Krahmer's studio with the same personnel, minus John Dankworth and Leon. On this we recorded "Arual" a bebop tune on the chords of Laura which came out quite well, except for the fact that at some time during the making there must have been an upsurge in the power supply which produced a marginal change of key!

Around this same period I started playing piano for a

bandleader called Jimmy Edwards and I made contact with him through Norman George's friend Charles Osborne who at that time was both playing for Jimmy and also assisting him in booking and running the band. A lot of his original work involved society gigs but the scope extended to dinner dances and working at the American Air Bases and playing at town hall functions with bands of all sizes. Unfortunately for Jimmy someone of the same name was making a big reputation as a comedian at the time and in 1949 he changed his name to Jimmy Evard as he was quite unable to take on some of the work he was being offered. Talking about town hall functions, we once played for a dance at Fulham Town Hall for the Labour Party attended by Dr. Edith Summerskill at which the first prize was a television set and at the time this was a very big deal indeed as very few people possessed one. One of the musicians had sent in a dep. as he was ill and would you believe not only was the replacement pretty awful at playing but he won the raffle. This was one way of losing what had been until then a regular engagement!

We once had a gig at the Dorchester and I had acquired a light brown Crombie overcoat from my father. On reflection I feel that possibly dad must have been offered this by a friend as there was absolutely no way that he would have bought it new himself. Anyway I strolled through the main entrance only for a voice to say "Musician's entrance is round the back" – now how did he know? I have to confess I was less happy playing the dinner music that was required at some of these functions but really enjoyed working at the American Camps where the opportunity to not only play jazz but have a more appreciative audience was most welcome. Indeed I can recall more than one occasion when having finished the official engagement we dragged the piano into the bar and had a jam session for another couple of hours.

On some of the big band dances at places like Walthamstow or Ealing Town Halls I had to accompany a singer called Wendy Brooks who I discovered only recently had previously sung with the great Joe Saye. Now Wendy was married to a chap called Leo Pollini who at one time was Tommy Steele's drummer. One Friday I received a phone call at the office to say that it was the last day of filming "The Little White Bull" and they wanted to have a jam session and party in the studio in the evening. Could I possibly make it and of course I did. When we started playing Tommy Steele suggested playing "Blue Lou" a well known jazz standard at the time and still played on occasion these days. What really got to me was the fact that Tommy didn't have a clue as to how the middle eight went and I was somewhat put out over this, Of course this was sheer naiveté on my part but nevertheless I never forgot my one session wit Tommy Steele! At the time there was a tenor player with Tommy Steele called Alan Stewart and in recent times he has been fronting an eight piece jazz group playing the clubs. I'm not sure that he was pleased to be reminded of the fact that he ended up with Tommy's group lying on his back with his legs kicking up in the air whilst still playing the sax.

One of the drummers who played with Jimmy Evard was called Dave Clifford and there is a wonderful story about his being booked to play for a society function. On arrival he discovered after a time that not only was he the only musician there, but that was all there would be. He asked the hostess what on earth was happening and found that he was to accompany gramophone records. Somewhat miffed he nevertheless did as requested. At the end of the evening the hostess asked for God Save the Queen and he enquired whether they had a recording. The hostess said – "No you'll have to sing it" and to his eternal credit – he did!

Another drummer of Jimmy's was Roy Sutton, a real character always good for a laugh. Mind you he had no sense of time (by the clock that is), and in those days I had no car and Roy lived nearby and often gave me a lift to the gig. The trouble was that he would always arrive at the very last minute and into the bargain would sometimes stop en-route to pick up a bottle of cider. He did a few trips on the Queen Mary and on one occasion he had been shopping in New York for a table lamp and was so late getting back to the ship that he had to fling himself on the very last gang plank. When he arrived home with his booty he plugged it in and it promptly blew up! On another occasion we were playing at an American Air Force Base, Bentwaters I believe, when one of the Americans insisted on getting on stage to sing at the mike and he was really diabolical. Suddenly I realised that we had no drummer and looking round I saw Roy down on the dance floor with a large broom – sweeping the floor. Of course we all collapsed!

In the course of doing the American Clubs we were required to accompany the cabaret and this really created some hairy moments. It was ridiculous to expect someone to do justice to parts which were either very complicated of so badly worn that it was almost impossible to follow them, particularly when repeats were required. I remember once we had to back Max and Harry Nesbitt and their act seemed to last forever, yet the run through comprised about a 10 minute talk-through back stage and I swear the dog had been chewing the music for ages.

I was generally able to cope but it really was an imposition and after the agents had exploited the bands and, I heard, following some real disasters, the Musician's Union stepped in and insisted that each cabaret at least had to provide a pianist and a drummer after which life became somewhat more relaxed.

It is generally accepted that all musicians thought the world of Tommy Cooper and I am no exception. On the other hand I use to have great admiration for Dickie Dawson, Diana Dor's second husband, who had a great personality and I never understood why he was not better known. Mind you I also remember walking down Jermyn Street one Sunday evening behind Diana Dors when she was very young and everything moved in a delightful way!

But I digress!

In those days the gig of the year was New Year's Eve when you would expect to receive at least double the normal rate and as time went on it escalated much further to the complete detriment of the performances. As a result in order to obtain the highest possible reward the regular line up of the band would change as some of the key figures decided to accept more lucrative offers and it was a very rare occasion that the dep, would be even equal to the regular. Thus the public were paying a lot more for very inferior musicians who in any event would not be familiar with the routines. In my case I was once booked for New Year at a hotel at Crystal Palace. The bandleader was a Scot who was almost out of this world when I arrived. Every one of the remainder of the band was depping for someone else and there was a not-too-good girl singer whom I had to accompany. Effectively I became the bandleader and then I discovered that the band had been booked to play for an all Polish organisation. They soon discovered that things were not as they should be and I ended up "taking the flak" and at the same time trying to prevent a lynching and I had to agree that they were very badly wronged. Shortly afterwards I decided that I would not partake in future unless I could guarantee the band would not allow deps.

Funnily enough on the run up to the Millennium, things got so far out of hand that a very large number of functions had to be cancelled through sheer greed. I heard of some completely ridiculous sums being quoted and simple mathematics would have told them that they were doomed from the start and I am not talking about the Dome! Of course that did not only apply to the musicians as everyone tried to get in on the act.

During the period from 1949 to 1950 Jean and I gradually got to know each other and sometime in 1950 we went to the London Palladium to see the Nat King Cole Trio and on that evening I proposed and she accepted. On our rare evenings off together I used to end up at her home in Brixton and soon discovered that all was not well between her mother and father. I mentioned before that her father had his own men's hairdressers in the City with a good class of clientele. Unfortunately during the blitz a landmine came down fairly close to his premises and he was kept out for quite a considerable period whilst this was being dealt with. When he returned it was to find that his premises had been ransacked and this had a very profound effect on him from which he never really recovered. He was a man of some considerable intelligence and in earlier days had been extremely supportive of some of the less fortunate members of his family. However this unsettled him and he turned to drinking which undoubtedly changed his character and by the time I arrived on the scene there was a very bad atmosphere in the house. In fact it was a very long time before I actually met him as I was generally taken up to the front room of their flat leaving him in the back when he was actually in the house. Jean's mother was very kind to me but it was obvious that the situation in the house was the cause of considerable distress to her as indeed it was to Jean. Of course I introduced her to my parents who made her more than welcome and mum just had to look up to Jean who was so much taller being around 5ft 9in then.

We had our first holiday alone together at a guest house in Brixham in Devon. The weather was superb and I very nearly became sunburned and all in all this was a very good holiday. On our way home we had to catch an early train from Newton Abbott and I remember standing on the station waiting for the train and noticing that someone had dragged the mouth of a fish from one of a number of crates that were awaiting the train and put a lighted cigarette in its mouth – this looked most bizarre!

Eventually we made plans to marry in a couple of years but meanwhile decided to buy some of the furniture which my parents agreed to store as they had extremely large rooms in Laitwood Road. Thus it was that we bought a dining room suite from Ercolani (now known as Ercol) and for our bedroom suite we went to Heal's in Tottenham Court Road when it was famous for the extensive range of furniture it had to offer. Now the Ercol suite was fairly traditional but Heal's was rather special although both were classed as utility furniture – it was so soon after the war. Heal's was made of French Walnut and Beech and comprised two wardrobes, one fitted, a chest of drawers, a dressing table of most unusual design, two bedside tables, and a bed all in the same wood. I still have the bill which totals 110 pounds 2 shillings and 3 pence and by modern terms seems very cheap but when we got married my salary at Barrow Hepburn was just £7.00 per week. All this time I was still working full time during the day and was getting familiar with what was to eventually prove a lifetime's occupation. After a time I noticed that on certain afternoons Douglas, and his father and an elderly chap called Bill Locket used to disappear and shortly after re-appear dressed and complete with the necessary regalia for a Masonic meeting after which they

91

were not seen again in the office that day. Bill Locket was in charge of what was known as the P.H. Department – this stood for Purchases Hides and in essence he bought and sold hides for as little as a farthing a pound which sounds quite absurd. Apart from this however he sold anything he could make a turn on and this at one time included a couple of taxis and elephant hides. Just before he retired I came across a very old ledger listing some of his transactions all set out in magnificent copperplate. As for the Masonic Lodge both Bob Banfield and I could not get enthusiastic about this activity and for that matter I personally was never keen to join the Scouts or Boy's Brigade in my youth. On a Friday it was customary for all the reps. living close to the office at Mitcham to report on the week's progress and afterwards most of them would go for a drink in the Bermondsey area, where our head office was situated and Bob and I joined them. On one such Friday, shortly after my parents had given me a very special 21st birthday present of a gold watch, I came to on the floor of the toilet in the pub with a lump on my head but minus the watch! In those days this area had a reputation of which I was not particularly aware at the time – but you live and learn.

Every Christmas we had a party in the works canteen and I volunteered to supply the band and I reckon we had one of the jazziest groups for those days and made a point of keeping it that way and nobody complained. Allan Ganley played for us when he was not otherwise engaged and we had a very fine semi-pro tenor sax player called Denny Rose who was not only better then a lot of pro musicians but had a wonderful fund of stories which he put over like a seasoned comedian. He was a senior buyer for Price's Candle Factory and when we attended his funeral a couple of years back I was asked to provide some tapes from the parties we held after getting married and we had about 10 minutes before the service and a further 10 minutes afterwards and it was rather like a farewell concert. One of the good things about being a musician is that many of them become comedians and whereas in the old days it was said that all jokes started at the stock exchange this is no longer the case.

Jean and I began looking for houses towards the end of 1951 and in one case we went to a house in Galpins Road near Mitcham which was in excellent decorative condition. Fortunately I decided to check with the neighbours who flatly refused to comment but referred me to a house further up the road who might be able to assist. Here we were told that there had been extensive woodworm which is why the skirting boards had been renewed, but in addition there were things growing up the plaster at an alarming rate, hence the decorations. This really put us off but ultimately I went to an agent near Clapham South who put me onto 8, Queensville and suggested I should be quick as someone else was interested. I tore off on my bicycle and met Miss Rankin who lived there with her sister. The asking price was £1700 Leasehold and with the help of a loan of £250 from my parents we were eventually able to do a deal. This was an area we had looked at for some time, never dreaming that we would be able to afford to live there. Incidentally the starting rate for the mortgage was just 4% and we were advised that it would have to be increased to 4.5% soon! We were allowed to maintain the original rate (all of £9 pounds 1 shilling and 4 pence) and to extend the period, but eventually we paid a further £550 for the freehold at which time we increased the payments and made one further adjustment much later ending up with a monthly charge of £24.80 – and we thought times were hard! It was to prove a very good investment and a wonderful place to live and we were there until a year after we both retired at the end of 1988.

The mortgage was taken out in our single names and although we had advised the building society that we had got married at a later date it did not register with them. In the end I had to write them a letter saying that the children were beginning to read and would they please amend their records. They asked for a copy of the wedding certificate and when it was returned it had the stamp on it saying "Received Abbey National Building Society" and we were not amused.

During this period London fogs were a fairly common experience and on one Saturday we had a big band gig at Ealing Town Hall and visibility was so bad that Roy Sutton and I did not arrive until the interval to find the saxes, who lived nearer, had soldiered on alone. After the gig we got home very slowly indeed with the window down and my head out of the window. When nearly home we suddenly found ourselves in a small access road across Clapham Common with a tree right in front of the car. Once indoors I discovered that I had joined the Black and White Minstrels!

Early in 1952 King George VI died and for some considerable time afterwards it was not considered to be good form to play "The Merry Widow" for an old fashioned waltz, which was a pity as we did not know that many. Mind you on one function for an Irish company, in my innocence, I played one of the few Irish tunes I knew at the time – "The Sash My Father Wore". It turned out that we were playing for "the other side" and at that time it meant absolutely nothing to me!

About the same time we made plans to get married in June and asked Allan Ganley to be our best man to which he agreed. Jean's mother organised the invitations and because of the situation at home she did not include Jean's father on them and this was to cause considerable problems ultimately. The reception was arranged at Landor Halls, Clapham North for June 7th, otherwise known as D-Day plus one. We had access to the house some time before the wedding and dad and I were able to do a certain amount of decorating and moved in some of our new possessions before the big day. The actual service took place in St Stephens in Atkins Road, just a stone's throw from our new house. The vicar was a large character who moved around on a bicycle and always tried to doff his hat if he passed someone he knew and actually fell off on several occasions. Quite obviously our new found religion did not fool anyone and the church was pulled down within a few years!

Just before the day Allan advised us that he had been offered and accepted one of his earliest engagements on our wedding day to be and he would have to leave immediately after the service. He was to be playing in the Festival Gardens in Battersea Park with a group called The Celestino Quintet and obviously could not turn down the opportunity. Came the day and Allan arrived in the band uniform, which was a very light blue with very large padded shoulders, and after the service we assembled outside the church for photographs. After those of the bride and groom and closest relatives, had been taken Allan bade us goodbye and made off for the gig in the car he had borrowed from his father. Alas this broke down and Norman George stepped in to get him there on time. Thus we lost another of our guests.

We had made arrangements for my Uncle Jess to take over the function of best man which he did admirably. At the reception there were quite a number of musicians including Norman George, and Ronnie Gleaves – a vibraphone player who was probably one of the first to play with Dave Shepherd who still runs a British Benny Goodman type sextet and I have frequently played with

Roger Nobes – his current vibes player. Apart from this there was a bass player called George Woodruffe who had a reputation of being able to down a pint faster than anyone else. The fact that he had a hare lip and a considerable deformity inside his mouth had everything to do with this "ability" but he won quite a few pints by keeping quiet about this!

Now I swear that I did book a piano player to be present but he did not turn up so guess who played the piano. Mind you I never was any good at dancing and always found it difficult to relate to some of the "Come dancing" efforts to the music we were playing. Anyway a good time was had by all and at the end of the afternoon I have a memory of Uncle Cecil and George Woodruffe looking slightly the worse for wear at the back of the hall.

Jean and I went straight from the reception to our new home where we changed and made our way to the West End. We had to get a taxi for the last part of the journey and he braked suddenly causing Jean to hit her head on the glass partition. This could have been one of the earliest manifestations of a headache. Oh! And the show we saw at the Saville Theatre had Leslie Henson in "And So to Bed!"

The following weekend a small newspaper cutting appeared stuck on the wallpaper just above the mantelpiece in Jean's mother's house. It related to the wedding of Roy Cook to Jean Bateman, daughter of Mrs. D Bateman and the late Mr. Bateman! Unfortunately the photographer had put one and one together and really should have asked a question or two. Needless to say this was a bone of contention for a very long time indeed and any hope of reconciliation was finished- -not that there was much chance by this time anyway.

Allan Ganley, Roy's Dad & Mum, Roy & Jean, Jean's Mum & Uncle, Pearl Lucas

NOW WE ARE MARRIED

We spent the honeymoon in our new house and used most of the time getting everything in the right place. On one side we had Terry and Daphne who were most helpful although I quickly learned not to rely on Terry for any advice as he turned out to be a D.I.Y. fanatic. When they moved elsewhere some years later the new occupants spent several years removing most of his handiwork. On the other side were a brother and sister, much older than us, who, I believe, were not too enamoured of their new neighbours. These were terraced houses which were very well constructed, we were to discover, but despite this I expect the arrival of a grand piano must have caused some consternation. They had been built around the 1920's during the general strike period and the General Secretary of the Amalgamated Builder's Union lived just a few doors away. The story goes that they took their time and produced the houses to a very good specification bearing in mind that they had earmarked one for their own personal use. There is something of a parallel between this and the way my grandfather acquired 43 Laitwood Road. The General Secretary, Sir Luke Fawcett, was a man of considerable importance and was also a part-time member of the Atomic Energy Committee for some time and he was always very charming and easy to talk to.

Later in the year we went to the Stoll Theatre in Kingsway to see the first production in this country of George Gershwin's "Porgy & Bess" which starred William Warfield as Porgy, Leontyne Price as Bess, and Cab Calloway, the bandleader, as Sportin' Life and to this day this has to rank as the finest show I have ever seen. It was so good that we went three times and that is something I have only twice done more, firstly for the "Guys and Dolls" revival at the National Theatre and secondly for Stephen Sondheim's "Sweeney Todd" at the Theatre Royal.

Since then we have seen other productions of "Porgy" and "Sweeney Todd", but none of them compares to the original versions that we saw despite the fact that we paid a fortune to see "Porgy" at The Royal Opera House a few years back.

In November Rosa Lewis died aged 85 and the hotel was carried on for another 10 years by her lifelong companion Edith Jeffery.

We spent Xmas day with my folks but later in the holiday period we invited Allan Ganley complete with drums and a vibraphone player called Allan Graham, who was at that time working with the Jerry Allan Trio in a West End show, to stay. We had one session which carried on until around 1.30am the following morning. Next day I had a phone call from the brother next door saying "I say old boy – dog doesn't eat dog" and I had to apologise rather profusely and I have to agree that it was possibly a bit over the top even though it was holiday time.

In February 1953 new neighbours moved in two doors away at No.4. in the shape of Ray and Bunty Brooks and over the years we developed a very close relationship with them and still see them from time to time. They had four children and our two had a lot of fun with them over the years. Part of the reason for this was Ray's father, Dickie Brooks, who lived with his wife Winn in a house backing on to No.4. He had run his own Insurance business but was also a member of the Magic Circle and you may find it hard to understand why a few years later Jean and I found ourselves playing cards with him on a Wednesday evening with various other partners. He started by teaching us Canasta and when we actually won a few games decided it was time to educate us into the game of Bridge. It was some time before I realised that none of his close family ever made up the fourth man! Nevertheless he was good fun, was very young in spirit, and every year he used to organise an outing for half the street and on many occasions we used to go in convoy to Trent Park, Victor Sassoon's former mansion, where we had a swimming pool, tennis courts, and lavish grounds all to ourselves. He was a tireless organiser for the local Catholic Church and quite frequently roped me in on the piano and all the family joined us in whatever the function. Now his son Ray was a very studious person and always seemed to be engrossed, whether sitting in the window at home or out in the open air, and he eventually became Professor Ray Brooks, who is one of the leading experts in this country on the Endocrinal Gland, and as such is an authority on the use of steroids by athletes and has attended most of the Olympics and other games all over the world in this capacity.

I once asked him if he was ever besieged by irate athletes but he replied that it was usually little men wanting to enhance their physique. When he retired some years back he was presented with a gold plated model of a steroid – now not too many people have one of those. Once or twice a year he would take our children and his to Brighton just to collect limpets from the beach and by so doing I understand he was able to save quite a lot of money for the hospital where he worked.

In 1958 Miss Tanner and her brother moved to Worthing but shortly after, the brother died and it was not long before Miss Tanner moved back into Queensville Road and married and became Lady Fawcett.

The new occupants of No.6, Pat and Terry Reid, were nearer our age and again we had a lot of fun with them over the years. Terry was always good for a story, he illustrated some children's books and was the life and soul of any party. He and Pat did a double act for which she played guitar and when I consider the hours I used to practise on the piano we were very fortunate to have them next to us. On occasion they would even phone up for requests!

I remember going on one of his parties and meeting a friend of theirs, Stan Britt and his wife Mary. Now Stan has been responsible for the notes on many a jazz record and often gave talks to jazz appreciation societies. At one stage I heard he had tried to work on a book about Frank Sinatra (whilst he was still alive) and as I understand it was warned off in no uncertain manner. Since writing about this I tried to verify the facts at our local 2nd hand bookshop who, surprisingly, informed me that one book on Sinatra was published in America in 1966 and is not available here, but that another book by Stan was published in 1998 and quickly withdrawn, As Sinatra died in May1998 this possibly could be the explanation. Stan's wife, Mary, told me that they went to Ronnie Scott's to do an interview with one of the musicians once and while Stan was backstage she was left watching the performance in the company of John Le Mesurier. He asked if he could hold her hand - as it's so much nicer to share these experiences! What a smoothie. Unfortunately Stan and Mary parted some time back and I am told she has taken up holy orders and become a nun.

Both Terry and Pat, like myself at times, suffered from very severe bouts of sneezing which shook the foundations and later in life Terry was involved with organising functions for Fina for whom he worked until he retired. One such function was a golf outing and on one momentous occasion as the Chairman was in the act of driving off the first tee to open the proceedings Terry gave out an enormous sneeze which resulted in a terribly embarrassing shank and the ball hardly moved more than 10 yards or so. After much consultation it was agreed that he should be allowed to drive off again and of course the second drive was only marginally better than the first. Thus the Chairman glowered at Terry and marched off down the fairway! I think it only fair to say that Terry did not play golf and had no clue as to the etiquette involved!

During these early years we had a coke burning boiler in the kitchen which used to smoke quite badly, as did the fireplace in the dining room. This entailed a lot of attention to both flu and chimney and ultimately we decided to have a new boiler – The Ideal Concorde boiler – what a misnomer!! It had a handle which fitted into the end of the grate bars which formed a right-angle to the bars and when opened there was absolutely no way to void bashing your knuckles against the thermostat. After strong representations we were presented with a new lever angled away from the boiler which alleviated the problem – for a time. Then the operative part of the lever wore so badly we had to have two more and by this time the aperture in the grate bars had also worn and we were supplied with two more replacement sets! I made a point of visiting the Ideal Home Exhibition to make my feelings known as of course this did not happen overnight.

I did not mind doing the decorating although I was inclined to go at it hammer and tongs working right through the day into the night. On the other hand as I have previously indicated I am not really a D.I.Y. man. However there was one notable exception when I took on the challenge of making fitted wardrobes in our bedroom, which was a very large room. The end result fitted from floor to ceiling and incorporated four full size doors with a central section with two specially fitted recesses to take a rather splendid pair of Minton figures of a lion and a panther each with a naked lady sitting on the back. These were made from Parian, a white marble-like material and measured approximately 18" X 11" and about 10" tall. Nobody knows the true history of these but it is generally believed that Jean's father accepted them as payment for a debt years before. As they looked out of place when we moved we had them auctioned at Sotheby's a year ago and they fetched £1150. As I recall the total cost of this large unit was £29.10.00 but I fear my grandfather would not have approved. The frames for the doors did not include proper joints as you could put your toe under the doors until you hit the cross joints. I had also fitted decorative beading around the actual doors and was quite proud of the finished article. Of course in those days a kitchen was a very basic affair and it took several years before we bought a second hand Bendix Washing machine for £25 – which was a lot of money then.

In researching old copies of The Melody Maker to pinpoint exactly when I was playing in the clubs I came across an advert for the Feldman Club dated 7th Feb.1953 in which I was included in a band led by Ronnie Scott with Ken Wray, Harry Klein, Arthur Watts and Dickie Devere. This was on a bill which included Mary Lou Williams, the Jimmy Deuchar sextet, the Ross McManus Quintet with Sammy Walker and Tubby Hayes and also Cab Kaye, and the compere was Maurice Burman who helped me considerably over the years. He had of course been drummer with Geraldo prior to Eric Delaney. Now I had completely forgotten having played with Ronnie after completing army service and had always felt that my inclusion in the band was purely through the absence of other players in the forces. As the war was long since finished it was nice to feel that perhaps I had made the grade after all.

Shortly after this, thanks to my acquaintance with Keith

Bird, I was offered the chance to play with Eric Delaney's Group, comprising two tenor saxes, two trombones, trumpet, piano, bass, and drums. Eric was still with Geraldo at the time and in the main the group comprised other members of the big band. This included Don Lusher, who has only recently led the reformed Ted Heath band in its farewell concert and Maurice Pratt who was the other trombone player. Albert Hall was on trumpet, Keith Bird on tenor, Frank Donnison on bass and of course Eric on drums. I did all the gigs I could get to without taking time off work and in the main this was no problem as we were mostly playing at places like the Feldman Club, the Flamingo, and the 51 Club. The reason they used me was that Sid Bright, Geraldo's pianist and brother was not into jazz. Geraldo's real name was Gerald Bright. On the odd occasion that I could not possibly make it the big band arranger Alan Roper would step in. Other musicians who played with the group from time to time included Douggie Robinson on alto, and from outside Jimmy Skidmore, Bob Efford, and Eddie Mordue on Tenors and on rare occasions Johnny Hawksworth on bass. The latter was quite a character and I remember once we were playing at Welwyn Garden City and in the interval we were having a cup of tea, yes it was not drugs and drink all the time, and he distributed the lump sugar all over the cups that were set out, from a great height and at random. Eric was one of the first drummers to have two bass drums and to show the action to everyone he had a revolving stand made which was quite effective. One occasion when I first recall its use was at the Lyceum, which was then a dance hall, but has now converted back to a theatre. One Sunday we had three gigs, starting with a pub in North London where Mattie Ross, the blind pianist brought along a tune he had just composed which had no name so I suggested "Matt Finish". Many years later Mattie and I attended a benefit somewhere in Surrey and whilst waiting for a changeover I noticed Mattie very close to hand and I played the tune to him and asked if he remembered it. When he said "No" I pointed out that it was his own composition! The second gig was at the 51 Club and before we went on we saw the great Phil Seaman in action and I recall Eric saying "he ought to be locked up". Finally we ended up at the Astor and thus ended my most prolific day in such exalted company. At one time during his career Phil Seaman was working in the pit during "West Side Story" and in an interlude between the musical items he fell asleep. One of his colleagues gave him a nudge and Phil rose to his feet, gave an almighty thwack at the largest cymbal available, and announced "dinner is served". This turned out to be his last performance! I realise this has no relevance to my story but could not resist including it.

During this period I got to know Don Lusher quite well as he lived just up the road in some flats at the junction of the South Circular and Streatham High Road. Sometime during this year he moved out to New Malden and he invited Jean and myself to dinner with his first wife Eileen who had sung with Lou Preager in the past. By this time Jean was pregnant and was not feeling very well. Eileen was very concerned and strongly urged us to seek medical help without delay and I believe she had some background knowledge on these matters. The outcome was to prove that she was absolutely correct in her advice as Jean ended up having an operation for an ectopic pregnancy – a very serious and painful condition.

During the year Maurice Burman asked me to play for the golden anniversary of one of his uncles, in a large hotel by Baker Street Station. During this they showed a home movie which Maurice had made in which he took the part of everyone in an orchestra including the lady cellist, which was hilarious. At a later date this was shown at the Feldman Club prior to the evening session. On another occasion Keith Bird's wife Sue had developed T.B. and he organised a concert in the hospital at which the main Geraldo Orchestra, complete with singers Anne Sheldon and Derek Francis took part and I played with the Eric Delaney Group. I also took part in a benefit held at Wimbledon Town Hall for Joe Ferrie, another of the Geraldo regulars, and this is where I first came across Stan Tracy playing with his own trio amid a whole host of different groups.

This was the year of the Coronation and we watched the ceremony next door with Daphne and Terry as we did not have a set at that time. We had our first married holiday together and went to Jersey by Dakota, and found Freddie Harfield, the singer, working at a large hotel in one of the bays. In the band was a drummer Jackie Dougan who had played with Ronnie for some time and a very fine pianist whose name escapes me, but I often saw him on television when on holiday in the West Country later. I was fascinated by the way all the bars and hotels remained open at all times, and the fact that they nearly all had Bar Billiard Tables, which I enjoyed so much that we purchased a smaller version when we got back to London.

In May 1954 Eric Delaney left Geraldo to form his own big band and that ended my association with him. He did ask if I would join him but I had no illusions as to the radical change of life this would entail and I had no hesitation in refusing. From a personal point of view I am sure I gained far more pleasure as I was, and as it would entail a lot of touring this was not a lot different to being a travelling salesman, a position I had already turned down. Nevertheless I look on that part of my musical career as having been something rather special and privileged. In December of this year the Feldman Club finally closed its doors.

In a very few years the advent of the Beatles and the new style of music affected the jazz scene very badly and I was grateful not to have to rely on it for a living.

During this year Jean and I went with Laurie and his wife Eileen by car to the South of France and just over the border along the coast into Italy. I was best man at their wedding sometime earlier. We stopped at one or two places on the way down before we arrived at a delightful place on the coast slightly west of Marseilles called Bandol. Here we stayed for a few days and I recall it was so hot that Laurie fried an egg on the front on the concrete! At various places we were allowed to sit in with local groups and this stood us in good stead as most of the drinks were on the house. We eventually drove along the coast as far as Viarregio in Italy. Perhaps it would be more correct to say that Laurie drove all the way as I did not get a licence until 1961. Overall it was a very good holiday only slightly marred towards the closing stages when we were pulled up and fined on the spot for overtaking on the main road. We had actually followed another car but they let him go and stopped us. This meant that by arrival at Calais we were nearly skint! I mentioned before that I proposed to devote a chapter to Laurie and I feel this is perhaps the right place to commence so here goes.

Don Lusher, Johnny Hawksworth (Standing), Jimmy
Skidmore, Jean Cook, Eric Delaney, David Jacobs, Roy
Cook, Eric's wife and a friend.

THE MELODY MAKER AND RHYTHM   August 26, 1944

SENCE

t at present are FRED
(of London), alto sax and
"POP" TONE (of Dar-
1; BILL TAYLOR (of Man-
rums; and ERIC PEARCE
npton), trumpet.
as got into conversation
ver in France with an
ho was guarding an im-
ce; conversation turned to
Tom discovered his com-
ance been with Charlie

●

(O, for a moment, to
ans whose homes in
England" have been
"doodlebugs" reminds
or two members of Buddy
raugh's Sextet have been
in this respect.
AFFER has lost a part of
collection, and has had
i furniture severely dam-

blow, however, was to
t. 4 in. drummer, MON-
ILEY WATSON, whose
Slingerland " drum kit
P. variance, " gone for a

by the way, is now work-
propaganda programmes
i jazz numbers for the
which the Sextet is to
h jive for the people of
a.
to " streamline " and
l of Spike Hughes' com-
hich he feels are still
most interesting of this

When he hit London, in 1941, after incredible adventures in the Merchant
Navy, drummer Cab Quaye, soon finding himself discharged from the Service
after his dreadful experiences at sea, settled down to organise a band and
get himself "back into the groove" again. The above picture explains how
well his ambition has succeeded, for it shows Cab with his Ministers of Swing
at the Orchard Club, Wigmore St., W., where he has been playing now for
nearly two and a half years. With Cab presiding at the drums and also
making a corner in the vocal department, remaining three boys in the photograph are Charles Scott (bass); Ronnie Scott—no relation—(tenor); and Dick
Katz (piano). Last named is not a "regular"; he joined the band for a week
whilst regular ivory-tickler, youthful South London boogie-woogie discovery
·Roy Cook, took his well-earned holiday.

LAURIE

Laurie had been a surveyor for the Air Ministry before being called up. His father had been a high ranking Police Officer and his mother was formerly a police driver but the father died very early aged about 42. As a result Laurie was convinced that he would also die early and he seemed to be trying to live life to the full with a sort of desperation to it. He was very strong willed and from an army point of view this sometimes made my life difficult, being responsible for him as far as the band was concerned. I should add that this is not just my opinion but others felt he was not easy to get on with but nevertheless at the time I did not make an issue of it in the interests of harmony. I was never a Benny Goodman who seemed to go out of his way to antagonise the players that worked for him. There are some priceless stories of the Goodman era and just to digress a moment here are a couple of them.

One day he heard some promising young musicians in a club and asked if they would care to do a recording with him to which they readily agreed. He then suggested 8.30 am. the following morning which they reluctantly accepted. The studio was extremely cold and after a couple of numbers one of the lads said "Hey Benny - -it's very cold in here" – in response to which Benny said "Yes you're right and he went and put a pullover on!

On another occasion Victor Feldman was touring with the Goodman Band in Russia and on one of their days off he spotted Benny giving some money to a beggar in Red Square and Victor had a cine camera with him and filmed the action. When they got back to the U.K. Victor had a great time playing it to the rest of the band – in reverse! I also gather that nobody in the band was ever

109

allowed to outshine Benny and if they did they did not last much longer!

Now we must get back to Laurie.

He was inclined to be extremely careful over money and always felt that Lyon's Corner House gave you the best value where food is concerned, based mainly on the fact that you could return for more as often as you cared to, (mostly salads), and in later life transferred his affection to the transport café's all round the country. The sports jacket he always wore was always the subject of debate as to which was older, the jacket or Laurie!!

When we were demobbed we saw a fair amount of each other and for a while he rejoined the Air Ministry. After he married he moved to a large house in Streatham. The marriage was not a great success and there were serious problems with Eileen's brothers who were very protective of her. They divorced towards the end of 1954. At some time during the next two years he remarried and then sold the house in Streatham to enable him to buy a small caravan site in Brean, Somerset. Here he volunteered his services to survey the site for the local council and in so doing I understand he contrived to get space for 4 of 5 more caravans than were legally justified. His next move was to install a unit to make fish and chips on site for which he invested in a very rapid cooker to ensure quick turnover and this was quite successful.

Following this he set up about 40 fruit machines on his site and in several other establishments in the district which he primed to pay out often and of course these were a great success and gave him a very good return. He was not afraid of hard work and he serviced all the machines himself.

Jean and I were invited to stay for a holiday during 1957 and we had to go by rail as I did not start driving until 1961. As it happens, when we arrived all the local buses were on strike and of course leaving ourselves aside this would have made things difficult for his holiday trade at the camp. Not to be deterred he hired a covered lorry with a drop down tailboard and open back, put a very old three seater settee in the back un-tethered, and ran a collection service to and from the station. Of course the strikers were incensed by this and there was considerable debate in the local press on the subject. However the local vicar came out in support of Laurie and he was able to ride the storm comfortably – but not in the lorry! At some time I cannot pinpoint he also ran a guest house in Looe, Cornwall, but we did not visit him there.

Undoubtedly the next major venture was when he moved to Kerry and bought a house there and opened up the only fish and chip shop in Killarney. Because of the success of the range he had used at Brean he bought an identical unit and then found he had problems fitting it in the space available although there was not much in it. He then began chipping away at the adjoining wall until a picture fell off the wall next door. Laurie, typically went round to apologise with a bottle of wine which apparently overcame the difficulty! Thereafter he enjoyed a steady trade although from what I was given to understand apart from chicken, whatever they asked for was supplied from whiting. Here again he worked extremely hard at making it a success and I was told that on the odd occasion that the chipping machine broke down Laurie could be seen working it manually with very raw hands, sometimes bleeding!

In 1970 we were all invited to stay with him at his house in Killarney for a holiday. The only problem was that by the time we were due to arrive he had already sold the house. In fairness he made arrangements for us to stay with a local doctor, a lady, who made us most welcome and this was a very pleasant holiday with large beaches all to ourselves. In the evening she would make recommendations as to which hostelry to visit and when we walked in the door someone would approach and say "Welcome Mr. Cook" – which took getting used to. Invariably I would end up on the piano and we seemed to be out all hours, bearing in mind that Linda would have been 15 and Gary only 10 at the time. There was nearly always music of one sort or another in these places and the atmosphere was unlike anything I have experienced elsewhere. Again, rather like Jersey, the pubs seemed to be open all day.

I cannot be sure but I believe he decided it was time to move when some of the troubles touched ever so slightly on the area in which he was living.

His next port of call was Majorca where he ran the original English Pub for some time. We did not visit him there but I do recall him saying that some of the local sherries were so strong that they would react on the lino if spilt!

Then he bought some flats in Fuengirola in Spain and we were asked over for a further holiday. Needless to say everything was pretty basic and on the second night I turned over in bed and one of the springs went straight through my pyjamas. He was watching local television and programs like "Poldark" in Spanish. This was before they were allowed to pick up English speaking programs from Gibraltar and frankly I did not give this project much hope and it was not long before he was back in the U.K.

Finally he started running The Mill House Hotel, an Ashley Courtenay recommended establishment in Sussex listed by Michelin, the A.A. and the R.A.C. He invited Jean and myself and Colin Rowe and his wife Betty for dinner one evening and we were highly amused that he should still show these accolades on his card when for example he would bring the whole plate to the table in one – no side plates or whatever. Michelin recommendations had no place in this establishment!!

We still saw him from time to time but I fear I got the stage when his constant preoccupation with quoting the prices of nearly everything he touched finally got to me. This reached a peak when we were about to enter a restaurant where I had already decided on a nice fillet steak and he turned to his partner, his second marriage having also broken up, and said to her – "we don't want to pay these prices for that do we" – and that was my dinner gone for the day. If that was not bad enough when Laurie talked he left no room for interruption and I can recall many an evening when, despite being really tired, I sometimes waited as long as forty minutes just to get an opening to say good night! It was a shame but there was absolutely no alternative and he is one of the few people I have ever felt the need to break away from.

In case I may have given the wrong impression I should emphasise that there was never any shortage of money on his side, and he was not ungenerous, but his budgetary control seemed to be in charge of him every minute of every day. Nevertheless a very complex and amazing character who, despite his fears, was still alive when I received my last Xmas card from him in his late seventies last year.

STARTING A FAMILY

Towards the end of 1954 Jean became pregnant again and because of the problems she had previously she was given very careful attention throughout. Once again things did not go smoothly and as a result she was admitted to hospital in St. James, Balham, well before her time, for close observation. I used to cycle in on my bike regularly after work until one day on entering the ward I saw the curtains were drawn around the bed. When I looked inside she was not to be seen and on making enquiries I discovered she had been transferred that day to The Weir Hospital which was much nearer to where we lived. Her condition had deteriorated and she had a severe case of toxaemia which causes increased blood pressure and considerable swelling because of water retention. When I arrived at the hospital I asked for Mrs. Cook and was directed to one of the wards. As I walked round I really could not see Jean at all. Then one of the patients suggested that there was a Mrs. Cook a little way down on the opposite side of the ward but when I walked past this woman was quite enormous and had it been Jean then there must have been a very radical change from the previous day. Nevertheless I was very concerned that I might be walking past her without realising it! Then it dawned on me what a common name we have and I eventually found her in another ward and, although she was undoubtedly quite swollen, thankfully I could at least recognise her, and she me. In all Jean was in hospital for something approaching two months and Linda was finally born five weeks premature, weighing 4lbs 7ozs, on April 1st 1955. From my point of view I was extremely grateful at the time as the early arrival meant I was entitled to a whole year's income tax rebate which at the full term would not have been permitted. Because of the problems they were both kept in the prem. unit for some considerable time after and I cannot speak too highly of the care and attention they received. We called her Linda believing that this was a name, rather like our own, that could not be easily corrupted. Why her friends call her Lin and Lu or Lindy I will never understand. When Gary was born 5 years later we adopted the same premise so why he is sometimes called Ga or Garth?

There was one tense moment in the hospital when the baby (Linda) suddenly turned blue, as can happen, but fortunately, Sister Stradwick who was in charge of the prem. unit knew exactly what to do and the emergency was over. Many years later Jean attended her retirement party together with another woman who had been in at the same time and lived very close to us.

Needless to say both Jean's mother and my parents were highly delighted and anxious to help – sometimes Jean would have preferred to cope on her own, but in the main there was no problem. Not being particularly religious neither Jean nor I were keen on having a church christening but after considerable pressure from both sides we finally yielded and arranged for my Aunt Ethel and Pam and Ray Gladwell to be Godparents. Pam had been a close friend of Jean's at school.

Thus began the era of sleepless nights, though to be honest I fear Jean took the brunt of these mainly because in those days I could sleep like a log and nothing disturbed me. How I wish I could say the same now that the positions are reversed! Five years later on 21st April 1960 Gary was born and this time things went a lot smoother than previously – thank goodness! For the christening we arranged for Jean and John Denny from Ipswich to be godparents.

Linda grew up to be a very likeable child who was very

easy to get on with. In addition when Gary came on the scene she looked after him from the very early days and a tremendous bond exists between them to this day. What is quite amazing is that the 5 year age gap between the two has been repeated now that Linda has become a mother to Emily and Thomas and a similar rapport exists there too. Both Linda and Gary were born in April, on the 1st and 22nd. Emily and Thomas were born in January on the 18th and the 10th. And but for the fact that Linda was born prematurely even the gap between the two would have been almost the same. Jean and I, both being only children feel that it perhaps would have been nicer to have a brother or sister to confide in, but on the other hand there are some advantages.

As I said before they both attended Cavendish Road School in the Infants first and then the Junior Section and were good at most subjects. In the junior section they had a very enthusiastic music teacher who organised a very good end of term concert when Linda was leaving. After the concert I gave him a piano copy of Oscar Petersen's "Canadia Suite" and I was delighted when attending a later concert to hear him perform with the orchestra one of the pieces from it which he had arranged himself. What a difference to my own experiences at Ipswich!

In November 1963 there was the fateful day when President Kennedy's shooting shocked the world and it has been customary to try to remember what happened to you personally that same day. When I was nearing home after work I came across the scene of an accident which had only just taken place involving a young schoolgirl at a junction of Thornton Road. As no medical help seemed to be available I drove straight on to the next turning where my doctor had his surgery, collected him very quickly and conveyed him back to the scene.

116

Unfortunately this story does not have a happy ending and as a result I always recall two needless deaths on that day.

It was around this period that Jean became a helper in a private school in a very large house just around the corner in Atkins Road and she was allowed to take Gary with her as he was not then old enough for proper schooling. In addition she decided to try to do something for mothers with young children, like herself, to give a couple of hours relief once a week. To this end she obtained permission to use the Church Hall on the corner of Laitwood Road, where my parents lived. With the help of Anne Masters, a close friend who lived not far away, they organised these meetings and started off wheeling two prams laden with toys to the hall, where both Jean's mother and mine gave a helping hand. They managed to get a speaker most weeks to address the parents whilst they entertained the children in a separate section.

Anne Masters met her husband Alan when they were in the Navy. At one time Alan was on the Royal Yacht – Britannia. He is a first class photographer and it you saw the film of Sir Francis Chichester crossing the Atlantic on television after the event that was all his own work. Chichester insisted on having Alan because he was an experienced seaman. Alan spent some time filming him during the preparation trials in the Carrick Roads and then filmed him from overhead by helicopter as he left these shores and later on arrival across the Atlantic.

In time the enterprise of Jean and Anne reached the ears of the Save the Children Fund organised in the area by a wonderful man called Ernie Randall. The hall itself was very run down and they firstly put the piano over a very large hole in the floor until Ernie not only covered it with linoleum, but also provided a lockable chest to store the toys and save all the carting about. This was in effect one of the very first pre-school playgroups and was very popular indeed. In later years Ernie was able to get Jean's help at a summer camp he was running to which she was able to take Gary, who, being the youngest present, was well and truly spoilt.

After a time her efforts came to the attention of the Junior Headmistress of Cavendish Road School, almost opposite, and she invited Jean to join the staff to help with the children which she did most successfully. After a while the Head persuaded Jean to go to college as a mature student so that once qualified she would receive proper remuneration for her abilities.

There followed 4 years of study at Phillipa Fawcett College in Streatham which was a very testing period indeed. Despite the hectic life involved Jean thoroughly enjoyed the experience and she had to choose a subject for intense study and this started us all on the road to becoming birdwatchers. She concentrated mainly on pigeons and also took up woodcarving and we still have several fine examples of her work around the house including a small cluster of four birds mounted on springs and a squirrel and a pottery pigeon. At one stage she also produced a set of chessmen in wood for which I provided squares in two shades of leather, dark and light, to form the basis of a chess board. One day on arrival at the college Jean saw a cardboard coffin emerging from the main doors and thought to herself that it must be student's rag day. Unfortunately nothing could have been further from the truth as one of the younger students had set himself on fire in the woodwork area and as a result the chessmen were no more which was a tragedy from two points of view.

Another first year student who joined at the same time as

Jean was a young, rather tall, Austrian girl named Ursula Kassin and one of the tutors asked Jean, as a mature student who was also quite tall, to keep a watchful eye on her and help where possible. The result was that she became a lifelong friend with whom we keep in touch regularly. Unfortunately she now resides in New Zealand with Judy Simpson, a New Zealander who befriended her in London when she first arrived here. Before they left this country we dined together almost every week and it was a real blow, in particular for Jean, when they left for good.

Ironically Ursula used to baby-sit for a couple where the wife was a quite well known concert pianist and many years later after we retired we decided to have a once-in-a-lifetime round the world holiday about which I intend to deal separately. By this time the boy had well and truly grown up – to become a Jazz pianist. His name is John Law and we were asked to get hold of a copy of a C.D. he had just produced to take to New Zealand, which we did. Unfortunately whilst he has tremendous technique his playing comes within the avant-garde variety and I fear this is not my cup of tea. Furthermore my experience is that there is a very limited audience for this type of jazz. I would like to think that maybe he will be tempted to modify his style as he has scope to do almost anything with his technique.

During their schooldays we once went just with Gary for a holiday just north of Ipswich at a place called Yoxford. On the first Sunday we decided to pay a visit to Easton Farm Park situated between these two places where they had all sorts of events specifically for children. In those days I had a Renault 12 with a centre armrest in the front and on arrival, after getting out of the car, I locked the front doors, whilst the rear doors were still open. I then decided it was too hot to wear a jacket and without thinking threw it into the car, shut the back doors, which had child-proof locks, and went off round the farm. Because it was a busy Sunday they had created extra space in the fields for use as car parks. It was to close around 6.30 pm and we went to leave at around 5.45 only to discover that I had, by merely closing the doors, locked my jacket, complete with car keys, inside the vehicle. Now this particular make of car had no quarter lights and was much more secure than most other similar vehicles. I was not too worried as I had seen similar situations overcome by the police in London who seemed to possess large bunches of keys covering every eventuality. First off we called out the R.A.C. who tried using lengths of wire but they could not help. Similarly when the local constabulary came I found that they were not so well equipped as in London and could not gain entry. By this time there were only a few cars left and the farmer started to let the cows back into the fields and in not time at all there were two or three trying to lick the paint off my car! I managed to get a few people to help me bounce it out of the area into a safe position and then went to phone my Uncle Cecil in Ipswich. His car was out of action at the time but he contacted his neighbour who happened to be a very well-known undertaker who sent one of his very best funeral cars to take us to our hotel! Once there I telephoned Linda to find out the key number from the spare set I had left at home. I then passed this on to Uncle Cecil who promised to go to the dealer in Ipswich next morning to get hold of a spare. I left Jean and Gary at the hotel and went alone to the farm to meet him. The garage sent him with an assortment of keys none of which did the trick. Uncle Cecil went back to the garage and finally they located the right key and he made his way back to us. Meantime they had set the sprinklers on in the field to which the car had been pushed and when my uncle arrived I was sitting cross-legged in an adjoining field trying to do the crossword in the Daily Telegraph. I have a photograph of the two of us in raincoats just about to gain access, by which time it was almost mid-day. Gary reminds me that I was not too happy especially as I developed a heavy cold as a result – still I suppose it could have been E-Coli or even B.S.E.

Having qualified Jean rejoined Cavendish Road School for a while until an opportunity arose for her to join Hyde Farm School which was not far away from home, close to Tooting Bec Common. This was a special school dealing with problem children having all kinds of difficulties. The classes comprised no more that 10 to 15 pupils and sometimes less and Jean gradually became very adept in dealing with these children. When the head, Gil Williams was promoted to a newly built school for similar children – Susan Isaacs – he took Jean with him and as this was on the other side of Clapham Common this created problems as, although it was not far away as the crow flies, it required two buses to get there, in which time it would have been easier to walk across the common. As we now know Clapham Common, day or night is not the place for an unaccompanied woman (or M.P.) so we had to get her a car and driving lessons.

I had done quite a few gigs with a fine Scottish alto player, Wally Glen, who also gave driving lessons and in the end he not only got Jean through, but later Linda and Gary, all first time. Jean passed her test just before Xmas and I could not resist pinning a large notice to the front door reading – THE FIRST NO L ! Little things....

In all Jean spent 19 years in education and a large part of this came at the end of the period when she was taken on as a teacher in the Wandsworth Child Guidance Clinic working with Psychiatrists and Psychotherapists and Social Workers, a very taxing occupation. The office was right in the centre of the Wandsworth one way system and took some reaching during the rush hour. I was highly amused when they held a meeting to discuss an ex pupil of Jean's who, despite having difficulties in some directions, had the ability to read almost anything at sight. When they asked Jean if this was true she pointed out that the first time he came across a Psychotherapist's title he read Psycho – the Rapist!

In most cases these children, aged anything from 7 to 16 years old, had very serious problems. One had pushed his teacher through a plate glass window. Another threatened to set fire to the house of a girl he was being prevented from seeing and in the end he did just that. We were really quite shocked when we read in the local paper that one of the ex-pupils had murdered another ex-pupil.

Despite these difficulties Jean had the right sort of approach to get results from most of her pupils. In many cases their inability to read was the main factor – something that most of us take for granted. To try to imagine what it must be like just to look round you almost anywhere – if you cannot read the signs or the instructions what on earth do you do – particularly if you do not possess the social graces to ask the right questions and could quite easily be looked upon by outsiders as peculiar – to say the least.

Over the years Jean created a series of games through which a very large percentage of her pupils learned to read and what's more to enjoy the method. These she also passed on to Ursula and Judy and several other teachers of her acquaintance all of whom found the most useful. Ursula is still teaching in New Zealand and continues to employ them. Now there was a period some 10 to 15 years ago when there was an outcry for some new ideas on the subject of reading and because of this we offered the scheme to every publisher we could think of.

As usual this coincided with a period when like most people they were having a hard time and nobody was prepared to take the risk. The Prince of Wales made lots of noises on the subject but when we wrote to his office we received the standard, fairly curt letter saying he could not possibly become involved, and I very much doubt whether it was even shown to him. I am quite certain that there are a lot ex-pupils who owe a lot to Jean who spent hours at home after school working on projects for the next day. For her part there was a great satisfaction in having achieved success with other people's failures. That she managed to achieve so much whilst still maintaining a very happy home life says a lot for her.

Turning to Linda, she took up the recorder at first and then had piano lessons from a Miss Jacks in the vicinity of Sistova Road. Later on she took up the flute and reached grade eight on both piano and flute – no mean achievement. After leaving Cavendish Road School she went to St. Martin in the Fields Secondary School in Tulse Hill which was a very fine school. There she played in the school orchestra and reached a standard which resulted in her being put forward for extra tuition on the flute at Pimlico School on Saturdays. This was where the London Schools Symphony Orchestra was created together with The London Schools Training Orchestra, and the London Schools Concert Band. Here they were treated as adults even though nobody over the age of 16 could remain in the School. The young musicians in these ensembles represented the cream of the London area and we were very proud that she managed to secure a place in the Training Orchestra playing both flute and piccolo. We went to all her concerts and those of the main orchestra which were held in The Festival Hall, The Barbican, St. John's, Smith Square, and other rather splendid locations such as The Banqueting House in Whitehall, scene of the execution of Charles the First. In those days the main

Orchestra was often conducted by Simon Rattle and I still recall a wonderful performance of Tchaikovsky's 4th Symphony at the Festival Hall which not only brought the house down but achieved rave reviews the next day.

St. Martin's of course had close affinity with the Church in Trafalgar Square and at a pre Xmas carol concert the school orchestra was joined by Cleo Laine and John Dankworth. Recently Linda attended a celebration at the school on its 300th anniversary together with several of her ex classmates. The concert given on this occasion was attended by the Queen and was most notable for the fact that the staging supporting the choir collapsed during the performance and we actually saw this on the T.V. News that evening. Fortunately nobody was hurt and they resumed after a short delay. So far this has not been shown again by Dennis Norden! Whilst at St. Martins Linda was taught sometimes in conjunction with a young very talented black piano player called Errol Reid who came from another school, St. Martins being a girl's school. He ultimately went on to perform with a pop group of the day "Mac and Katie Kassoon" and sometimes came to our jazz parties at home and provided an interlude to our regular jazz. I have not heard anything further about him since those days.

For a while we shared the services of an elderly lady with one of our near neighbours to clean the house and on occasion stay with Linda and Gary until we arrived home. On a few occasions we were both late coming home and I took Josie home by car to the block of flats where she lived just north of Clapham North. It was a very tall block and when I walked her to her flat several floors up I was astonished to see that the front door to each apartment was behind a very substantial metal security barrier.

At the time I had not appreciated the need for such

precautions but of course in April 1981 we heard from a distance the noise of police cars during Brixton riots.

When still at St. Martins Linda also played with the Streatham Philharmonic Orchestra led by Edward Bloomfield and on another occasion by Dave Crawley. I recall one occasion when they asked to rehearse in our house and we had no less than 17 string instruments in our lounge which only measured 15ft by 14ft overall. I swear I saw a bow coming through the keyhole in the door on one occasion – but perhaps I exaggerate a little!

Linda gained 7 ½ O levels, and 2 A levels in Music and English and passed with very good grades. For her 18th birthday we had a wonderful day starting with lunch at the Anchor at Bankside, a very famous London landmark and the food was excellent. Later we all went to Covent Garden to see a program starting with Elgar's Enigma Variations followed by The Concert, a really hilarious ballet with Wayne Sleep, and rounding off with my personal favourite Daphnis and Chloe – a sumptuous feast for the eye and ear. And the icing on the cake was a visit to Ronnie Scott's where the Bill Evans Trio was starring with a girl singer and separate trio but for good measure and I believe it was only a one off situation we had John Williams playing solo classic guitar in between. A most memorable day!

Linda obtained a place at Newton Park College, just outside Bath, but for the first year she stayed at accommodation on one of the main roads leading into Bath proper. Recently she was invited to a restaurant called The Olive Tree, attached to a new hotel called The Queensbury and suddenly realised this was where she spent her first year at college!

The next two years were spent living in at college during

which she was very active with the orchestra and played at concerts in the Cathedral and the Pump House amongst others. She finally graduated with a B.Ed. Hons. And we attended the ceremony at Bristol University.

Unfortunately this was a time when there was a huge shortage of places for new teachers and she finally obtained a position at a school in Sutton-on-Sea in Lincolnshire where there were no fewer than 307 applicants – a pretty good result by any standards.

The downside of this was Sutton-on-Sea, a more bleak uninteresting place you cannot imagine. We visited her on a Bank Holiday and even the birds had gone somewhere else and I vaguely recall reading an article which suggested that the main activity in the town for holidaymakers was a succession of people wearing cagouls promenading down one side of the main street and back on the other. In a lighter vein Ronnie Scott once wrote about Lincolnshire that the pigeons flew upside down because there was nothing worth s......g on!

She did her best to fit in and joined a local choir where she was the youngest member by a country mile! However after a while even the Headmaster encouraged her to look elsewhere for a teaching job as he thought it was quite unsuitable and after 18 months she landed a job back in Trowbridge, Somerset and she bought a flat on a new estate in Frome which was not too far away. Of course this put her back amongst a lot of friends form college days and she had quite a good social life here. On one of her birthdays (i.e. April 1st) she passed by the White Horse at Westbury, one of those enormous figures carved into the hillside, to find that by the judicious use of a lot of black plastic bags it had been turned into a zebra overnight. She joined an Inter Varsity Club and through this she met Colin Blackman who was then working in Bath for the Ministry of Defence as naval architect. All went well until Colin was posted to Gosport in Hampshire and it was this that triggered the wedding in August 1988.

This was held at a delightful registry office in Merton alongside which was a working waterwheel in almost open country – i.e. Morden Hall Park. Jack, my cousin Kath's husband was brought up very close to here and I do not think that there can be another similar place in the country. This was the year I was preparing for retirement and we decided that the reception should be held at our house, which was terraced, and the back garden was very small indeed measuring approximately 20ft x 40ft.

We hired a small marquee which was fitted directly on to the back of the house with a wooden floor which butted on to the French windows level with the dining room floor and this left a tiny border all round and could not have worked out better. Needless to say some of my musician friends supplied the music and it was generally rated as a complete success. I drove Linda to the ceremony and Colin went there in his own car and drove his bride back to the reception – and the chap with the white Rolls Royce shed a few tears!

They spent their honeymoon in the Seychelles and came back to a small modern house in Gosport that Colin had purchased.

Turning to Gary, after leaving Henry Cavendish School he qualified to get to Emanuel School in Battersea, another school with a fine reputation. He, like Linda, had become very proficient on the piano with another teacher who called at the house, and whilst at his new school he also took up the recorder, followed by the oboe. Much later he was co-opted to play the Racket with the schools early music group alongside the Headmaster and they

127

performed amongst other places at the Victoria and Albert Museum. Mind you the Racket is a most unusual instrument comprising a wooden cylinder some six inches long and having an enormous reed on top, almost an inch wide, making a very low and rather dirty noise, one of the earlier forms of bass instruments. He also took part in a light operetta on one occasion.

In his early years at the school he was relatively small and compact for his age and ended up being in great demand as a Cox for the rowing crews for which the school was quite famous. Around this time one of their former pupils took part in the Oxford and Cambridge Boat Race as Cox and on occasion Gary was called upon to act for various rowing clubs not connected with schools. Quinton Boat Club asked for his services at Marlow Regatta and we all went to see the fun. I did not realise then that the Cox has to be weighed in, rather like a jockey, and at that time he weighed so little that they gave him a bag of sand to make up the weight. Trouble was the sand was so heavy he had problems lifting it. Anyway they lined up for the start and the race began. As he had been trained to do at Emanuel Gary issued a command – something like "Touch em two!" and the chap rowing immediately in front of Gary said "Shirrup!" However the joke was on him as the crew were so bad that the umpire's launch overtook them and I do not remember seeing this happen anywhere else. I must say it was a really glorious day and during his time at Emanuel we enjoyed many an outing, especially at Henley where his school's first eight usually put up a good performance. On another occasion he was asked to attend a Regatta being held for the first time for years on the Serpentine in Hyde Park sponsored by one of the big banks. I believe this was also for Quinton and Gary turned up in a very tatty track suit the bottoms of which looked almost petal shaped and this time he was with a four who actually won. Now Gary did not expect to have to get out of the boat but the prizes were presented by the Chairman's wife, who for some reason did not want to lean over the boat – I can't think why – and of course Gary was revealed in all his glory – and – yes – I have a photo to prove it!

On another occasion they were practising for the Head of the River Race on the Thames, this being an annual event in which several hundred teams are timed over a set course at intervals. As I understand it they came across either the Oxford Crew or Cambridge, but either way Gary was instructed to tell them to "get out of the way" or words to that effect! Towards the end of his days at Emanuel he had begun to put on both height and weight and he took part on what is known as the Boston Marathon. This takes place from Lincoln to Boston on a 32 mile course which took several hours and when he finally got out of the boat at the end he almost fell into the water. This was a tremendous achievement and we were very proud to see how well he had done.

He made good progress in most subjects and had started taking A levels when he got up one morning complaining of being unwell. I suggested he should try putting his fingers down his throat to make himself sick (a time honoured system as far as I personally was concerned). I have to say I thought it could have been a question of exam nerves and I left for work hoping all would be well. When I got home I was most upset to learn that far from being better he had been whisked of to the hospital in preparation for an emergency appendix operation. I arrived just in time to walk alongside him to the theatre and he was almost green in the face by then. In contrast I was red in the face. So much for the sympathetic father! They were very good at the school and made arrangements for him to take the remaining exams in the hospital and fortunately he gained the necessary grades to get to college. He gained a place at Exeter to study Maths, Statistics, and Operational Research and became Captain of his house and from then on has never looked back. He is a great organiser and to this day is still in contact with some of his college colleagues and indeed people from every organisation he has worked with ever since. At college some of the tutors told him that with a little more effort he could have achieved grade one passes. Gary told them he was more interested in leading a balanced life and this has stood him in very good stead, and there is absolutely nothing wrong with his abilities. He has of course been involved with computers ever since.

For a time he lived with a partner in Putney but unfortunately she was so highly motivated to try to achieve great things – which she did – that it just did not work out. Apart from the work aspect she had once swum for Wales and she became involved in a little known sport called Octopush which is a sort of underwater hockey and ended up playing for the British ladies team both in this country and abroad. They were together for eight years overall.

Gary has always been good with people and in the last few years he has been studying counselling at weekends and evenings. In the last few months he has negotiated a four day week so that he can take on the necessary clients to achieve the requirements of the course on the odd day. He has recently met a very nice girl who seems to be more on his wave length and we have high hopes that this will develop into something positive.

I mentioned his organising abilities and one of his achievements is the cycling group that has grown up over several years which include people from his various contacts over the years. Every year they visit another country on trips which he organised and they have a tee-shirt on the back of which they list every one. I believe the last one was attended by fourteen of the gang, male and female, and a good time was had by all. So you see we have even been lucky with our children – or perhaps we can take some credit for the way things have turned out.

Gary, Colin Roy, Emily, Jean, Linda & Thomas

BACK TO THE FACTORY

Working with Barrow Hepburn I gradually made steady progress and was made overall manager in charge of both production and sales and indeed every possible aspect was my province and this I found very rewarding. At the time I often likened my position to an advert which was current at the time which spoke of "Having the strength of the insurance companies around you". In fact over the years the leather department, size for size, in most years gave a far better return, albeit on a smaller turnover, than most other departments. I recall one particular year when the return on capital employed reached 80%.The job required careful attention to detail as everything had to be produced exactly to fairly close limits and unless made correctly the finished article would not work. In many cases the customers would be in a breakdown situation and this required to be dealt with both promptly and accurately. Now I had no problem with this but, because of the attention to detail required, I found many of my assistants gave up after a very short period and frankly I found this hard to comprehend. Mind you in the years that followed there was many an occasion that my brighter assistants, and even some of the secretaries I had were snaffled for the conveyor side of the business – and I really could not stand in their way.

The factory had been moved from Bermondsey to Mitcham during the early part of the war and was located both sides of a fairly busy road. Originally the conveyor side of the business was on one side only but with the developments which had taken place requiring larger and more up to date equipment there came a time when it was necessary to find space for a rotocure to produce conveyor belting continuously and not in 30ft. press lengths. This was built on the other side of the road but certain preparatory processes still had to take place on the opposite side. This meant that huge rolls of material weighing several tons had to cross the road from time to time with obvious disadvantages. A later development was our venture into manufacturing Steel Cord reinforced Conveyor Belting. This required the steel cords to be tensioned at both ends and the press was on rails and moved along vulcanising a press length at a time. This took up quite an area on the original side. For many years we held a very small part of the N.C.B. Conveyor Belt Contract – tendered for annually, and we were up against all the major producers such as Dunlop and Goodyear and at an obvious disadvantage. Finally a decision was taken to opt out and use our capacity for more lucrative quarry business and the like, but even this was very competitive.

In my early days we also manufactured rubber flooring tiles and mouldings and also sponge sheeting including Church Kneelers and to this day I have one of these for use when gardening – certainly not for any other use! Mind you I feel it is perhaps time to buy a new one. (Did I ever mention that I was once taken for a Jew in Palestine!) Anyway because of the problems with conveyors it was decided to give up manufacture and leave Mitcham and make arrangements to carry stocks of finished belting in the popular sizes purchased from our former competitors. After many meetings we were told that sufficient space could be found back at Bermondsey and I had to draw up plans for the removal and re-installation of all our equipment, including thousands of moulds. At the same time it was essential to keep some of the production going at both ends and I am pleased to say that on the first day in our new premises we had almost half of the major items of machinery up and running.

I had a very serious problem however. By this time Joe Weight had retired and because our trade required someone with intimate knowledge of the customer's needs, and the tooling, I had been compelled to appoint Jock Bruce, his assistant, as foreman, the person with most of the knowledge required, to replace him. Until then Jock had been the shop steward, which he had since given up, but apart from this his wife was working under him in the leather department. Now I was under strict instructions to tell no one in the factory what was to happen, until the official announcement, and to make matters worse I also knew that Jock and his wife, who lived in Bermondsey, had made plans to move out to Epsom! Knowing him, I had to agree that it would have been fatal to forewarn him, and I certainly did not endear myself to him when he went ahead and moved! At this moment I find it hard to recall how I managed to draw up detailed plans for the move without giving the game away – largely at home I suspect!

From my personal point of view the change of address meant that I was going slightly further in the opposite direction but there was much more traffic about – nevertheless my luck was still holding – it could have been much worse. Over the years we acquired several other manufacturers apart from J.H. Fenner including Edgar Vaughan, Rose, Downs & Thompson, and Nobes & Hunt whose filing cabinet appeared to be an open top tea chest! At the same time the conveyor side was also taking over various former competitors. One of the first of these was W.T. Lambourne Co., run by Leslie Lambourne, a thorough gentleman. The story I like best is when he had to officiate at the retirement of his warehouse foreman who had been with the company for many, many years. Believe it or not they had to introduce him to the man first! Now that's what I call a gentleman!!

It was during the six years we remained at Bermondsey that new faces in the from of Michael Horsman and the playboy John Bentley (he of Mynah Bird fame) came on the scene as non executive directors on the main board. I spent all of fifteen minutes walking through my department with John Bentley once and he showed absolutely no interest in what was going on, and O.K. it was not the most up to date looking place, but his sole concern was whether we had any patents of value.

During our time at Bermondsey a regular visitor was the Reverend Percy Gray who was vicar of St. Crispin's, the patron saint of shoemakers. I understand that George Odey had supplied him with a small car and he used to call on the various parts of the company just in time for a gin & tonic – or whatever. He had been in the Paratroop Regiment and was often in the news following arguments with the Bishop of Southwark. He was of course available for counselling when required but on one occasion he used his former army experience to help promote some of the safety equipment made by our associate company. One New Year's Day he jumped off London Bridge wearing climbing equipment and a full photo occupying half the back page appeared in the Evening News – a very large picture indeed. I'm told that as he jumped one of the helpers called out "Hey Vicar – you're going the wrong way!"

Whilst we were at Bermondsey we had a chap in the office who had recently married and got into problems with his accommodation and I tried to help. My mother knew a lady in her road, Laitwood Road, who had rooms to offer and we were able to get them fixed up. Now a very few years later Rosemary Brown, the landlady, achieved considerable fame when she claimed to have psychic powers and that some of the great composers had dictated new compositions to her.

This caused quite a furore at the time and ultimately concerts were held by some very famous musicians playing these new works which were assessed by those in the know as being very plausible. I am the last person to have any such beliefs but the fact is that my mother had known this person for many years. She could play the piano but was by no means a virtuoso and yet she was capable of putting extremely complicated parts on paper which she herself could not play easily. Furthermore because her husband had been unwell for some time she had been working at Cavendish Road School, as a dinner lady and there was certainly nothing to suggest that she was remotely capable of carrying out such a massive fraud, that is if fraud is the correct word.

Eventually, by 1972, it was decided that there was a need to move the whole of the factory including Barrow Hepburn Equipment, who had been there throughout the war, to separate premises. After many attempts to find a suitable place it was decided that we would go to Battersea on the premises formerly occupied by a firm of builders, surrounded on two sides at right angles by the railways. The Equipment Company had a separate building and we were in two other buildings at the far end of a large courtyard all of which was sealed off from the road by a large gate. The part the leather department was to occupy was on two floors and the moment I went upstairs I discovered that the floor was wooden and I could bounce up and down on it, it was so springy. As the gin leather section would have to be here we quickly decided that a new concrete floor would have to be floated and in fact this was not completed until a few weeks before we were due to move. I meantime had planned where the machinery was to go based on the drawings showing the support pillars for the new floor, helped of course by the experience of the earlier move, enabling us to avoid the odd pitfall we had come across on that occasion. When we were able to go into the completed building I then discovered to my horror that two of our presses on the ground floor were too tall, and that the ceiling had been made lower than had been agreed. To overcome this we had two square holes cut to accommodate the machinery in question. Then I found that the supporting pillars were also not where the drawing showed and this meant a lot of hasty re-arrangement. On the ground floor there was the need for a large soaking tank with overflow into the drains which had to be specially dug for the purpose. When they were completed I took one look at the floor and got a bucket of water and poured it towards the drain and – guess what – it went the other way! Somehow the gods were against us. In the other building, which housed a huge overhead crane and was being converted to hold large rolls of belting, they had put down a new concrete floor. The same night we were broken into and they not only stole a large amount of copper which was crucial to the workings of the crane but made all sorts of footprints and depressions in the floor which had not properly set. Despite the clues I do not remember anyone being arrested for this.

The factory at Bermondsey had enjoyed the presence of a live-in caretaker and this could not be continued at Battersea. During the move it was decided to employ security guards at night and we ended up with two Pakistani guards and a dog costing £100 each per night which in those days was a lot of money. They came from a reputable company but I was very amused one morning when Dan Powell, who was then in charge of the Equipment Company asked one of the guards whether they had any problems. The answer was "Vell it was velly difficult – ve didn't know the name of the dog!!"

In these very early days at the new premises, the senior

management had to attend courses held at the Midland Hotel, Manchester. I believe Dick Odey had instigated these, which were organised by the Manchester Business School run by Professor Roland Smith, who ultimately was to become Chairman. I can never understand why anyone believes it is possible to take in a mass of new information if you work them from nine in the morning until ten o'clock at night with minimal breaks for food etc. By the end of the day we used to go out for a run round the building just to get some fresh air. One of the lecturers told us that if we did not have the ability to make a living in more than one way we ought to seriously think about it. Later I found out that he practised what he preached and regularly ran a series of adverts for Nude Jigsaw Puzzles in one of the Sunday papers!! When we returned to the factory I'm afraid most of the theory did not seem to work in practice and overall I for one developed a certain mistrust of consultants. (Nothing personal Gwynn!)

My journey to the factory when we first moved took around 15 to 20 minutes and by the time I retired it could take as long as 45 minutes. I was the nearest executive to the factory and became the key-holder for emergencies, not only for our part of the group but also for the Equipment Company, under certain circumstances. I always stopped at the local police station for an escort and frankly the police were not at all happy to go there when the alarm had been raised, which initially happened far too often. At night I could be there, door to door, within about 5 minutes. Later someone had the bright idea of installing a fire alarm system connected directly to the Fire Station and this too gave problems. It went off for no reason at all and the firemen actually broke into the building on two occasions in one week thereby setting off the security alarm. I had to present them with a cheque for their Christmas party to placate them and we decided that enough was enough and we took out the direct link. On another occasion we could not stop the alarm from ringing and I ended up on a ladder, about 12 feet up, at one o'clock in the morning, unscrewing the bell which was about 16" in diameter. In the very next road there was a large block of flats and I learned from the police that quite a number of villains lived here and this explained their reluctance to accompany me. There were two occasions when Jean came by bus to the factory and I had to warn her that if anyone asked the time whilst walking down the road, she was to say she did not have a watch – and it happened both times!

The wages for both sections of the company were delivered every Friday by Securicor and the van was driven into the courtyard and the main gates were locked whilst the money was unloaded. On two consecutive Fridays the company secretary had been out on business and returned whilst the gates were locked so he left his car outside in the street and came in via a wicket gate. On both occasions his radio was stolen. At weekends when nobody was working the place was really vulnerable and any noise that might be created was easily drowned by the trains running past from time to time. Backing on to our courtyard was the premises of a scrap metal merchant and one weekend a gang came over the wall from the railway side, created a hole in the metal merchant's wall that was about 30" square and no less than 24" deep, stole a van belonging to the equipment company, took £7000 of scrap metal, and broke out of the main gates and made off – that's how isolated it was.

A few years later it was decided to make some alterations to the conveyor store involving concreting some new bases for rolls of belting just in front of the building where the roof provided an overhang for protection. One

139

evening after the builders had left I went to see how far they had progressed only to discover that they had managed to concrete in the sliding doors which were abut 12 feet high, I quickly had this cleared before it could set. Perhaps I should add that I had absolutely nothing to do with taking on these builders.

The piece-de-resistance occurred a little later when they were demolishing a small building close to the railway which was protected by a very tall wall which concealed all activity from us. I was urgently summoned to the scene when they accidentally nudged the railway wall and it ended up hanging out over the line at an angle of about 30 degrees from the upright position. Now before I reached the scene I was not too alarmed as this line that continued in the open past our building, had never to my knowledge had a train on it. However, now we could see the line it became obvious that it was well used where the accident occurred as a very short distance along, the line took a fairly sharp half-right turn. What is more the rush hour was less than two hours away. Returning to my office I phoned Waterloo Station to ask for help which they promised. After 45 minutes I phoned again as nobody had arrived and it should not have taken more than 20 minutes to get to us from Waterloo. Then I was assured that help was on the way – coming from Croydon by train!!! In the meantime the builders put a rope around the problem area and attached it to the J.C.B. that had done the damage and sat back and hoped. Eventually Sir Galahad arrived and it was decided that they would trundle a large grab through the streets at night with a view to clawing it back to safety. I had to return at midnight complete with camera to record the action for the ensuing court case. Somehow all this just did not seem to tie in with our sojourn at Manchester!

Of course one of the problems of moving factories is an

inevitable loss of some staff and whilst the move from Mitcham to Bermondsey went fairly smoothly the second move, coming so soon after left us with several vacancies. Our main requirement was for men of reasonable physical fitness who were able to carry out accurate measurements of the large stock of rings we employed in moulding leather seals. By asking for men I incurred the wrath of the local job centre who wanted to insist on equality for women. When a small party from the centre visited us, I showed them that a lot of our moulds were made from mild steel and when used for wet blocking the operative would inevitably end up with discoloured hands. We supplied barrier creams but these soon came off in the operations involved. Sometimes they also had to be heated, some were extremely heavy, and this frankly was never a job for a woman, but they stuck to their guns and even sent one woman along, who very soon left when I showed her what was wanted. One of the first men I interviewed was a wizened old black man who claimed to be capable of measuring. I then asked him to point out three and three eighths of an inch on a ruler and he pointed with his finger and said "dere's de three & dere's de eight". Asking the same of another applicant also claiming to be capable the reply was "a bit dodgy on the little uns governor!" After this I phoned the local job centre and explained that our requirements were fitness and measuring ability and surely they could vet them before wasting everyone's time. The reply came in a plummy accent saying "I say old boy. Is it really necessary". Another misfit I do believe! Eventually we found a man who could fit the bill, so I gave him the standard application form to fill in and alongside Nationality – he wrote – Church of England! Well you can't have everything – can you!

We had one Jamaican called Basil who was a very good worker but seemed always to have to complain about something, which entailed interviewing him in the foreman's office. Invariably these discussions would take quite a while and when I mentioned this to Jean at home one evening she said that I should avoid direct eye to eye contact as this would be interpreted as being a threat in Jamaica. On the next occasion I sat there looking out of the window whilst talking to him and I suppose it did shorten the encounter a little. I got the feeling he just enjoyed a break, although the subject of one of his complaints was that he had been paid incorrectly. Now the rate for National Insurance had been altered as from the week in question and the difference was minute – but he was dead right – and I do not know another man in the factory who would have been aware of the change.

Round about this period we were offered a leather for sealing purposes which had been impregnated at the tannery with a synthetic rubber called Thiokol. Some of you may recall that the Apollo disaster was attributed to the failure of the huge "O" rings that were used which were made by the Thiokol Corporation. For more normal applications this was extremely useful material and this opened up several avenues to us. Many of the oils in use in modern hydraulic systems would leach out the impregnations that we had used until now whereas we were now able to counter with a seal which combined the virtues of both types. One of our first successes came following a visit to an exhibition at Earls Court where I came across a company called Kinetrol. At the time they were having great difficulty with seals of their own manufacture. After some discussion they let me have a tiny mould approximately 1" long x 1/2 " wide of rectangular shape and I promised to endeavour to produce a seal in "Thitan" as we called it. To start with this in itself was fairly unusual as, with the possible exception of the early golf bag bottoms that we made for our Equipment Company, every other moulded seal was of circular construction. Not only was it of uneven shape but the base was not flat either. With our very rough sample they found they had to re-calibrate their test equipment and the interest was immediate. The first reaction of some of my colleagues was that it was hardly worth the effort. In time I was able to justify my position as we gradually worked throughout the range of sizes they produced until we reached the largest measuring 15" x 9" and this was a very valuable customer. The function of these was to provide the seals in actuators which, for example, could control valves from remote positions and because of the unique contours of the seals we had a lot of assistance from the customer's engineers, incorporating techniques unknown to us to produce suitable moulds.

In the years that followed we extended the use to a large range of spray equipment of American origin and many other applications. Unfortunately the tannery in question became involved in receivership proceedings on two occasions, and this was I believe the only time I encountered this problem. At one stage they had materials ready for impregnation but were lacking a small quantity of an accelerator needed to proceed. I think the value was around £15 but although I volunteered to pay for this the Receiver was adamant I could not do so. We eventually were given further supplies but serious problems arose and it was a long time before we discovered that because of the noxious nature of the process, most of our leather was being treated after hours by the chief chemist. When this tannery finally ceased production it was transferred to another tannery, but shortly after I retired it was banned on health and safety grounds.

During my last years with the company we were offered the chance of supplying a complicated set of packings which were used on an Ethylene Cracker by one of the oil companies in Scotland. The company was purchasing direct from America and we were dealing through an intermediary. The specification was the most exacting I have ever come across. One set comprised 7 Vee leathers with one 3 ply solid header plus one 5 ply base ring. This was required to complete 250,000 cycles on a 30" stroke in 14 days. At one end of the stroke it was in liquid at minus 40 degrees C and at the other it was a gas at plus 70 degrees C, and the pressure involved was 35,000 P.S.I. Before they would put them into service they had to pass in test gauges giving a tolerance of plus or minus 5 thou. on the outer and inner sealing surfaces. Now it is a fact that all leather is hygroscopic (i.e. it will absorb moisture and in so doing is liable to swell under most conditions). We had to bake the un-impregnated leather to remove most of the moisture and then impregnate in a very hard, very expensive wax, and then seal the finished sets in polythene once they met the specification. Needless to say there was always a percentage of rejects, but this was also the case with the American supplies. I was very proud of our efforts which would have been regarded as quite impossible in my early years with the company. Unfortunately we had barely enjoyed the fruits of our labours for more than a couple of years when the end customer scrapped the machines and that was that! Nevertheless this was proof if any was needed that leather is an amazing sealing material and the satisfaction that we all achieved in the department was tremendous.

We were unfortunate in that we arrived at Battersea at around the time there was a fatal accident at the fairground nearby. The district surveyor at the time was a rather short little man called Ball. From our first meeting he made it quite clear that under no circumstances was he going to suffer the fate that had befallen one of his colleagues who had been blamed for not preventing the accident. As a result we received the most thorough going over, looking at every possible aspect for problem areas. This cost us a substantial amount of money, and whilst I have no quarrel with this in principle, I found it decidedly irksome that when we visited some of our competitors prior to takeovers there was such a lack of safety everywhere we went and it was anything but a level playing field.

When George Odey retired in 1974, his son Dick was Chief Executive of the group, and Professor Roland Smith was appointed Chairman and my understanding is that this came about at the behest of the city. Douglas was still at the helm and in 1977 we acquired Southern Industrial Rubber who specialised in a wide range of hoses and allied materials. One of their practices was to save all the incoming envelopes for use as scrap and whilst this may sound a laudable proposition I would imagine that one gin and tonic less a day could have saved them the effort, but this is the way the minds worked on occasion. Earlier I can remember being told to dispense with the man who swept the factory when times were difficult, which usually meant that a much higher paid individual had to do it.. With this latest acquisition we were introduced to one Paul Alliston and his father Harry who had founded the business, and from my personal point of view, and also that of many others in the company, the arrival of Paul was not one of our better days!! It was not long before Harry retired and Paul was put in charge of the S.I.R. section.

Then followed a period of adjustment which also included the acquisition of another company "The Outra Belting & Rubber Co." and as a result it was felt expedient to put representatives from each company on the board and eventually I was included as a director and at the same time made Managing Director of the Leather Department.

In 1980 Douglas Dew retired and it was then that we were to meet David Woodcraft, of whom I have written separately in the next chapter concerning "The Industrial Leathers Federation" because of the advance information I received prior to actually meeting him. The events that followed will be outlined in a later chapter headed "Under New Management".

THE INDUSTRIAL LEATHERS FEDERATION

When I first joined the company there were two separate trade organisations, one covering Leather Belting Manufacture and the other Hydraulic and Pneumatic packings. Douglas Dew, my boss was Chairman of both of these on more than one occasion, and for a very long time he was Chairman of the Wages Committee. On several meetings I accompanied him and got to meet the members form other companies and also took part in the sporting activities which involved playing golf, crown bowls and putting and at Douglas's suggestion I purchased a half set of golf clubs and became hooked for life. I was never very good to start with but invariably won the booby prizes until they stopped awarding them!

Eventually, I believe it was during 1959, I attended one of these meetings on my own and at that time there were still separate meetings for the two sides, mostly held in Harrogate. At this particular weekend, at lunch, I sat next to a chap who seemed to be about my age and he asked me how long I had been in the trade to which I replied "About 10 years". I then asked him how long he had been working for the company and his reply was quite amazing – "I start next week!" I believe they call it nepotism. This was Bill Richardson who was to become Captain of Derbyshire Cricket Club, whose family are very wealthy and own a lot of property in Derby, apart from running their own tannery which has since closed. I quite liked Bill who was also a very good golfer. Since the tannery closed James Richardson, his cousin, has continued to run their hydraulic leather business, similar to my own department but considerably smaller. In the ensuing years the Leather trade had very hard times indeed as a result of which the number of members dropped to such a degree that it was decided to amalgamate the two sections and thus was created the Industrial Leathers Federation. One of the problems facing the industry was the fact that hides are, like copper, sold on the open market and are thus subject to market forces which, for example, at the time of the Korean War resulted in increases of up to 45%. More recently when there was a slightly smaller adjustment I was able to negotiate a 17 ½% increase from the National Coal Board – without even paying them a visit – as they were well aware of market conditions. Bearing in mind the fact that despite using modern methods to speed up the tanning process you will still have equipment tied up for weeks on end the effect of these huge increases was very difficult to control with such a large amount of capital involved. Needless to say the prices did not always increase thus creating further problems. On this subject I do believe that as a trade we have suffered partly because of the actions of some of our customers, mostly in the shoe trade. For example I got to know Allan Elwood who was Managing Director of William Walker's of Bolton, who became part of the Barrow Hepburn Group at one stage. During lunch I asked him what would be the value of the leather used in the production of a top quality pair of shoes which at that time were selling for around £25 and his reply was "£3,50". Now when the trade had to increase prices as I have outlined above, too often the shoe manufacturers would use this as an excuse to get a similar – but not justifiable increase.

Over the years I eventually became a long standing member of the Federation and during the first part I was very much the junior member dealing in the main with people generally much older than myself, mainly contemporaries of Douglas Dew. This included Alan Elwood, Harold Birkin, Tom Entwhistle, Edmund Cotton, Bob Hope (no, another one!), and Hamish Hendry who was nearer to my age than the remainder. During the latter part of my membership I became the permanent treasurer and this continued until 9 years after my retirement. In this period, apart from Hamish, I became very friendly with Roger Birkin and David Cotton and our various outings were most enjoyable.

Earlier in the book I mentioned going out with Roger Birkin to the New Cavendish Hotel. In earlier years his father Harold used to take Jean and myself out once a year and we dined at Simpson's and Brown's and many other well known establishments. One year he took us to see Flanders and Swann before the meal and I felt that the time had come to reciprocate so I booked seats to see Marcelle Marceau at the Arts Theatre after we had eaten. I soon wished the earth would open up as he sat there completely mystified and kept asking me what on earth the fellow was supposed to be doing. Another example of the great North/South divide!

Also in the earlier years we were sometimes invited as guests to outings organised by the tanners as some of these were members of both organisations. One sub section was known as the Hairy Belly Tanners Association, the secretary of which was a Gwen Stapleton who also covered one of the main tanning sections. Gwen received an award for services rendered and had to attend Buckingham Palace in her car to receive it. Unfortunately when they inspected the boot she had only just collected a bulk delivery of toilet rolls for the office – a very large quantity - and this caused some amusement all round!

In 1974 I was appointed to the executive of the Federation and in 1976 I was made Chairman (that indicates just how much our numbers had diminished!) – not that it was a very onerous task. In most years the meetings were held in the North-West in places such as

Morecambe, Grange-over-Sands, Southport and Blackpool, but on this occasion we went to Scarborough and had a really glorious weekend. Normally the business meeting took place prior to the dinner and on one occasion, and it could have been at Scarborough, we got behind on schedule and postponed one item involving the introduction of new basic price lists for both hydraulic leathers and leather belting until after dinner. This meant that the second part of the meeting started around 10 o'clock and the result was quite hilarious. As I recall I had produced the figures for the Leather Packings and Tom Entwhistle those for the Leather Belting and between us we had to deal with a very disinterested bunch of people who had consumed rather a lot of alcohol. In fact one or two actually dropped off during the proceedings - we were so riveting! In the end I believe we decided to give up and negotiate by phone with the interested parties. Perhaps I should add that this was not a price fixing ring but merely a necessary adjustment to two extremely ancient lists which were in many cases out of kilter with costs, particularly at the lower end of the size range. Members were free to offer such discounts as they wished and in fact were not compelled to use them at all.

I used to attend the wages meetings with Douglas and these were strange rituals bearing in mind that the terms we were agreeing were in our case only used as a basis for overtime premiums and were considerably lower than the actual rates paid for normal hours. Here again most members had an entirely different method of calculation. However other factors such as holiday entitlements, shorter working weeks etc. and any new safety regulations which may have arisen were an essential part of these meetings and this is where we all relied heavily on the advice of the Federation Secretary. In the early days this was John Cox, and more recently Jack Purves ably assisted by Joyce Strong. At the end of one such meeting,

150

the unions having left the room I wandered across to their side and picked up a piece of paper left by their chairman and read – "Mr.Dew, Committees Members, I should like to say on behalf of my members etc.etc." He virtually had everything set out in black and white.

Mind you, many years later after we acquired one particular company dealing in Conveyor belting it was thought necessary to appoint one of their managers to the board. Apparently he used to rehearse his statements at home with his wife the night before. On this particular day he was asked to give his statement, but before he had gone very far the Group Chairman butted in with a question which he had difficulty in dealing with. Having done so he looked really put out and insisted on going right back to the start which caused some amusement round the table.

Over the years the number of members playing golf shrunk considerably and when the amalgamation of the two separate sections took place we then played for the cup which originated with the Belting Federation and which was only slightly smaller than the F.A. Cup. In the end there were only six players taking part (in pairs) on the last time it was presented and I was lucky enough to get David Cotton, the only decent player amongst us as partner – and we won. In the evening we each did a lap of honour around the dinner table clutching the trophy.

Douglas Dew, my boss for so many years, was scheduled for retirement in 1980, and had long since ceased to attend most of the general meetings, other than the wages committee, and when I attended the next meeting everyone wanted to know who his replacement would be. At that stage he had not taken over but had been introduced to the guests at a group dinner in London a few weeks previously. I was several tables away from him and when he stood up I saw this very large figure looming over the table and this was David Woodcraft, whose arrival at Barrow Hepburn Group changed the way we were to live for ever after! When I mentioned his name I was asked to describe him by one of the federation members and having done so he said "You poor b....." or words to that effect.

David Woodcraft had been a near neighbour of this man and had moved into the same area just after him. He was invited for drinks at Xmas and I am assured that before he left he made a statement to his own wife on the lines of – I hope we don't have the same problem here as we had at the last place when people were putting notices in the windows saying – Woodcraft must go!" Now I have to say I found this hard to believe but Hamish assured me that he had heard this story a long time back. There were other stories confirming that he was anything but an easy man to get on with. As a result you can imagine I did not exactly welcome him with open arms and he probably found it hard to understand my attitude towards him.

At the very first meeting with all the senior staff he left us in no doubt as to who was now in charge and that he would brook absolutely no opposition. You could be forgiven for thinking that I am gilding the lily somewhat. However we had been investigating the possibility of manufacturing synthetic packings at the instigation of our new Group Chief Executive, Ray Way. We had previously taken over the manufacture of the Leather Packings Division of Edgar Vaughan who also made synthetics. One of their managers, Cyril Hawke, had set up on his own in a small way with synthetics but had retained the right to control the purchases of the leathers from us that they had previously produced. Ray asked me to take Woodcraft to see at first hand what was on offer and when they met this very soon established that they had both worked for another company at some time in the past. After a very short while Cyril turned to David in my presence and said "You are just a hatchet man!" Somehow I do not think David appreciated that remark, but it did me a power of good.

Reverting to the Federation I must say I enjoyed meeting up now and then to exchange views with people engaged in similar occupations. This was particularly useful as the numbers decreased as, by then, we had mostly achieved our own niche from the original cake and were no longer seriously competing with each other.

Perhaps this is a suitable time to give the promised chapter on Gin Leather and the Sudan as this was one of the first topics discussed when David Woodcraft took charge.

GIN LEATHER & SUDAN

I doubt whether many readers would know of the existence or usage of Gin Leather and I feel this is deserving of a separate chapter. The term Gin Leather covers the use of leather for ginning cotton. Most of the cotton produced in the Middle East comes from cotton gins – machines for separating the lint from the seed in the raw cotton as taken from the fields. The machines were originally called "engines" and this became shortened in speech to "gin" and the factory in which they operated became a "ginnery".

Barrow Hepburn started in this business around 1926, the year I was born, and from the earliest days it was produced from the thickest part of the Bull shoulders varying in thickness from 3/8" to 5/8", and later from Buffalo. The material was made into rolls finishing 1.1/8" wide each weighing approximately 18 lbs using scarfed joints cemented together in similar style to flat leather belting. The working surface of the leather is the cut edge and when fitted to the cotton gin it is wound spirally onto a wooden roller about 4" diameter approximately 36" wide. The roller is first covered with a very thin leather which is glued into place and then the gin leather is glued to that and to itself on edge until the roller is completely covered and is now 6 ½ " in diameter and covered in glue.

The roller is then faced off leaving the fibres of leather exposed and when the raw cotton is fed into the gin it is to this surface that the cotton fibres attach themselves and the remainder falls away against a stationary knife placed at the rear of the machine. This produces the long staple cotton which enables the producer to get a premium price for his output. In America they use Saw

Gins for the same purpose – these being produced on rollers made up of circular saw blades. This of course inevitably tears the cotton and their standard product does not command the same price. At one stage the Americans tried to persuade the Sudanese to change to a synthetic type of material and actually gave them 5 tons free of charge. Fortunately it is not possible to recreate the fibrous construction necessary to achieve the desired result and this project came to a swift end. Whilst on this subject I should perhaps point out that Buffalo does not produce the thickest finished leather. I was once the proud possessor of a piece of walrus hide which had been beautifully mounted on a leather base and this was two inches thick and in retrospect should have been kept in the safe. This type of leather was and possibly still use for polishing bobs in the steel industry. On the other hand, despite its size Elephant hide is much thinner and more variable.

When I first joined the company the bulk of our output went to Egypt and a certain amount to Sudan. Unfortunately Anthony Eden decided to invade Egypt at the time of the Suez problem in October 1956 and with immediate effect that was the end of our business in Egypt. Our agent in London – Richard Grieve – controlled Insurance Companies in both Egypt and Sudan who had people on the spot who could negotiate for the business. We then concentrated our efforts on Sudan with very good effect. In the years that followed we were eventually tendering on an annual basis for as much as 90 tons a year. Now to produce that amount would require 135 tons of raw material – and that's a lot of bull! – if you'll pardon the expression. Just to complicate matters further along came artificial insemination and there were just not enough Bulls to cater for our needs – let alone theirs!

We then turned to using buffalo, which gave an even

greater substance being between 3/8" and ¾" thick.

From my early years with the company we always produced Gin Leather in anticipation of the annual tender on the instructions of George Odey, the Group Chairman, and this was indeed a very risky business, particularly so because the tanning process took several months and our only customers, but for a few minor orders, came from Egypt & Sudan. Against this we were originally dealing particularly in Sudan, with the Sudan Gezira Board which was then run almost entirely by British people – and only a relatively small number of people at that. In the event the management was taken over by the Sudanese and inevitably there was a huge escalation in numbers and from then on everything took twice as long to settle. Despite this we continued to supply on open account for many years until – at their behest – we worked on more satisfactory terms ending up with Confirmed Irrevocable Letters of Credit. The problem then was that after making an offer in May it would sometimes take until the following February before the first shipment could take place whilst payment was being arranged. Because of the quality we produced we were always able to command a premium price which was essential as, of course, the local Egyptian Tanneries were using more readily available Buffalo with cheap labour which together amounted to a much inferior product. Our hides came from the Far East and were on average much thicker. There was hardly any Gin Leather production in Sudan. Then came the period when inflation hit our country and all of a sudden it looked to the Sudanese that their old friends were taking advantage ot their position.

Now for many years we had a strict policy that no one was allowed to tour the Gin Leather department. Unfortunately the Chairman's right hand man at the time, David Clifton, insisted on showing two Syrian Brothers around the factory despite all our protestations and surprise – surprise – within a very few years they began quoting for the annual tender. What's more for 3 or 4 years in a row they maintained the same price which was much lower than ours to start with – and we still had problems with inflation. Now I don't pretend that they would not have done so without the visit but I firmly believe they must have gained some useful ideas from us and thus speeded up the inevitable. Events came to a head in 1981 when we had some 45 tons of finished product and no orders and it was decided that I should visit Sudan to try to find solution.

For many years when the children asked what I would like for my birthday or Xmas I would always ask for a Pentax camera. As I was to visit a place not normally part of the tourist scene I decided to invest in one complete with a 70/210 Zoom lens with a two times converter and various other attachments. I already had an excellent pair of binoculars for bird-watching given to me by the company to celebrate 30 years service and of course the opportunities for this in Sudan are endless.

I left London on the 6th March 1981 at 17.45 by British Airways – First Class – (the one and only time!) arriving in Khartoum at 3.40 am, and emerged into a temperature of 80 degrees F. I was met by one of our two agents on the spot – Mohamed Nazeer. He was a Sudanese and his partner Fawzi was an Egyptian. I was grateful for his attendance as he helped me through customs which was proving a little difficult at one stage. He then conveyed me to the Hilton Hotel, which overlooks the Blue Nile at the front and the White Nile at the back, and this was without doubt the finest hotel in Sudan. The following day we went to the offices of Khartoum Trading & Insurance Agencies and had general discussions on the situation and later went to the government offices in Khartoum. From then

157

on everything seemed to slow down – but this is the pace at which they operate all the time. However that is not to say that they were discourteous as that is just not true. From 2 pm it becomes much too hot and this is siesta time and I returned to the hotel and was collected in the evening by Mohamed and taken to one of several restaurants we visited during the course of the week. I was fortunate in that they really liked to eat a lot of meat in the form of steaks and chops and never once did I encounter the dreaded Garlic or Onions. We started with a local speciality called Sudan Foul Soup which, despite the name, was very much to my taste being basically produced with peanuts and I was delighted to have something to enthuse about. Next morning when Mohamed picked me up at the hotel there were 5 large bags of peanuts on the back seat for me to take home.

Because of the heat we had to drink a lot and they had fridges in most offices full of Coca-Cola. On our travels it was necessary to stop for a drink fairly often and some of the places we came across were particularly unsavoury to say the least. So much so that on the 3rd or 4th night I collapsed at the dinner table in an outdoor restaurant, for a very short time, much to my embarrassment. I should also mention that there was probably only one occasion that there was not a power cut when we were dining out, sometimes two.

We made arrangements to visit the Sudan Gezira Board at their headquarters at Barakat, about 2 1/2 hours journey south of Khartoum. Because of the heat we left very early in the morning and on the way passed several petrol stations outside of which were dozens of yellow taxis who had been queuing all night for 4 gallons of petrol. The route follows the Blue Nile fairly closely and on occasion you would see the river being used as a car or lorry wash. I saw very few camels the whole of my stay there and I saw only a couple of trains – both stationary – on the journey. Everything was flat apart from a few sand dunes and the roads were frighteningly narrow and rough and to stray on to the surrounding areas was not a good idea. Sudan is the largest country in Africa occupying nearly a million square miles varying from desert in the north-west giving way to a vast clay plain part of which is irrigated by gravity by the Blue Nile on which farming is carried out. Further south comes the Savannah and a considerable increase in rainfall. However this is seasonal and cotton needs water every 10 to 20 days and because of this they constructed the Sennar Dam which raised the level of the Blue Nile to cater for the slope of the land from North to South of the scheme which covered 5 CMS per kilometre making this one of the cheapest irrigation schemes ever attempted at that time.

Now the Sudan Gezira Board is the largest farm in the world. The word Gezira means island in Arabic and it is an island between the Blue and White Niles. As you approach you see a steady increase in growth alongside the route and they grow wheat, groundnuts and dura – a form of cereal – as well as the cotton which accounts for the bulk of their output. We were well received at Barakat by the management and given a conducted tour during which they had organised a demonstration of the production of a gin roller from start to finish. Unfortunately it proved impossible to make any headway during the visit and they tried to illustrate that the alternative material they were testing was not all that inferior, a point on which we did not reach agreement. However the main stumbling block as always was finance for which they were largely dependant on the I.M.F (The International Monetary Fund). There was nothing more we could achieve at this time apart from making contact with some of the authorities in Khartoum which we did on the following day. From then on I was taken to see some of the sights and because Mohamed was aware of my interest in bird-watching he took me to the local Natural History Museum which was run by their own television equivalent of Armand and Denis who were most helpful and showed us a wide range of birds mostly in glass cases. When we emerged I could see that Mohamed was rather agitated and he suddenly turned to me and said "Why didn't you use your camera whilst you had an opportunity". It took some time to persuade him that the idea was to film them whilst still alive in the open air. I was taken to the now dilapidated former Gezira residential club at Wad Medani which had obviously been the centre of activity in years past. Here I spent some time chasing a most attractive bird all round the area – no not that type of bird! This one had a glossy dark blue coat – O.K. I give up - let's change the subject. In the afternoons, despite the heat, I used to go out of the front of the hotel complex with the camera and binoculars to get photos of the area and reasonable shots of Bee-Eaters, Sacred Ibis, Kites, Spur Winged Plovers, and many others I could not identify.

What was quite amazing was that I was completely on my own at these times and carrying valuable equipment, yet at no time did I feel under threat from the natives. In fact their main interest was to have their own picture taken. In talking to one of the guests at the hotel I discovered that he was based in Cairo, working for a British Pump manufacturer, and had to visit every country in Africa on a regular basis. He told me that he would go anywhere in Sudan on his own, day or night, whereas he would never venture out in Egypt by night as it was too dangerous. I've no doubt the situation is entirely different now and you have to feel sorry for people like Mohamed who have to endure the imposition of Sharia Law. One day he stopped the car and excused himself for a short while and on his return he was carrying a crate of whisky – 12 bottles in all! I

160

believe this was entirely for his personal consumption and I have never seen anyone in our country make such a purchase. I was also taken to see the Republican Palace by the Blue Nile at Khartoum where Gordon died and also the Sudan museum made up of items salvaged from places that were flooded to create the Aswan Dam. Included amongst the exhibits were some Christian frescoes dating from the seventh and eleventh centuries. To remove them from the walls they invented a special technique. On site the archaeologists spread beeswax and cheesecloth over each fresco and built a frame on it. When hardened the fresco, attached to the frame, was sawn in one piece out of the mud brick wall.

We also saw the point at which the Blue Nile and White Nile meet. The flow of the Blue Nile is considerably greater than that of the White Nile. At the time the weather became overcast and it was difficult to detect the considerable difference in colour which I was told existed when visibility was good.

In the hotel there was a Grand Piano and they had a local pianist who was really painful to listen to. Mind you he did not stand much chance as the local piano was dreadfully out of tune and although I managed to try it out for myself one day I was very glad to give up despite suffering from withdrawal symptoms. This is one country where the modern electronic keyboard would be ideal as they cannot possibly keep a steam version in tune!

At the end of the week I flew back to Britain feeling a little like Neville Chamberlain and not having achieved very much although I was in possession of a rather nice Ebony walking stick with a Buffalo Horn handle as a present from Mohamed. From this I appreciated for the first time that Ebony wood is not black through and through and this is one of my proudest possessions and it probably will come in useful in a few years from now!

During the next six months or so Mohamed and Fawzi came to this country with proposals which of course entailed a considerable reduction in price and I had to take them to meet Dick Odey the Chairman's son who by now was chief executive for the group. Frankly I never had a very high opinion of him as he was only there by virtue of his parentage and many years previously I had to meet him on a stand at the Leather Show at Earl's Court to discuss the supply position re Gin Leather. We sat at opposite ends of a table behind the stand and the man could not look me in the eye which I found rather disconcerting. Anyway we had to meet him at his room at the Inn on the Park Hotel as he had broken his leg in a boating accident. He looked up and said "Please excuse my position here but as you can see I'm mechanically damaged!" I'm afraid I have no time for such posturing. In addition he was once put in charge of a new venture making plastics in Hull and I was told by several people working there most of the production went straight into the furnace. Almost everyone else was sacked but not Dick. I suppose it was ever thus but it does not make it right. Mind you he eventually died in hospital shortly before he was to stand trial for fraud. I fear his father must have turned in his grave when this happened. Although George Odey was autocratic I must say that as far as I was concerned he gave me a very free hand. For example our own tanneries produced a wide range of materials which we could have used for hydraulic leathers but whilst he would mention the possibility I was under no compunction to order from them and in fact in the main I went elsewhere because of quality.

During their visit to London I was invited to go with them to a reception at the flat of the man in charge of the Sudan Embassy in London which turned out to be a very pleasant occasion. Our normal commission on sales to the S.G.B. was 5% which was distributed by Richard Grieve but I was quite astonished to hear Mohamed suggest that we ought to give them 7 ½% when our host could not help but overhear. However they do things very differently to us but we were not prepared to follow this route.

Mohamed and Fawzi returned to Sudan and there were many exchanges of correspondence culminating the following year in a suggestion that I should pay a further visit almost a year after the first. It was recommended that before proceeding I should contact the Embassy to ensure that the Chief Purchasing Officer would see me and this I did. We were told that he was in America having talks with the I.M.F. and that he had agreed to see me if I went.

On arrival at Khartoum Airport I asked Mohamed when we were to meet and he told me that on arrival back from America the C.P.O. had reported to the government in Khartoum and then made his way to Barakat. On his arrival everyone he met was expressing great sympathy at the news and he finally learnt that whilst he was en route for Barakat it was announced over the radio that he had been sacked – but they omitted to tell him first! I gather that politicians are often dealt with in this way – at least it was the custom in those days. As a result I never did get to see the man and from this point of view it was a most unsatisfactory situation. Nevertheless we had discussions with other officials and tried to get our proposals over but without a person at the helm it was an impossible situation.

During this visit Fawzi was taken ill with malaria and we had to visit him at his house in Khartoum. When we arrived he was up but Mohamed insisted that I see his bed which had been specially ordered as a duplicate of the one originally made for King Farouk of Egypt. Very unfortunately I only had my zoom lens with me so I was only able to film it in sections. There were mirrors everywhere, even at the outside of the foot of the bed. The basic wood was like mahogany, and it was decorated in silver and gold and there was some lighting as well. Apparently Fawzi was a hypochondriac and the pills on his side table had to be seen to be believed. This was the last time I saw Fawzi whom I found to be quite charming and extremely helpful.

On another day I was invited to lunch with one of Mohamed's neighbours but before this I was taken inside Mohamed's house which he had built back in 1954. It was built three storeys high and both upper storeys had fairly large open areas to accommodate them at night. Mohamed had two wives, one of whom had died fairly recently and thirteen children Because of the heat at night time they all slept outdoors, some in the courtyard alongside, and the remainder on the upper levels. Most of the furniture inside the house had arms which were covered in Formica and seemed very basic by our standards.

After a little while I was introduced to an older man who was Mohamed's uncle and he produced a roll of white cotton, and asked me to stand up whereby he got me to put my arm out at full stretch and as a measure he marked the length by wiping the cotton on the sweat of his brow. He used the same procedure to cater for my height and then disappeared. We then went to the neighbour's house and I was introduced to 9 or 10 people of varying occupations. One was introduced as "The Tailor" and I discovered that he made tents for the army. The Doctor was a very engaging character with a good sense of humour. Another turned out to be a nephew of Mohamed who was a fighter pilot. He related a tale of journeying down the Nile and sleeping on deck, men and women side by side, and how if one were to take advantage of such a situation one could end up being knifed. Unless I misunderstood him he seemed to suggest that he himself had been very fortunate on one such journey and you can read that both ways! We sat in the garden having drinks before the meal and I was astonished when one of the party opened the conversation with "Do you think Liverpool will win this Saturday?" They were very well informed on the subject and despite the intense heat I passed by numerous games in progress during my stay and it is obviously a very popular sport there. I managed to do some justice to the meal but this really was not my favourite repast. Eventually I bade farewell to my host and we returned to Mohamed's house where his Uncle was waiting with what I believe is known as a djellaba (or galabieh) produced while we were eating from the white cotton material with which he had taken my measurements earlier. There was also an open work headpiece. I thought that was pretty quick work. The next time we're invited to a fancy dress party I will be alright, but musicians very rarely get involved in such events.

Once we were in their offices when they had a visitor who was introduced as the former Grand Mufti of Sudan, a charming man who, when I requested permission to take his photograph, insisted on putting on his turban first. He was collecting for charity and when I asked who had taken his place he revealed with a smile that there were now 27 Grand Muftis.

When we were stationary in traffic one day I took a photo of what looked to be a carpet hung up but I was later informed that it was in fact a tent. Another day we visited the local tannery where I saw a large splitting machine which had been purchased from one of our Italian associate companies – Rizzi.

In our travels I took a photograph of a eucalyptus tree – in full blossom – something I do not recall seeing anywhere else. We also came across a couple of Haboobs which is the name for a very fine sandstorm during which visibility drops dramatically and the temperature rises rapidly. The native dress provides good cover for the eyes in those conditions. Talking of dress reminds me that during our visits to some of the offices I was quite surprised to see some of the ladies adjusting their dresses, which I have since discovered are called taubs, and are made from a single sweep of cloth, and on one occasion the result was quite revealing. I have since read that this is a fairly common occurrence.

On my last day, the Friday, I was to dine with Mohamed at his house and he sent his eldest son in his Mercedes to pick me up. Whereas Mohamed had worn western dress all the time previously this was their Sabbath and he was wearing his robes. I was ushered into the courtyard which had been cleared of all the bed frames which had been there on my earlier visit and there was just one low table on either side of which there were two armchairs. On the table were two glasses, a bottle each of whisky and gin, and one small bottle of tonic!

I had learned previously that Mohamed was fond of classical music and I took him a couple of tapes, one of which was Elgar's Enigma Variations. On a separate table he had his Hi-Fi equipment and this was blaring out to all and sundry – a most bizarre experience.

Then I was to meet almost his entire family one by one as they came out bearing all manner of gifts. First in line was his youngest son who presented me with yet another walking stick, the handle of which was circular and large, and below this was a finely carved head of a bird. When

Jean went to college as a mature student she took up wood carving and I must have mentioned this to Mohamed on my previous visit and this was the very welcome outcome. Mind you when I boarded the plane the following day I found it a bit disconcerting standing alongside a Sudanese gentleman in full robes carrying an almost identical stick. Anyway I can now have one in each hand! Every so often another of his offspring would emerge and make a presentation and one of his daughters who had been at Cairo University gave me a "tapestry by numbers" of a woman's head that she had produced there and I found this most embarrassing. Then followed two matching well used ash-trays one having a female figure arms-akimbo as decoration, the other being a helmeted male figure. Also two metal pots with heavy lids, decorated in green and gold, again much used, and the piece-de-resistance was a very weighty glass dog about 8" long, 6" tall and nearly 3" wide which was almost transparent but had vivid red eyes, nose and tongue. Lastly I was given a framed picture of three dogs made from plastic raised from the surface in what I believe is termed bas-relief. This measured some 12" by 8" overall and was very unlikely to be shown at the Royal Academy.

Whilst we were talking I asked Mohamed how long it would be before they settled their differences with Israel. At the time you dare not use any vessel for shipment to Sudan if it was likely to call at Israel. His reply was simple "never. It is written in the Koran".

During all this time I managed to phase my drinks with the one bottle of tonic water used sparingly, although I am not too keen on almost neat gin, and then we were called to eat. There was plate after plate of chops and steaks far in excess, I felt, of the numbers sitting down and this was only for the adults. I fear I must have been a disappointment but I did what justice I could to their very generous fare and finally we arrived at the coffee stage which was poured out from a very attractive earthenware vessel with the spout coming out from the side at an angle from a large bowl. Inside the spout was some coir like substance and when I went to remove it Mohamed pointed out that this was the filter! We then had coffee from tiny white cups with gold decoration and when we were finished I was presented with three of these cups, made in China, and the pot which are really quite splendid.

All this time I had not been introduced to his wife but just as I was about to leave this lady who had been providing a slap up meal for us was brought in for a very brief hallo. When I arrived back at the Hilton I was carrying this large plastic bag full of my ill-gotten gains and I met a chap in the lift and said "This is a picture of a man who cannot say No".

Next morning Mohamed took me to the Airport and in view of the problems I nearly encountered on my arrival I was compelled to bring every single item in case it should have been necessary to open my luggage. On the way home I vowed that if ever there was a likelihood that Mohamed would come to my house I would hide everything I possibly could and go to a car boot sale for replacements. They really are incredibly generous and would be just as likely to give you the last mouthful of food they possess if the occasion arose.

After all this it took a very long time before we received a telex from Mohamed and the necessary covering Letter of Credit which enabled me to enter the boss's office crying "Eureka" thus ending nearly 60 years of continuous trading.

Fitting Buffalo Leather to a Cotton Gin Roller in Sudan

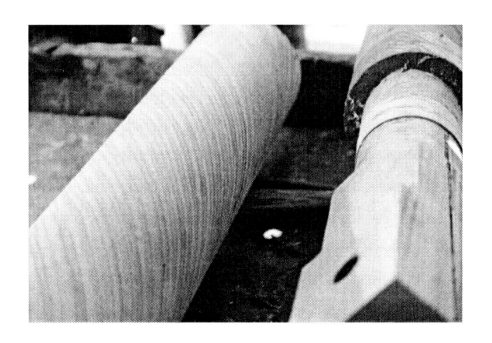

171

LIFE AT QUEENSVILLE

I have endeavoured not to overlap where possible but it is preferable, I believe, to maintain a steady thread throughout, otherwise this just becomes too complicated to absorb. This chapter does slightly cover some of the chapter set out in the chapter headed "Starting a Family" which of necessity dealt with Linda and Gary through their schooldays and well into their careers. This was a time when I was too tied up with events at the factory to do anything else and it coincided with both children learning the piano which meant that even at home I did not get much of a look in.

In 1966 we decided to have a holiday in France at a place called Rotheneuf. Unfortunately we overlooked the fact that this was a French holiday period and we had planned to spend the night in Le Havre after crossing on the ferry but found all the hotels fully booked. However we met up with an English girl, married to a Frenchman who used to meet the ferries just to keep her language going, and having tried to help us unsuccessfully, she invited us to stay with them at their house in a little place called St.Addresse, just on the outskirts. When we arrived we found the house was at the top of a very long row of steps – there must have been 60 if not more. It was really beautiful inside and her husband Jean-Pierre was an expert at carving both wood and stone and the house was full of his work. They made us most welcome and in the morning the views from the house were spectacular. As I recall we visited St.Malo the following year and on both occasions stayed overnight when travelling in each direction. The end result is that they visited us in England and we have a couple of examples of Jean-Pierre's carving in the house of which we are very proud. When they came over with their young son Arnold we took them to Wisley Gardens and in the rockery, which is enormous, there were several small pools, one of which was completely covered in green algae, and poor Arnold thought it was grass. Now it may have been only about 30 inches in diameter but it was so deep that the lad went right under. I quickly hauled him out but his parents were having convulsions, almost out of control. Mind you with his newly acquired green hair he did look rather odd, and it has become a bit of folklore whenever we see them or even write to them.

In 1974 Dad died, to be followed within a year by my mother, and of course this kept us very busy trying to keep an eye on mum to start with and dealing with all the legal matters involved. During this period Jean's mother used to visit Laitwood Road fairly frequently and so got to meet one of mum's neighbours which turned out to be quite useful, as after mum's death we arranged for Jean's parents to move into Laitwood. From then on we saw much more of Jean's father and the relationship improved somewhat. Eventually he died in 1979 and Jean's mother survived until 1982. We eventually became unwilling experts in dealing with bereavement as, in what seemed a very short space of time, my aunt and uncle, Edie & Cecil passed away, and Jean's Uncle Olly from Southend also died.

My parents had had two sets of lodgers for many years but unfortunately they were on extremely low rents which could not be adjusted to a realistic figure – and they were quite demanding as far as their rights were concerned. Furthermore new regulations governing safety were issued which meant that my mother would have been required to carry out a large number of modifications, at great expense, had she remained alive. Ironically if the other people in the house had been related the act would not have been applicable. I had the alternative of having the work done myself, with no guarantee that I could adjust the rents afterwards, or to sell to the council, which I did, for around £15,000. I have been told recently that they are now selling for over £400,000! Despite this I neither had the money, the inclination, or the time to carry this through satisfactorily and of course it is very easy to be wise after the event.

This was the period when, Jean having commenced full-time teaching in 1969, we were also in regular contact with Ursula & Judy who now reside in New Zealand. Until the time they both retired early, and went for a while to Menorca to run a bar with some friends, we used to dine with them at least once a fortnight. In the same period I met up with a very fine drummer called Graham Morley who at one time used to present drum clinics for the Premier Drum Company. He also wrote the drum feature in a magazine called Crescendo for some time. We did quite a few gigs together including two trial evenings at the Leather Bottle in Merton. On the first of these England were playing Brazil at Wembley which did us no favours at all! Apart from the Drum Clinics he used to go to schools along with a multi-instrumentalist called Malcolm Illingworth who hailed from the West Country to demonstrate something in the region of 47 instruments. He had a shooting brake and the mere fact of packing them in securely was something of a feat. He usually began playing part of the Artie Shaw clarinet concerto and went through nearly all the strings, woodwind and saxes, and brass, ending up with a piece of rubber tubing and a funnel with which he made a very acceptable noise. The children were then expected to choose the instrument they would then be taught. I joined in on a couple of occasions when they also had a girl singer with them.

Now Graham was very good at organising and I once attended a drum clinic at which he presented Louis

Bellson the great American drummer who married Pearl Bailey. In fact when they were married at Caxton Hall Registry Office the newspapers showed them as they came out being serenaded by a jazz group with Allan Ganley on drums prominent in the foreground of the picture.

In researching for this book I came across a draft for a program, by Graham, in which we were to play the first half of a concert, the last part of which was to be performed by Pam Ayres, whom Graham was apparently dating at the time. I had forgotten it because it never actually took place. Unfortunately there came a time when I felt the need to extract myself from his company as he could be very moody and upset me very much with comments he made to an old friend of mine whom he had just met at one of our parties. He also seemed to have a bad back more often then not and I ended up carrying his gear around which didn't seem right considering the age difference. There were one or two other problems which finally made me decide. Mind you I have recently been given to understand that he has since had a sex change operation so maybe that was the root of his troubles.

Our best man Allan Ganley, had married a girl called June, who became quite well known in the early 60's to all and sundry as Mrs. 1970, being the face on many full page advertisements for oil fired central heating. In fact there was a time when she was in nearly every paper at least once a week. Unfortunately the marriage did not work out for the simple reason that they rarely met. She was out all day opening new housing estates etc., whilst Allan's work took over in the evenings and also involved quite a lot of travelling. In fact I never actually met her. The upshot was that Allan took a up a job in Bermuda playing in one or two large hotels and stayed there for 11 years, returning in 1977. Whilst there he frequently accompanied visiting American artists in cabaret and he struck up a friendship with the great guitarist Jim Hall. In addition he spent several months at Berkeley in America studying arranging and composition and as a result is now heavily in demand for the wonderful music he produces. Mind you when I first met Allan we used to practice at his parent's house in Largewood Road, Tolworth, and he had a huge pile of books on drumming which he went through time and time again and thoroughly deserves the success he has enjoyed since.

Anyway in the meantime Allan was to meet yet another June whilst in Bermuda and they married and have a lovely daughter called Allison. I don't know if he talks in his sleep but it wouldn't matter would it? Now I come to think about it the words to the song "Making whoopee" contain the line "Another bride, another June, another sunny honeymoon". So that's what it was all about! Sorry – no offence intended.

It was when Allan returned to the U.K. that we went to see him playing at The Leather Bottle at Merton, a famous Jazz venue for many years where Tony Lee, (England's Errol Garner) was resident for a long period. This meeting was our first for many years, but as always, then and even now, he is very little changed from the person who had one of his first professional gigs on our wedding day.

June 7th 1977 was our 25th Wedding Anniversary and we were rather put out when the Queen and Prince Phillip decided to adopt it to celebrate her 25 years on the throne. Nevertheless we had a splendid street party in Queensville for which we were fortunate enough to have two first class chefs living in the road. I provided a small group playing the piano on the back of a small open backed truck whilst the drums and bass were just behind in an open garage. Terry and Pat our next door neighbours also provided all sorts of entertainment as did several other people. The street was decorated from one end to the other and we decided to have another house party in our house for those that were most involved in the preparations at which we were presented with a pair of candelabra for the piano, a la Liberace.

The co-operation amongst the neighbours was tremendous and on one occasion around ten of us, some in Queensville, and some backing onto our gardens, decided that we would get together and replace all the fencing. From then on every evening after work we would all descend on one area and after a couple of hours we ended up having a barbeque and drinks wherever we might be. This must have taken about three weeks, or more, to complete and we were all very sorry when it came to an end.

Very occasionally I would meet up with Norman George whom I last mentioned some while ago. In the interim he had parted from Mary and ultimately married Billie George, who of course became Susan George's mother. This upset Mary tremendously and at some time later she married someone else but this ended up in divorce after a short time. Over the years she used to see Norman's old friend, guitarist Charles Osborne, and they used to spend their weekends together whilst maintaining separate households and there was quite a strong bond there.

Meantime Linda and Gary decided to surprise us with the present of a weekend at the Ritz which was on special offer at the time. We were quite delighted with this and booked in on the Friday lunchtime and enjoyed an afternoon performance of "Les Miserables". In the evening we invited Ursula and Judy to join us for dinner which was excellent, as of course were the rooms. The following morning we got into the lift to go down for breakfast and when we looked at the only two other people in the lift who should they be but Mary and her sister! We had breakfast together and marvelled at the co-incidence, as neither of us expected to be making a return visit. Next evening we had invited Linda and Gary for dinner and this too was most enjoyable. We had to leave by lunchtime on Sunday, but before we did so we asked to look at one of the more luxury apartments which was being made ready for new guests and which overlooked Green Park. There stretched out on the grass was a tramp who had obviously slept there all night and I must say the contrast made me feel somewhat uneasy. Then came the crunch. Although bed and breakfast was included we had incurred the cost of eight dinners, which produced a bill for over £400.

Nevertheless it was an experience I would not have wanted to miss. When we arrived home we discovered that the toilet rolls had been folded to a point and our shoes were outside the bedroom – unfortunately it didn't last!

In the years that were to follow we were invited to dinner by Betty Evard, as Jimmy had died some time back, and Charles and Mary were there as well and we later reciprocated. A couple of years back we were told that Charles had died and that when Mary's niece called to take her to the funeral she found her dead in bed from natural causes. Isn't that quite remarkable?

Talking of Betty Evard I must mention that Jimmy was seriously ill for many years and this put a tremendous burden on her and she took up decorating, for which she still enjoys quite a reputation, and has only recently stopped outside work – and she is I believe well into her seventies. If that's not enough she also does a lot of work for U.N.I.C.E.F. and regularly helps with Meals on Wheels. And she started out as a dancer. Why does "This is your life" concentrate basically on so called stars from the soaps who have not lived long enough to have much say? – no need to answer – it is mainly publicity.

In our early married life, because of the estrangement of Jean's parents, we saw very little of Jean's various cousins! This changed around the early 70's and was triggered by an offer to join a car rally organised by cousins Audrey and Harry which was most enjoyable. Ultimately they organised many more outings of various types and it suddenly became clear to me that there could have been a lot more of the family at our wedding if the situation had been different. Much later a further development made some of the absences crystal clear in that Jean's cousin Eileen had married another Harry on the same day – June 7th 1952. Since her husband had died a few years back we have seen her every couple of weeks or so and she is very good company indeed. She has a reputation for being a very fine writer of short stories for which she has won many prizes, the best being a cruise in the Caribbean. She has also recently won first prize in a limerick competition in a writer's magazine. During the war she worked at the Foreign Office in Downing Street, on codes and ciphers and she has been a valuable help to me in my attempts to write this book.

Around 1985 I saw that Allan Ganley was playing at Shepperton Jazz Club and decided to pay him a visit, probably the first since seeing him at the Leather Bottle after his return from Bermuda. As a result we joined the club and remain members to this day and it has opened up a veritable stream of friendships apart from providing some of the finest Jazz in the country. It is run by Harriet and Allan Coleman and has survived despite a fire which destroyed the piano in the original location in the early days. It has since moved to four other venues, and in the last of these has moved from the smaller room to a much larger one to cater for demand. Originally the concentration was on having a guest star with a local rhythm section and I was fortunate enough to take part quite often during the early years. Harriet is a fine singer and she spent many years with one of the founder members of the club, pianist Rex Cull playing in a restaurant near Twickenham and in recent years has made several appearances at the Pizza on the Park. Harriet, who is American,, specialises in singing the verse as well as the chorus and of course Rex has been responsible for the bulk of her arrangements. Rex is a very fine pianist who, unlike me , had a thorough grounding in music and theory at the Royal College of Music, where he emerged with very good grades. In his earlier years he played for a long time at the Playboy Club. He is quite an enigma however, in that he is probably the only piano player I know who does not possess a piano at home. Despite this when another vocalist wanted to sing a particularly complicated tune in an unusual key, he disappeared into the toilet for about 10 minutes and came out with parts for himself and the bass player and it sounded great. So you see it is all in the mind.

As time went on the musicians insisted on having their own backing groups and this has developed to the point where we have many artists who also appear at Ronnie Scott's. From America we have had the late Gene Harris and Oliver Jones, Ken Peplowski, now acknowledged as the modern day Benny Goodman, Harry Allen, Scott Hamilton, Spike Robinson, Warren Vache, Ricky Woodard and many more. On the home front we have had Dave Newton, a pianist up there with the best of them, the Allan Ganley Big Band, Dave Green, Roger Nobes, John Pearce, Martin Drew formerly and still occasionally drummer with Oscar Peterson, and the very cream of

British modern jazz – but not avant-garde – thank the Lord! The real difference in this club is the fact that, with a few exceptions, nearly everyone knows each other and they often meet outside the club. For this Harriet and Allan have to take full credit – it doesn't just happen.

For me one of the great attractions is that the club has a beautiful Yamaha Grand piano, supplied by Sylvia and Brian Ford, also members of the club, and we discovered that, as a child, Sylvia lived within 200 yards of Jean near Brixton. We regard them as great friends and see them quite often.

As I neared retirement I was playing with one or two of the local groups and through these I met a wonderful singer called Annie Noel and we seemed to hit it off from the start. Annie had won a place in the grand final of London Weekend's "Search for a Star" in 1981 and spent several years as a resident vocalist on Radio 2 on "Nightride", and "You are the Night and the Music" and appeared as guest vocalist with the B.B.C. Radio Orchestra.

As a result I was asked to accompany her at Shepperton Jazz Club on several occasions. And these events were most enjoyable because people came specifically to listen, I had a very fine piano to play and conditions were as good as you can get. For these we generally got together to sort out a program and include some new material. This is where the fun began as had any casual observer listened to what took place he might have thought Annie was on drugs of some sort. Unfortunately she has no knowledge whatsoever of music and had developed her own shorthand system of notation, involving "uppers" and "downers" – if you see what I mean! Most of the arrangements we had were initially improvised on the spot and if considered O.K. would be incorporated for the future programs. Only very few were written first and performed afterwards. I found this most rewarding and enjoyable and was devastated when she decided, for very good reasons, to move back to her native Torquay some years back.

I was given the opportunity of backing Roger Nobes, the vibraphone player who has been with Dave Shepherd's Benny Goodman type band for some time. As it happens both he and I were very fond of the record "Soul Fusion" performed by Milt Jackson and Monty Alexander – one of my Desert Island Disc choices – not that I have been asked! As a result we played several of the pieces giving a complete contrast to Mr.B.G. and, again it seemed to go well from the start – and I have a tape to prove it!

Similarly we seemed to achieve an immediate rapport when I played with Julian Stringle a young clarinettist who has since gone from strength to strength. However, in recent years, he was asked to record an album consisting solely of Latin American Music, and although he plays very fine Jazz he was not allowed to put in a single note additional to the melody, which must have been quite frustrating. However the company financing this deal had a 17 1/2% interest in Japan and as the Japanese could not pronounce "Stringle" they insisted on calling him "Julian Marc" thus making use of his middle name only! I understand that it is selling particularly well in India amongst other places and I can only think Edmundo Ros must wonder where he went wrong. Please don't misunderstand me, there is nothing wrong with the playing, it is quite immaculate, but for my money, a waste of good talent. Fortunately, since writing this paragraph he has just produced a new Jazz C.D. which displays his talents to the full.

I was playing in a wine bar in Windsor once, when an American lady came across before we started and asked us to play the "Penthouse Serenade" for her. When I asked if there was any special reason, she said that her brother wrote it. As it happened I was the only one who knew it well but after a brief discussion we managed to put on a reasonable performance. A little while later she left whilst we were actually playing, leant across and thanked me and put a £5 note in my pocket. In the interval I decided to use it to get us all a drink, and everybody had halves – mostly non alcoholic – and the bill came to £7.50!! and there were only five of us involved, and this was in the eighties!

Sometime later we put on a George Shearing evening at which I told a few stories about the Feldman Club and the Coliseum Concert, and I also related the wine bar incident, quite forgetting that one of the audience had made a request for "Skylark" which, as it happened, I intended to play solo, incorporating a slight reference to "Gymnopedies", similar, but nothing like the way the great man might have done. Anyway, came the interval and this lady came up and thrust a £10 note into my hand, to my great embarrassment!

Whilst trying to decide what to write next I have today received a letter from Geoff Banks whom you will remember played tenor sax with me during my army career and I quote – "I enclose a side A tape of a few Shearing 47/47 creations. Do listen to track 5 – Poinciana. If I needed a case against drummers it would suffice. Is he in the same studio? It's Norman Burns by the way with Jack Fallon on bass. Both to be reckoned with in their day". Now this is quite an amazing coincidence and takes me back to an incident which happened to me when this record first came out. At the time I was doing occasional gigs with a very well known South London Bandleader who shall be nameless. He had a reputation of being the last man to the bar during the interval and in fact never actually reached it most of the time. In addition he owned a record shop to which I used to go occasionally. I had heard that this record had been issued and said I would like to hear it, so he ordered a copy specially. When I went to the shop and heard just how overbearing the drums were I said to him that I really did not fancy it as it was so out of balance. Whereupon this very "careful" man picked up the record saying "well it's no good to me either" and promptly smashed it to pieces on the counter!

On the subject of drummers I have fairly strong opinions and I have on occasion suggested that "Drummers should be felt and not heard". Do please use the correct interpretation of the word "felt". Too often these days we are subject to a veritable battery, even when someone is taking a delicate solo and it does absolutely nothing for me – and a lot of other people I know. Neither do I feel is it essential if you have a quartet, to have a drum solo during every single number as happens in a large percentage of cases. Let's face it the primary purpose of the drums is to keep the whole thing swinging along and whilst on occasion it may sound musical it is not exactly a melody instrument. I believe Allan would agree with me on this point. One, or maximum of two solos in each half is quite sufficient in my opinion. If you listen to records of small groups you find that there are nothing like the number of drum features that the same group would play in public. I rest my case!

Having mentioned coincidences, we once had a holiday in Anglesey and visited a very remote beach with only the one lane for access. This was very popular and we found that there was only one parking space available which we took. On emerging from the car I was amazed to find that our number plate – 279 NPE, was right next to 278 NPE. – "In all the bars........." We used to try to remember our car number plates using mnemonics and the best we achieved only required us to remember 6Y – The full number was PYW 416Y – or Pay your way for once 6Y.

On another holiday in Scotland, a place called Lochgoilhead, I went fishing in a boat, on a lake, early one morning with Linda and Gary and I'm afraid when it comes to intricate knots and the like, I am not very handy. At one stage I said between gritted teeth, "where's the b...... float". Of course the b..... float was what caused me to grit my teeth! I have not been allowed to forget that one.

When staying in the region of Newmarket we decided to take Gary to the races to try to demonstrate what a waste of money gambling is. Needless to say he won overall although I'm pleased to say he did not develop the habit. I cannot believe the way people imagine they are going to win when the odds are 14 million to one and it would grieve me to see all my hard earned money going down the drain. I must confess to being partly influenced by one of my leather workers who had to pay back a large portion of his wage packet on pay day, only to borrow it all again the following Monday! And his wife also worked in the department and used to create merry hell with him. To this day I have never taken part in the lottery and would not know how to go about it. I do indulge in investing via unit trusts as there is some hope there and in the main I have been lucky. Mind you I should have sold those Technology shares but then so should a lot of people.

Because Jean had made a study of pigeons at teacher training college we all became interested in bird watching and where possible this was a feature of most holidays. This can be quite frustrating at times and invariably you see the unusual ones when you are least prepared, such as the Sparrowhawk which landed about

185

20 yards from the bottom of my garden and stayed there for around 20 minutes one day. I did see a Bittern, a very rare bird in flight at Minsmere once and very early on a Bearded Tit about 6 ft outside one of the hides there, but that was a long time ago. After I retired and moved to Gt.Bookham, in the early days I recorded no less than 19 different types of birds in our garden during one lunch period. I have not seen a Coal Tit, or a Siskin for many years and even more common birds are definitely in decline – here at least.

On two occasions I was called upon for jury service and the first time was at Newington Butts, near Elephant & Castle. The magistrate was a relative, brother, I believe, of George Robey, and apart from this I recall the comment made by one of the police saying, "I raised my truncheon and aimed for his shoulder – but I hit him on the head!"

On one of my gigs in the mid eighties Jean used to sit next to a chap in the audience who really preferred Jazz as played until the early 30's and one day gave her a tape comprising all his favourite piano players for me to listen to at leisure. In the car on the way home we listened to several American pianists, and then there was a comment from this fan that "Now for a change here is British pianist Gerry Moore" and of course this brought back very fond memories of his kindness to me as a lad. The next week I took along a tape of some of my own playing but the chap was not there. There was a different tenor player depping for our regular man and he heard me relating this tale and he turned round and said that he had been best man for Gerry when he married for the second time a few years earlier. I was astonished that he was still alive as he must have been approaching 80 by then. I learnt that although their home was well up country, Gerry had a flat in London and was still playing solo several nights a week at a large hotel. I asked the tenor player to give him my regards and the following week I had a phone call from the man himself, and he was still enthusing about jazz in such a way that he could almost have been a newcomer to jazz! There is undoubtedly something about jazz that enables musicians to co-exist regardless of age.

Every Xmas we invited a number of the neighbours in for drinks before dinner on Xmas day, which was always an enjoyable occasion. On one of these we had been discussing bird watching and after everyone had left I had a phone call from Terry, next door, suggesting I should look out of the window as there was a "Black arsed vulture" in the garden, which caused some merriment in our slightly inebriated state. The following year we were again phoned and told to look on the top of Terry's shed and lo and behold, there was a sizeable black chicken – it was a model that our other neighbours had brought back from holiday in Spain.

Sometime, I believe it was in the early 80's, Denny Rose invited us to a musician's get together run by Len Smith, a drummer, who had a business making furniture for M.F.I. He lived in a large house with a small swimming pool and snooker table in the Kenley area. He and his wife Jay used to have open house to what I have come to term the older gang of musicians, and their wives, one Sunday every month. The main players had formed part of a very successful commercial band. We normally took some food and drink along, but once a year, around Xmas time he would put on a lavish spread. It was not particularly Jazz orientated but what was interesting was the way they could dig up really good tunes that not too many people had heard of, which should have been far more popular then they were. Denny would play saxophone and sometimes a very good electric guitar and he liked to sing and had a very good voice into the bargain.

Frank Roberts was another of the regulars on Jazz violin and I once met Ronnie Gleaves, who had played at our wedding, at one of these sessions. Unfortunately when he lost the contract Len was compelled to move and I believe the house became a nursing home or something similar. From then on the occasions were few and far between.

During the last two years before retiring we used to spend many of our weekends touring any of the areas of Surrey where we thought we might like to spend our retirement. I must confess that for many years I was fairly adamant that I never intended moving but as time elapsed conditions in London, plus one or two road schemes that were in the pipeline, made us review the position. Over this period we would visit each district several times and get information on the houses that were available at the time and we had a folder for each district. By the time we had finished we had an apple box full of folders many covering the same house at different levels of price. This proved quite useful as it gave us time to build up a picture of the pro's and con's of each area and made the final decision that much easier. Now I intend to deal with "Moving House" in a later chapter in the book, but meanwhile perhaps a little light relief on some of my medical experiences would be a good idea.

Roy at a garden Jazz Party 1985

MATTERS MEDICAL
(OR TOUCHING ON THE HUMERUS)

My earliest recollection of anything to do with hospital came when I caught Scarlet Fever at around the age of 6 or 7. In those days the treatment required being sent to an isolation hospital out of contact with the family and I was certainly away for around five of six weeks which at that age is not a pleasant experience. Somehow I always tie this in with a round scar on the inside of my right kneecap, although I cannot remember for the life of me how I got it. Other than this I seemed to be fairly prone to getting a bad cough far too often and this turned into whooping cough on several occasions. This apart I enjoyed a reasonably healthy childhood with the odd bout of flu occurring but not on an annual basis. On the whole with three major exceptions I rarely had time off work for illness but I did suffer very considerably with Hay Fever. This kicked in sometime in my late twenties or early thirties and went on for quite a while until it went as quickly as it had arrived. I must have had many doses of Piriton tablets and other remedies which did have the effect of making you quite drowsy.

Now in 1964 we had a holiday in Anglesey on a farmhouse where one of the standard meals was tinned salmon and chips which is what made it memorable! They had a kitten to which our daughter Linda became very attached – she would have been 9 years old at the time. Anyway we were persuaded, against our better judgement, to take the cat home, hence the arrival of Toffee in Clapham. Believe you me we should have checked her pedigree (chum) for she definitely qualified as maladjusted. When racing from the garden she used to hit the step so hard that she would somersault into the kitchen and several times she jumped from the upstairs window. Trouble was she survived every time. That wasn't so bad but then she took to going out for long, very long walks. She had a collar with our phone number round her neck and the first call I remember came from the Streatham Bus Garage. I'm not sure whether she jumped on the No.37 or just walked there but yours truly had to fetch her. This happened at several other places and the next notable occasion was a call from the local Catholic Church where she had been found near the altar. Here it is perhaps worth explaining that we were probably the only non–Catholics in Queensville Road and we later discovered that for this reason it was also known as Pope's Row! So obviously our cat was trying to ingratiate herself with the neighbours.

The next thing that happened was that, one by one, we all got Chicken Pox and I was the worst affected. My father used to come to look at us through the front room window but, effectively, we were in isolation for quite a long period. Then we received phone calls from the area of Balham Station saying that our cat had arrived at a nearby shop and what were we going to do about it. We could only ask them to put her out again and subsequently there were two further calls from the same area. On receipt of this last message we asked them to kindly remove the name tag and phone number before releasing her and finally we were on our own once more – which goes to prove that every cloud has a silver lining! Earlier in 1961 I suddenly experienced the most excruciating pain which literally drove me up the wall – I certainly found it impossible to lie still at the time and it was fairly soon diagnosed as Renal colic caused by kidney stones. I was then sent to hospital for confirmation where I was injected with Pethidine in both buttocks on a very regular basis. I believe that this helped me to overcome some of my previous aversion to the needle.

After a few days they managed to get it under control but by this time I had managed to get a virus which meant they were unable to operate so I was sent home to get well enough for the op. Amazingly my driving test came up during this period and to my surprise I passed first time helped in no uncertain manner by the chap who actually overtook on the outside of me as I was halfway across a right turn. As I took this in my stride I am sure this was a deciding factor.

Anyway shortly afterwards I returned for the operation and 24 hours after the deed had been done I was still unable to pass water and I recall saying to the nurse "If my waters don't break soon you will have to give me a Caesarean". This operation kept me off work for six weeks involving quite a large incision which took some time to heal. Eventually we returned to see the surgeon who showed me a really tiny stone which had obstructed a ledge in the kidney. I asked him what the cause was and he said "You have been easting too many strawberries". Now as it happens strawberries are possibly my most favourite fruit as for example you will never see me eat a raw apple or orange and I mostly prefer the berries and currant fruits after cooking. The result was that for the next 16 years I avoided strawberries, except for the time that Jean tried to serve them up minus the pips which was a complete disaster not to be recommended.

In 1977 would you believe I had a repeat performance and yet another long incision crossing over the first near the waistline on the left hand side of the body. Unfortunately keyhole surgery had yet to arrive and this meant another seven weeks off. At this stage I felt that a zip fastener might have been a good idea. Then we went for the diagnosis, only to be told that I had been eating too much cheese and drinking too much milk which was fair comment although I was not aware that this could be a problem. I said immediately "What about strawberries?" and the reply was "I wouldn't worry too much about them, the season is too short!" I have to confess that since then and despite the fact that the strawberry season is possibly three times as long these days as it was then I never pass up an opportunity to indulge myself. Mind you I was somewhat apprehensive until 1993 came and went, especially as I have heard that Bing Crosby had five such operations.

In 1993 I was lined up for a prostate operation following extensive tests and this was to take place in May. I was told that after the operation, involving a very old procedure, I would not be allowed to drive for two weeks and could not play golf for six weeks but at the last moment it was postponed for lack of a bed. Eventually I was taken in in July by which time they were in a position to treat me with a more up-to-date method which was quicker to heal. In fact when I returned to the hospital less than 2 weeks after the op. they first made sure I was firing on all cylinders – so to speak – then discharged me. I asked when I would be allowed to drive and was told that I could drive home immediately if I felt like it. I asked about playing golf and again was told I could play the following day and I played just nine holes – somewhat gingerly I must admit. Thereafter I played twice a week until I took part in the senior's tournament five weeks after the operation and not only won it with a score of 47 Stapleford points but this was then the record score for the 10 year period that the seniors section had been in existence.

I was somewhat embarrassed by the fact that Peter Day, who helped me to attain a handicap when I first joined the club, came into the clubhouse after me, beaming all over his face, only to discover that his 46 points was not quite good enough. The following week was time for the usual 6 week check up and when I went into see the surgeon he said "Tell me Mr.Cook – have you noticed any improvement" to which I just had to respond "yes – my golf is a hell of a sight better – and you can expect a queue of seniors who will try anything to improve their game!" I believe that I was so successful simply because I was afraid of hurting myself by trying too hard – as we all seem to do most of the time.

The following year I had an operation for Haemorrhoids about which the less said the better - it is painful enough trying to spell the blessed name.

Around 1996 I began to experience a touch of Arthritis in my left thumb and I saw a specialist who initially gave me an injection which he later repeated but this did not improve matters. This is one way of emulating Oscar Peterson that I could well do without. He also pointed out that the little finger on the left hand needed an operation for what is called Duypuytron's Contraction – alias Trigger Finger – which was successfully performed in January 1998. Somewhat later I decided to try Acupuncture and was very impressed with the initial hour long session covering my previous medical history complete with check-up which revealed to my complete amazement that I was suffering from high blood pressure. I argued strongly that I could not believe this, all to no avail. After 6 hour long sessions I decided that I was wasting my time and money and called it quits, not before asking her to re-check my blood pressure again. The result confirmed her original findings and I decided it was necessary to consult my own doctor for his opinion. Surprise, surprise, I was completely normal and I took the opportunity of phoning the lady and suggested she should perhaps have her equipment checked over! So much for the "thorough" check.

Much later I was persuaded by the wife of a very good friend to see an osteopath who had a very good reputation in his field. In talking to him about how it was affecting my jazz playing he volunteered the fact that some years previously he had treated Ronnie Scott at his club for severe back problems. I told him that Ronnie had in fact mentioned in one of his books that his trouble had been caused by bending over backwards trying to please Stan Getz.

In this connection I once heard a story about one of Stan Getz's ardent followers in this country who invited him to come to dinner at his house one evening. Apparently he stayed with him for two weeks, made numerous expensive phone calls to America and left without paying a penny. He certainly was a strange man. I gather that the fan eventually went to America some two years later and did eventually get paid for the phone calls, which I suppose is something!

Coming back to the subject the osteopath was unable to do much other than to recommend that I should immerse my hands in water as hot as I could bear and to manipulate them in a manner he showed me. I mentioned that I had been using a spray containing Ibuprofen on my thumb before playing and his advice was to use it afterwards. From my point of view it is very difficult to be specific as to whether this gives some relief as there is always some feeling of pain, however slight, and it is very frustrating not being able to do certain simple actions. The one good thing about playing jazz is that you can tailor your improvisation to your physical capabilities and as the right hand is generally more dominant – so far – so good!

In the last two years or so I have had a worrying tendency towards an almost permanent cough, combined with serious nasal problems, which I have variously attributed to having had whooping cough in my youth, my own smoking – long since given up, and having shared an office with a 60 a day smoker. Apart, of course, from playing in smoky atmospheres. This became so acute that it affected me simply when talking to people and became a real embarrassment. My doctor tried various nasal sprays, none of which worked, and I eventually saw a specialist who diagnosed an acute allergy to grass and tree pollen and possibly an allergy to milk and wheat. Now to a keen gardener and golfer this was a bit too much and I eventually decided when I suffered throughout the winter that pollen could not be the answer. Then I discovered that I could obtain regular supplies of Goat's milk from our milkman and was astonished to find an almost immediate improvement. This has only been going for about four months and although I still cough sometimes all my friends have noticed quite a difference to my voice. This is still a source of wonderment to me although I have to say that I miss the range of cheeses I used to enjoy as goat's cheese is very limited. Re reading this chapter I find that I should have mentioned that I positively refused to give up eating cheese despite the problems with stones on the grounds that I would rather have the latest operation when they "Zap" them rather than suffer from brittle bones and be unable to "golf" or "garden". Overall I cannot complain at my state of health and I don't!

ABOUT PIANOS

The first piano we had at Laitwood Road was an upright Chappell which was bought for me to learn on by my parents. It was fairly old but served the purpose in those early days. As I progressed I felt the need for a better instrument and at great expense I purchased a second hand Spencer Baby Grand from the piano department in Bon Marche in Brixton. I entered into a hire purchase agreement for the princely sum of 192 guineas – a lot of money in those days. I should perhaps add that I was firmly convinced that if I did not get a grand piano before getting married I would never have one. Fortunately our front room in Balham was very large and could take this quite easily.

In the years that followed there was a period when you could hardly give a piano away and if one had the space for storage there were many bargains to be had. However be that as it may I eventually married and moved into a more modern, but somewhat smaller property where the piano eventually took pride of place on the immediate left of the fireplace where I sat back to the door. We had parties fairly frequently and as I was generally the only pianist I would be "in situ" for most of the evening. On more than one occasion I said to Jean the following morning that I was surprised that "so & so didn't come" only to discover that they had been there all the time and in fact I was not much of a host!

After some 25 years or so the instrument had performed pretty well but the action was beginning to be rather noisy. Then one day, I believe in 1974, I went to Ronnie Scott's to see Oscar Peterson perform and I came away thinking that I might be able to make a better showing with a more modern piano. The very next day I went to

Fischer's in Streatham, long since departed, and came away having paid £1350 for a 5ft 9in Kawai grand piano and getting £320 in part exchange for the Spencer. This turned out to be a very good buy as apart from being a far superior instrument, my timing was pretty good as I have to insure it for £9000 today.

Frankly, the modern piano is in my opinion much better than some of the earlier Steinways and Bechsteins because of the types of glues now used and the treatment of the timber, and the Japanese have made great advances in this field. Certainly my Kawai is still in very good condition and only requires tuning twice yearly – with the odd attention for a special party.

When the early Yamaha pianos first arrived I felt that they were inclined to be rather harsh and strident in tone and I felt that the Kawai was much better from this point of view. Some time ago I heard that Yamaha had opened a new showroom somewhere behind Oxford Circus and decided to pay a visit. I got lost on the way and ended up outside Bluthner's showroom and when I asked them where Yamaha was located they insisted on showing me their products. Rightly or wrongly I have always regarded Bluthner's as suppliers of ladies pianos having a softer, gentler touch and sound. To my amazement the instruments I tried were quite raucous and nothing like my previous recollections.

I thanked them and moved on to Yamaha and related my findings to the salesman there. He told me that the original Yamaha was produced, not unreasonably, with the Japanese idea of sound in mind. They had since discovered that there was a need to tone the instrument down a bit for the export models and as he demonstrated they had made a considerable improvement. Unfortunately for Bluthner's they had lost a lot of business

198

at the hands of Yamaha and had tried to emulate them and in so doing had lost the tone for which they were famous and for which I am sure there is still a demand.

In the chapter dealing with my army service I referred to playing a ship's piano on board the S.S.Samaria. These pianos are especially produced with a keyboard which folds up almost flush to the body of the piano and this is presumably done to avoid possible damage to the action when there is a storm at sea by disconnecting the horizontal from the vertical parts of the action. The one in question was quite amazing in that there was no ivory "or whatever" on the surface of most of the keys and furthermore on those most used the wood of the key had been worn down revealing the metal spike beneath which guided the key. Fortunately the wear produced a sort of crater in the wood which prevented damage to one's fingertips and yet, despite all this, it produced a very acceptable sound and I can honestly say I have had to play far worse instruments. It did require a slight adjustment to achieve a good sound but as all pianos vary considerably this was no problem – just very unusual!

I remember in my early married days when we went on holiday one of the first things I would do on my arrival was to find a pub with a piano to avoid the withdrawal symptoms I suffered otherwise. Nowadays of course there is no point in looking.

With very few exceptions for the past 12 years or so I have become a "Keyboard Player" when playing away from home and as I mentioned earlier on in the book this is a more tedious and time consuming business giving far less satisfaction. I am now on my second instrument having changed for one with much better sound quality and equally important one having a good weighted key action. Some of the keyboards are so light to the fingertips that if used to the exclusion of the steam piano for any length of time would make it difficult to revert. Even this action bears no comparison to the feel of a good grand piano. They will of course tell you that it does not require tuning – which is true. On the other hand a few weeks back I set up the keyboard and switched on only to find that I could not produce a sound from it. Fortunately a very good friend had once offered to let me have his keyboard in an emergency and he arrived to my very great relief and undying gratitude within 40 minutes of phoning, When I put the instrument in the repairer's hands he had great difficulty tracing the problem which turned out to be a capacitor smaller than my little finger but the time element produced a bill for £100. This is equivalent to two years tuning on my Kawai.

On of the joys of life in London used to be a visit to Harrod's piano department when it occupied one of the large central showrooms. It was almost like visiting a museum, and I suppose if I am honest that applies to the store as a whole, as I believe a large number of the items on sale will probably feature in the Antiques Road Show in the year 2100. Now at one stage of my career working for Barrow Hepburn our chairman was Professor Roland Smith in his early days. I have always resented the fact that not long after taking over and having his famous battle for control of Harrods with Tiny Rowlands – remember the phrase – "get your tanks off my lawn" – he relegated the pianos to a much smaller side showroom.

O.K. it is business I know but I spent many an enjoyable hour or so there originally. Mind you I also resent the way they change the football strip so often now that he is in charge of merchandise at Manchester United P.L.C. and find it hard to believe that this could be anyone else's decision but his own. If I am wrong I apologise!

The strangest gig that came my way was depping for someone at a club called The Pink Elephant. I was quite pleased to learn that there was a grand piano to play but when I arrived I discovered that the lid was down and the reason for this was that the drummer sat on top of the piano. This might be termed economic use of space but for all the sound coming from it it could have been an upright.

On another occasion I was playing at a pub in Putney where there was a very old upright which created an awful lot of noise quite apart from notes. Before we started we went through it very carefully and ended up with a beer mug on top of the piano full of bits and pieces and invited anyone who wanted a piece of the action to come forward!

One Sunday, Jean and I went to the Dog & Fox in Wimbledon to see Max Brittain playing with Dick Charlesworth and his group. There was a grand piano on the stand but no pianist and I was invited to sit in after the interval. When I sat on the piano stool I realised that there was hardly any room to move as the piano was extremely close to the edge of the platform which was about 20" high. There was no room for any adjustment without having a major upheaval so I soldiered on with great difficulty. However I have always had a tendency to rock backwards and forwards whilst playing and this literally proved my downfall as I went over backwards and performed a back somersault, rising to my feet to great applause which had nothing to do with my piano playing! This of course became known as the piano roll!

There is a piano player called "Cross Hands Pete" whom I met some years back and believe it or not he earned the name because that is how he plays – with one hand crossing over the other. The simple explanation of this unusual phenomenon is that he learned to play on a piano-accordion – and strapped it on the wrong way round!! Now Pete Waters – to use his full name – had a heart attack several years back and a lot of musicians got together to arrange a benefit night for him. This was a job for an electric piano and when one group vacated the stand Angela Christian, who used to sing with The Big Radio Band, got up together with Alan Berry, a fine pianist and Lennie Best, a fine vibraphone player mentioned earlier in the book and accompanied her singing "They can't take that away from me" in the key of B flat. All went well until Lennie tried to take a chorus on vibes and experienced the greatest difficulty. What none of us knew was that someone who shall be nameless had taken it up a semi-tone, as you can with the modern keyboard, and left him in the key of B – i.e. in 5 sharps, which is not exactly playing the game. I can now never think of the tune without referring to "They can't take that away from B"!!

There are some musicians who have what is known as perfect pitch and are able to tell in what key any tune is being performed. Personally I feel that because there are so slight variations from the "perfect" level this must surely be an irritation at times. On the other hand a very good friend of ours Frank Roberts, who plays a very fine jazz violin, and once played for the Malcolm Mitchell Trio has told me a rather nice story about his own perfect pitch. Apparently his wife, Diana, woke him up one night and said I believe someone is stealing our car" and Frank, without moving a muscle, was able to say "No that's not our car – ours in second gear plays in the key of A so it's nothing to do with us – goodnight!"

There was a very long period soon after our children, Linda and Gary, were born in 1955 & 1960 when I opted out of playing mainly because of pressure of work in my day job and also when they were having piano lessons it was difficult to get on the piano at home. Eventually the need to play became more and more urgent and in 1976 we found a pub in Ashtead where there was a regular Sunday evening Jazz session with some very fine musicians and although there was a piano they had no one to play it. From then on I used to play for nothing just to keep my hand in. There was a fine bevy of musicians including Brian White who runs several bands playing mainly Dixieland style and his clarinet playing is good enough for anyone. He tours all round these days and is I believe a regular visitor to the Acapulco Jazz Festival. In addition, there was Gough Dubber another sax player mainly in the same bracket as far as style is concerned. This is where I met up with Max Brittain an excellent modern guitarist with whom I still play occasionally. In addition, the drummer was also from the trad jazz side and there was another guitarist and a tenor sax player more in the modern style. The leader of this somewhat mixed bag of musicians was a trumpet player called Tony Malcolm who used to burst into song with "I'm the king of the swingers" complete with lots of actions. The place was packed out week after week and had a really good atmosphere until the day come when Tony had a very serious illness and the band performed without him. They made the discovery that Tony had been subsidising the gig for some considerable time as they received only a third of the amount he had previously paid them! What's more on one occasion he had brought in Humphrey Littleton to mark some anniversary and I shudder to think what this must have cost him. This is even more proof that people who like playing jazz do it primarily for their own pleasure and not for monetary reward – with the exception of course of a very small minority.

Finally, I must mention the day when I was booked to play for a wedding at a hall in Tooting. On arrival, I went to find out what sort of instrument was on offer only to find that absolutely no musical sounds came out whatsoever when

I ran my fingers over the keys. I then took the front off, it was an upright, and discovered that all those tiny ribbons which bring the keys back into position were non-existent or broken. After some thought I asked someone to provide me with a long piece of string which I then placed around all the keys in the hope that those that were activated would be brought back by the others. Unfortunately this did not work. I then realised that we had two piano stools on offer and we placed these in front of the piano at either end and tilted the instrument forward to get a gravity feed and to my amazement this worked. I then sat on an ordinary chair and started to play whilst wondering whether I should have taken out an insurance policy, although I had never heard of anyone being killed by a piano – yet. The lead instrument in the group on this occasion was a vibraphone and – would you believe it – the blessed piano was exactly a semitone out!

Now for any other occasion I think I would have been entitled to call it a day but for someone's wedding we had to soldier on. As I recall we spent most of the evening with me playing in A flat and the vibes player was in the key of G and the written key for the majority of the tunes we played was neither of these. This was well before the electric keyboard was available and is a very major plus point in its favour.

Saying this has reminded me of the gig I went to in Surrey when living in Clapham Park and as I was setting up I discovered that I had left the bag with all the cables and connections at home. I phoned Jean and got her out of the bath and, bless her cotton socks, she came charging down in her Mini but of course did not arrive until interval time. For some strange reason we did not get asked back here and I am pleased to say that it has so far not happened again.

There is a certain challenge involved in trying to get the best results out of different pianos and you have to adapt very considerably to the varied actions that you have to play. In some ways there is a parallel with the leather industry in that no two pieces or pianos are the same – even if they come from the same producer.

AROUND THE WORLD IN 40 DAYS

Jean and I were never that keen on holidays abroad but when we retired, after having moved to Bookham, we spent sometime sorting out the new house and then decided on a once In a lifetime trip around the world but with the emphasis on spending a large proportion of the time in New Zealand with our friends Ursula and Judy.

On the 18th February we left Heathrow on a Cathay Pacific flight bound for a 3 day stopover in Hong Kong where we stayed at the Century Hotel, from which we had a restricted view over the harbour. We were most impressed with the facilities and the general air of bustle in the city. Mind you we very soon realised that owning a car here must be a nightmare but this is very much offset by the proliferation of taxis which were available all the time. What is amazing is the number of shops, in many cases next door to each other selling jewellery. These all seem to be family businesses and one wonders how they can all survive.

Just before we left we had been to a musical party of the older gang at Derek and Honorie's house in Bromley. Their grand-daughter was playing cello and had been asked to try to get a better instrument and my help in locating one was requested. I then phoned Malcolm Creese, who was then John Dankworth's regular bass player, for assistance, and was answered by a female voice who told me that Malcolm was just reaching the end of a tour of Australia and New Zealand with Stan Tracey and was in Hong-Kong at the time, where the tour would end the following Sunday, the day after our arrival. She spoke with Malcolm and we were instructed to visit "The Jazz Club" in Hong Kong without fail, which of course we did. Apart from Stan and Malcolm the group included Clark Tracey,

Stan's son and Art Themen a tenor player with whom I had played at Shepperton Jazz Club a couple of times. This of course was a wonderful start to our tour and apart from having a brief chat with Stan for the first time ever, Malcolm also introduced us to Warren Vache, a very fine American flugelhorn player who like us was there to watch, after having played elsewhere earlier on.

The following day we took the Star Ferry across to Kowloon and the Peak tram to overlook the city from the heights. We also discovered the very modern shopping precincts which from the outside looked more like banks as their presence did not seem to be advertised in any way. I was highly amused on visiting a men's toilet in one such centre to see that a number of the individual urinals were supposedly reserved exclusively for customers of one particular shop, the rest being for general use. Now just how do you enforce that one! Well I could not see a camera anywhere. We travelled on their underground metro system which was absolutely spotless, but of course of very recent origin compared to our own. It was fascinating watching the enormous amount of building work being carried out, constantly shrinking the waterway between H.K. and Kowloon, there being nowhere else to expand. The result is that the hotel overlooking the harbour that you visit one year could well be in a back street within a very few years. At Malcolm's behest we visited Delaney's, an Irish Bar, to see an amazing Banjo player playing with a small group and although this is not one of my favourite instruments I have to concede this chap was rather special.

Next day we took an organised coach trip which called at a Buddhist Temple, a large market where most of the produce was still alive, a very quaint walled village where a number of the local ladies wore hats with extremely large brims – especially for the tourist photographers – for a fee, and ended up overlooking the border with China. Unfortunately it was a very misty day and my photo could have been taken anywhere. It was during this trip that we kept seeing weddings being performed anywhere and everywhere, sometimes in the most public places. We bade farewell to Hong Kong the next day and were pleased to have been here before the colony was handed over to China the following year. An impressive start to our trip!

We again travelled on Cathay Pacific which I believe was the finest of the various airlines we were to use in the ensuing weeks. On arrival at Sydney we booked in to the Holiday Inn Menzies which was within easy walking distance of most places including the Opera House which we were unlucky not to be able to tour on the days we visited it. We did take a cruise around the harbour which was notable for being devoid not only of graffiti, but also advertisements, and you realise how much nicer some of our towns would be without the obligatory hoardings everywhere and anywhere. I must confess that the older I get the more obnoxious I find adverts, particularly those associated with television and radio. These days apparently we are incapable of taking the point unless the decibels are raised quite offensively, and in my case at least when I do listen I rarely know or remember what the end product is that is on offer. If I could find a programs giving a reasonable choice of good music, not necessarily jazz, I would be prepare to pay if there were no ads. We took a trip across to Manley and also went on the mono-rail which runs around the city. In places this runs through streets high up within just a few feet of shop windows and when it was built it must have been a nightmare. It is a very good way to view the city and includes a running commentary telling you all the important places. When we came off we found our way to Sydney Aquarium, which was most impressive, and of course, similar places can now be found over here. As we walked away from the aquarium I noticed an odd looking building not far away and the sign outside indicated that this was housing a display of Chinese Ice Sculptures and we went inside to investigate. The exhibition was due to close the following week but had been there continuously since before Xmas. This was a very large area and inside there were rows of refrigeration units closely packed together all round the unit. They provided warm coats to combat the drop in temperature we were to undergo. The sculptures were quite out of this world covering elaborate ships, bridges, figures of people and animals and temples. The item that took my breath away, situated behind a large figure of a shark, was what I can only describe as a screen roughly 8ft tall and around 20ft long so intricately carved it was like filigree work – if that is the right description. There was a life size figure of a woman which I ascribe to being Jean after 20 minutes inside – or Lot's wife! I have the photo to prove it. On the Saturday we went up their equivalent of the Post Office Tower which is 1000ft. tall. The view at that height was spectacular particularly as Sydney Harbour was a mass of small boats, it being the weekend. In the hotel, after dinner on the first night we discovered there was a piano bar and the sight of a grand piano was like a magnet. The pianist, a chap called Tim Foot, had a style I can only describe as being a cross between Elton John and Barry Manilow. He had a very good voice and the piano was surrounded with tall stools occupied by his girl friend and several of their friends who joined in most of the songs, and very pleasant it was too. Eventually when he realised that I was also a pianist he invited me to play a few pieces. Then he came across and said he had always wanted to sing Sinatra's songs but did not know how to accompany them – would I mind backing him. After hesitating for all of two seconds we were away for almost 45 minutes and it worked very well indeed. The following night, our last night, the same thing happened and was well received by the audience who gathered round.

Before going down to dinner that evening I suddenly recalled that amongst the names uncovered in our family tree there was a Shimell living somewhere near Sydney and I found a local telephone directory and there, sure enough, living in Avalon a little north of Sydney I came across Sven Shimell and his wife Gae. They answered and I tried to get them to join us for dinner but unfortunately they had already made other arrangements for that evening and we had to leave the following day. Nevertheless we had a short interesting conversation although I was annoyed with myself for not thinking of this earlier.

When we first arrived we went straight to a chemist for protection from the sun which was very hot indeed. I asked for 25 factor cream such as we had bought previously in England only to be told that 15 factor was the maximum and in effect 25 was just not possible! You have to believe that with their vast experience on the subject they ought to know. It came as a surprise that tipping was not expected, excepting in the more expensive establishments. Summing up we were very impressed with this city and by the end of our travels we decided it had the finest harbour of those we came across. Next day we took a cab to the airport passing the large sign we had seen on our arrival saying "Go home pommes!" and went to Auckland, this time by Air New Zealand, who although very good could not quite match up to Cathay Pacific – well that's our opinion.

Ursula and Judy were waiting for us at Auckland and the most surprising feature of the Airport was the lack of huge crowds such as we had experienced elsewhere, but of course this is virtually the end of the line – so to speak. The journey to Tauranga, overlooking The Bay of Plenty, where they live, took just over two hours and was quite spectacular. Everywhere was lush and green and there seemed to be an awful lot of fairly gentle slopes or hillocks for a large part of the journey with plenty of sheep about. When we finally reached their house it was on a two acre site, the nearest neighbour being a few hundred yards away. The house was built on the highest point on the plot and commanded a wonderful view over the Bay of Plenty and the garden. There was a very large decking balcony, on stilts because of the slope, and high enough for a cherry picker to pass under when they needed some repairs to be carried out. It was very well appointed and we frequently ate outside on the decking. Immediately beneath this there were all sorts of trees and shrubs, in the centre of which was a small swimming pool, and this gave a very good opportunity for bird watching and of course there were plenty of them. Australian Magpies are completely different to our own and during our stay we also saw Pied Stilts, Bellbirds, Welcome Swallows, Spur Wing Plovers, as I had seen before in Sudan, and New Zealand Pigeons, California Quail and the Pukeko.

Outside and below our bedroom was a "Swan Plant" and whilst there we were fortunate enough to see several Monarch Butterflies emerge from the chrysalis and they are very spectacular indeed. This plant is a favourite breeding ground for the butterfly. However I do not recall seeing too many other varieties during our travels.

Ursula and Judy were excellent hosts and knowing my distaste for onions and garlic they managed to provide superb fare without once digressing and I know that on their own they would have most certainly indulged. They had two pets. One, a very attractive Siamese cat appropriately named Chocolate (plain not milk) and Bella, an enormous Newfoundland dog, who was very affectionate and a joy to be with. The girls, as we always refer to them, took us everywhere by car and this included a long weekend in Auckland including a trip across the harbour and a visit to the museum where I was inveigled into joining in a demonstration of Maori dancing involving swinging a white ball, similar to a tennis ball, on the end of a piece of cord. Poetry in motion it was not! Whilst there we visited some friends of theirs on the outskirts who were in the course of building a new house very high up with a central courtyard and they made us most welcome. We saw some of the yachts that had taken part in the America's Cup in the harbour and got some photos of the centre of Auckland one of which, The Mayoral Tower, had an extremely old fashioned entrance façade, above which are 12 or 13 floors of typical modern all glass skyscraper – most odd. We drove a little way north from the city to some cliff and rocky outcrops which were smothered in gannets and I have not seen as many in one place before, and that includes Bempton Cliffs just north of Scarborough which has quite a few. Our friends took us on the coastal road home which made it a considerably longer journey than otherwise. After a while I was about to comment on the lack of birds on the shore when we rounded a bend to see a large number of birds in one area on the beach and observing them through a powerful telescope was another tourist. We parked and approached very quietly and he was good enough to let us use his telescope. He told us that these were wry birds, only found in the North Island, and there must have been nearly a thousand of them. The name refers to the fact that these birds have bills all of which veer to the left and I suppose the names derive from being awry. That's my guess anyway! We stopped at one or two small towns for refreshment and it really was like being in a time warp once we left Auckland. Many of the churches were

212

wooden buildings but they, and all the shops and houses, seemed to have been painted very recently and could have come from an old film set. Their nearest neighbours were a very nice couple called Chris and Adrienne, Chris being headmaster of a local school and they could not have been more helpful. He even brought home from school one of their electric pianos for me to keep my hand in and I gave an impromptu performance for his parents who were with them. The old couple kept pigeons and because they worried about possible attacks from the predators circling overhead from time to time they had painted the upper surface of the wings with coloured circles rather like the R.A.,F. emblem. I have heard of this before but this was the first time I had actually seen it for myself. One day we all joined Chris and Adrienne for lunch at a local Vineyard where there was a jazz trio playing. The son of the guitarist went to Chris's' school and he had arranged for me to sit in between courses which was great.

Knowing that, apart from being involved in Jazz, we were quite keen on bird watching Ursula had been in touch with the local expert for guidance as to the best habitat to visit. He recommended an area where there were two large lakes, separated from the coast by a narrow strip of land called Matata, and we went there, binoculars at the ready. The first lake was surrounded by caravans and lots of people so I suggested to Ursula that we should explore the second lake as there was less disturbance nearby. We saw quite a number of birds including variable oystercatchers, paradise shelduck, New Zealand kingfishers, white heron and Indian Mynah birds. Now in the U.K. you have to have very sharp reactions to catch sight of a kingfisher but in New Zealand they tend to behave like swallows over here, often resting on telephone wires. On the subject of mynah birds I once had an amazing experience with one in the entrance to an aviary, I cannot remember where. This bird said "what's your name" to which I replied "My name is Cook" and the response came back "Cookie naughty boy!" The rest of the family will confirm this! Anyway, back to New Zealand – as we were returning to Jean and Judy, who had stayed in the car, we looked behind us, away from the lake, and caught sight of a disused bird hide which was covered in graffiti, mostly in Maori dialect, but there was just one part that was clearly readable which stated "F... the Cooks". Needless to say we were in stitches all the way back! And I have a photograph to prove it – We'll keep a welcome in the hillside!!! Captain Cook does seem to have a lot to answer for. Talking of the Maoris I often wondered why some of the other place names throughout the Island were so long and convoluted. Later during the trip I found out that there are only 19 letters in the Maori alphabet which limits quite severely the number of alternatives. Furthermore when we went to Hawaii we discovered that they only have 12 letters to work with and a similar problem arises with their names, only much worse.

On another occasion we were taken to Wai-O-Tapu which is a very colourful volcanic area just south of Rotorua created in 1886 by the eruption of Mount Tarawera. Here there were pools in a wide range of brilliant colours, red, green, yellow, some boiling mud pools, silica streams looking quite smooth and solid, and a veritable wonderland all in a fairly confined area. We also went down the Waitomo Caves which was rather like visiting an underground cathedral it was so huge. We were fortunate to be there with a visiting choir who gave an impromptu performance and the sound was magnificent. In some areas there were fireflies in large numbers and this was very impressive. The only time I had seen one previously was in Italy when I managed to catch one loosely inside a handkerchief where it looked like a

214

small lamp. We also visited a wildlife park where we saw a kiwi in a special enclosure designed to simulate their nocturnal habitat. Apparently they had several birds which were kept on different shifts to ensure that at least one was awake during visiting hours. In Rotorua itself, quite a sizeable town, there were hot vapours coming out of the ground all over the place and frankly it was none too pleasant and I would not want to live there. On our way to some of theses places we went alongside the Waikato River and it was possible to see how the course of this mighty river had been changed by the eruption I mentioned earlier. You could see a huge ridge several hundred yards away form its new path. We visited Huka Falls where the river narrows to only 15 metres and the power generated at this spot is awesome.

One day Judy took us to see her parents who lived at Matamata, not far from Tauranga and we were entertained to tea. In recent times Matamata has been immortalised during the filming of the "Lord of the Rings". Judy's father was one of the founders of the village and had been a farmer of considerable repute and one of his sons still runs a farm in the area. They were very hospitable and we had had in fact met them in London previously when they were on holiday. Since our visit they have both died, Mac one year, and his wife May the following year. However there is apparently a custom in New Zealand to put some favourite item in the coffin and in Mac's case they included his best pipe and his slippers. In May's case they included some earrings, her slippers and the book she was reading at the time. Some little time after the funeral they discovered that it was a library book they had buried with her! Fortunately the librarian saw the funny side of this.

On a visit to Hamilton we had a trip up the Waikato River on a paddle boat and visited a museum which contains a large number of Maori carvings, mostly larger than life size, and designed to make most men feel inferior. Outside there was a very clever series of small and large silver rings apparently suspended in space quite high up. It took very close scrutiny to detect the support wires. On another weekend we were taken to the Coramandel, a very picturesque peninsula to the east of Auckland, full of magnificent beaches with clean white sands, including one called The Hot Water Beach for obvious reasons. Whilst out one evening, at a place called Cook's Beach, Mercury Bay, we were struck by the sheer intensity of the whiteness in the passing clouds, quite unlike anything I've seen elsewhere. We saw the famous Kauri Trees which are very tall and as I understand it were taken in great quantity in the early days to be used as masts on sailing ships. They are trying to restore the numbers but of course trees like this take many years to mature.

At Whitianga there is a very exclusive area full of expensive properties, all possessing their own man made moorings, and having its own airport, which is used for long weekends by the more affluent New Zealander.

One small town was full of large murals which in one case depicted a schoolhouse with the children assembled in front, a motorist's workshop which was very realistic, and a pair of horses emerging from an area full of fallen trees. They were displayed so well that you had to look twice to take it all in. The whole of New Zealand, or perhaps I should say, what we saw of it, gave an air of cleanliness. The grass appeared to have been mown that day, the buildings painted that year, but despite this we came away from the Coramandel feeling that this was rather special even by their standards.

When we told Judy and Ursula about our trip they also contacted the chap who gave a weekly broadcast of

Jazz records every Sunday and told him of my interest in the subject. The result was an invitation to attend a rehearsal of a big band the following week in a nearby pub. Now I have to say the quality of the playing left a lot to be desired but we met up with Gary Osborne the D.J. and one or two others in the band and were invited back to Gary's place afterwards. Here he invited me to be his first overseas guest the following Sunday when I would be able to play some records of my choice and we would talk about my jazz background in England. When I asked if I could choose from some of his records he amazed me by saying that he had hardly any C.D.s and yet that was the only means he had of transmitting the program – two C.D. players side by side in the studio. I gather that this was a relatively recent addition to the radio program, but had not realised just how expensive and hard to find C.D.s were at the time in New Zealand. He suggested I should get in touch with Cedric Sutherland who was the best piano player in the district who had a collection of C.D.s and we phoned and arranged to visit him the following day. At first he seemed slightly bemused but invited me to play one of his instruments and within a very short space of time we were playing duets and both enjoying the experience. When it came to his "collection" this comprised all of 14 C.D.s. Now can you imagine just how difficult it is to fill out an hour long program, in which there was quite a lot of talking, from such a meagre assortment. In the event I succeeded in cobbling together a program starting with Benny Goodman, Zoot Sims, George Shearing, Monty Alexander and Bill Evans finishing with Dave Grusin and including one or two others. However with only one disc for each of these it was difficult to get a representative sample of what I liked about them. In fact we had to endure quite a lot of a jazz violinist before we arrived at Monty Alexander. On the day we arrived at the studio as a local Maori M.P. was being interviewed and we were next in line. Now this was to be my one and only

217

broadcast and was purely in a speaking role so experience was not on my side. As it turned out there were some moments when it became quite hilarious when Gary made no fewer than four attempts to get the right track on the Shearing record. We have a tape of the first part of this which Ursula did for us at home. Unfortunately the phone rang when she should have turned the tape over so we lost the last part. Overall it was a good experience and a lot of my friends have enjoyed listening to poor Gary's misfortunes.

As a result of meeting Cedric he invited me to attend a weekly jazz session held at The Falcon's Nest restaurant in Tauranga once a week and volunteered to bring his electric piano along. There I met Trevor Bolling (known as Dr. Jazz) and Jeff Smith who was the piano player from the wine bar and several others who gave us a very warm welcome and this was a very enjoyable evening. The owner of the restaurant presented me with a bottle of wine which came in handy as in nearly all their restaurants it is customary to take your own wine for which there is no charge. Now just imagine what difference that would make to the cost of eating out in England!

The girls invited one of Judy's cousins, Jan, for dinner one evening with her husband Rex who turned out to be a musician playing keyboards and we got on famously well. As it happened it was to be Jan's 40th birthday shortly and we were asked to join them. It was to be a musical event with a lot of local musicians and was held in a large circular building on Matamata racecourse starting at 8PM. We arrived shortly afterwards and were confronted with a lot of musical equipment. Then I noticed that high on the shelves around the edge of the room were two large television sets which were being watched by nearly everyone there. New Zealand were playing Australia at Rugby and this is a nation very much obsessed with sport, to such a degree that not one note of music was played until 10pm after the game was over. Frankly I was astounded and felt rather sorry for Jan, being upstaged by a game of rugby but I tell it as it happened.

When things were underway I had a very enjoyable session with a guitarist whose name escapes me. We were certainly made to feel most welcome by everyone we came into contact with throughout our stay. I played a couple of games of golf with another near neighbour Ray, and he and his wife Thelma entertained us on several occasions. I was quite surprised that we were able to play by placing money in an honesty box on the side of the clubhouse – I can't somehow see that catching on over here!

Towards the end of our stay we visited Bethlehem (There's two of them I've been told), witnessed a bungee jump of some considerable height over water, and saw some of the few remaining Kiwi fruit farms. Unfortunately many of these are in the process of being turned into building sites, which we also visited, only to discover that the prices were a fraction of what we would have to pay here, for truly magnificent properties.

I think that sums up our stay in this country and much as we enjoyed every minute we could never stay there on a long term basis. Mind you if we have many more winters and summers like the last ones I might be persuaded to change my mind! On the 23rd March we said farewell to Ursula and Judy at Auckland airport and started off on the next leg of our tour.

Once again we went by Air New Zealand with a short stop at Fiji to drop a few passengers and pick up a few more. Once airborne again we encountered a strange period when we were flying with daylight to our right but darkness to our left hand side of the plane for quite a long period. This was a flight that left Auckland at 16.15 hrs but was due in Honolulu at 4.45 hrs the same day thus crossing the date line. When we cleared customs, bearing in mind it was still only 5.30 a.m., there were not many people about, but as our flight included transfers we looked for the chap holding the board for the Outrigger East Hotel and he quickly approached and according to local custom placed a garland of flowers, or lei around our necks and bade us to follow him. There seemed no reason why his car should not have been immediately outside until he ushered us both into a 58 seater coach – and we were the only passengers! Once in our rooms, still garlanded, we decided to take our own photographs in the mirror, there being no one else about at this time. After a short rest and breakfast, for which some reason we had to go to the hotel next door, we decided to explore the town on our own. Here and there it was obvious that, as in Auckland, a number of the hotels had been dramatically increased in size and modernised at the same time, but without making it look too obvious. Waikiki Beach was very sandy indeed but I understand it is entirely artificial and is topped up from time to time. We were in fact on the Island of Oahu, one of the many Hawaiian Islands, and this is by far the most developed of them all. I would have liked to have seen the rest but we had only 3 days here and the only way would have been by helicopter which, apart from being extremely expensive, would not have afforded sufficient time to take it all in. That day we took an afternoon tour around Honolulu and the waterfront with a party of about 24 people in a small coach. The driver was only around 25-30 years of age but his father and grandfather had preceded him in the job and he had a fabulous way of telling the history of the place and lacing it with a lot of humour. We went into the grounds of the Old Palace where the Americans deposed their Royal Family a century ago and I was astonished to find myself standing within 12 feet of a Golden Plover. Whenever I have seen them before in the U.K. it has always been through binoculars a long, long way away. In the same grounds there were some very tall trees the like of which I have never seen before and the notice alongside said – "Do not swing from the roots!" These roots came from branches in the tree and must have been nearly 30 ft. high and there were lots of them. By this time Jean was having problems with walking and she decided to stay with the coach whereupon the driver produced a ukulele and proceeded to serenade her. There was also a Bougainvillea tree, (not a bush), in the grounds which was very spectacular. During the tour it was made clear that there was great dissatisfaction at the treatment the locals had received at the hands of the Americans. Promises that had been made years back relating to payments in compensation were still considered to be valid but not much was ever forthcoming.

The next day we booked for an all day tour of the Island which took in Diamond Head Crater, the famous surf beaches which hold world championships in winter and which looked relatively peaceful but quite beautiful to us, and the Waimea Valley which is absolutely spectacular. This is a world famous botanical garden which slopes upwards through lush vegetation, full of unusual bird life, at the top of which there is a waterfall and from time to time divers jump from the top into the lake below. It was here that I first saw a Jacaranda Tree and many more exotic bushes the names of which I was unable to discover. Half way up there was an open hut with a thatched roof where you could be married if you wished and it is no small wonder that the church seems to be losing out fast to all these exotic locations. We were also taken to see pineapples growing in the fields in the centre of the islands and I had not realised that they grew on low bushes rather than on trees. I seem to recall reading somewhere that it takes almost 12 months to produce one pineapple on a plant and a second smaller fruit on the same plant after a further 11 months or so but my efforts to confirm this have been fruitless ---- sorry!

We stopped on the coast overlooking Hanauma Bay which was festooned with palm trees. This was very beautiful and was formed by the collapse of a volcano many years ago. There were a large number of people in the water under which was a coral reef which had since died. When I used my binoculars I could see large numbers of fish of all sizes which were coming inshore to take food from the visitors. This was quite unlike anything I had ever seen before. I gather the fish were of quite an exotic nature but only continued to come here because they were now fed artificially now their original source of nourishment was no more. There were several stops overlooking some superb golf courses and other places of interest in the mountains, and Honolulu itself, and we were also shown a special landing pad which had been set up for emergencies for the shuttle. We also paid a visit to a Buddhist Shrine which had been recreated specially but this seemed somewhat out of place. The only place we did not visit was Pearl Harbour as we had heard the queues were always very long and Jean was still having some problems with her legs and this would not have helped. On the Saturday, our last day, we booked a luncheon cruise on a modern Catamaran which firstly took us along the coastline and then took us whale watching. We saw quite a lot of activity although they were very careful not to get too close as there were a few very young whales about. This was where I needed a video camera as nearly every time I spotted a whale, by the time I took the photo it was no longer there. Nevertheless this was a most enjoyable trip and during lunch on board we were serenaded by a typical Hawaiian group. Although this country is part of the United

States this was the one place we visited where we did not encounter any jazz – at least if it was there it was not given any publicity. Perhaps this is why many of today's American Jazz Players spend a lot of time in the U.K. After the cruise we were having a last walk along the front when we came across a fire in a small hotel and shortly afterwards the fire tender complete with ladder arrived. Now this took me back to some of the early Keystone comedy films as the turntable and ladder were hinged to the main engine and were actually steered independently from the rear. I would have liked to spend longer here but in the time at our disposal we covered it fairly well. It is almost impossible to take a duff photograph. Once again we witnessed weddings taking place anywhere and everywhere, including the grounds of the Buddhist Shrine – and they were not of the faith as far as I could see. Early next morning we went to the Airport to make our last port of call – San Francisco. Despite all my endeavours when booking the trip I was unable to get a direct connection and we were compelled go via Los Angeles where we had to transfer to the local United Airways for the last leg of this journey. This was a real pain as they made us physically take our luggage from the Air New Zealand plane and manhandle it on to one of the small buses to get to the correct terminal. We were rather tired at this stage of our holiday and the cases were extremely heavy. I was miffed to say the least! However the plus side was that instead of flying at 30,000 ft we were much lower and flew all the way along the coast from L.A. to S.F. with a magnificent view on a brilliant sunny day. We were booked to stay at the Sheraton Hotel, in Fisherman's Wharf but there was no transfer service and we tried to get a taxi and ended up sharing one of those elongated limousines with several other people. It looked fine from the outside but Jean and I virtually crawled across the floor to reach the back seats, the door being so far away, and this rather took the edge off the luxury appearance. Fisherman's Wharf is a most attractive area and we had a good stroll from our hotel and saw the seals which swarm all over one particular part. Why go fishing when you can get the scraps from the numerous Fish Restaurants surrounding the area and on the numerous piers which seem full of life (quite unlike some of our piers). We then booked a coach tour of the city which, of all the tours we had been on so far, turned out to be the least enjoyable. This was undoubtedly due to the fact that the coach driver had absolutely no personality, but worse still, spoke in an accent that was for the most part unintelligible. We went to the Golden Gate Bridge and were taken to a vantage point above the bridge giving splendid views all round. The tour also took in the Bay Bridge, which seems never ending, and a trip through some spectacular parks and coast lines. In the middle of the built up area was a very imposing Russian Church which looked of fairly recent origin. If our guide had been more lucid I might have been able to be more specific. The following day we took our customary cruise round the bay which of course took in Alcatraz and decided not to spend what little time we had going on to the island. We saw a very attractive Japanese Garden and of course marvelled at the gradients of some of the roads, made familiar in countless car chases on American films.

A large percentage of the houses are of wooden construction and there are a lot of turncocks on the streets and there are gaps between most buildings to allow access for the hoses in emergency.

The next day we decided to take a walk to try to locate the house of a local British pianist who has spent a lot of time in San Francisco. He lived at 2875 Greenwich Street and once we found the street we started walking in the right direction. The combination of gradients, distance and time, eventually beat us and we finally hailed a taxi to find that this was the very last building in the road. It took us some time to raise anyone at home in this block of flats, because of the security in place, and when we did, it was to discover that he had long since left.

Before leaving the U.K. I made enquiries of Al Merrit from our local Jazz Club, both drummer and record critic, as to where we could best see some jazz and he suggested both the 36 Club and Jazz at Pearl's. The 36 Club was on the 36th floor of the Marriott Hotel and I was rather disappointed to find that the jazz comprised solo piano – a very good solo piano mind you, from a chap called Larry Vucovitch. Now this was one of the most modern looking hotels in the area, which tapered gradually from top to bottom and overlooked the bay. During the interval I asked him why he was alone and he told me they sacked the bass player last year and this in a huge hotel where the drinks were very expensive! Larry had actually played at Ronnie Scott's years ago and was most accomplished but there is nothing in my mind to beat a good piano trio – biased though I may be. When I asked him where I might go on the following night, the last of our holiday, he suggested Jazz at Pearl's where there would be a good guitar trio.

We had previously found a very nice restaurant in the theatre area of the city which was within easy reach of both places so after a splendid meal and a few glasses of wine we headed to Pearls' where a group was listed as the Vince Lateano Trio featuring Bruce Forman – the guitarist, Vince being the drummer and the bassist was Scott Steed. Now Bruce Forman had been to this country for jazz festivals previously and is a fine player. Whilst the drummer was setting up I ventured across to enquire about the pianist we had searched for without success and although he seemed to recognise the name he had no idea where he might be at that time. He then asked where I stood in all this and when I told him that I, too, was a pianist, he immediately invited me to sit in for the second set, there being a fine Yamaha Grand standing idle beside him. Now I was absolutely flabbergasted as this man did not know me from Adam. There is absolutely no way that this would happen over here in such circumstances and in such a place. Nevertheless this was a really spectacular way to end our tour, and although I was given a very good reception and stayed on for the whole session, I did feel afterwards that I might have been that little bit sharper if I had not had that last glass of wine. How could I possibly predict what was to happen?

We reported to the airport at 13.30 hrs the next day and at the check-in desk they were full of apologies for the fact that we did not have a window seat. What they did not explain was the fact that there was no window at all where we sat. This might not have been too bad if, firstly, the seats had been a little farther apart, and secondly if they had not decided to give individual televisions on top of every seat so there was no view, or air, coming over the top. It was claustrophobic to say the least and rather like being in an angled coffin with the side off. It didn't help that one of the passengers was taken ill and we were then delayed an hour whilst their luggage was located. Obviously this had to be done for security but then we faced 12 hours in solitary – or as good as.

Arriving back at Heathrow there was a little delay waiting for our luggage and a rather amusing incident at the conveyor concerning an earlier arrival. This particular plane load of luggage had arrived in dribs and drabs and when there were very few items in view one case had obviously come slightly apart and a young chap took it off the conveyor. When the conveyor came around next time there was nothing on it but a pair of knickers – and no-one seemed to want to claim them, certainly not the young man who was still trying to fix his case!!!

Summing up, we had a marvellous time, were treated extremely well in each of the countries we visited, give Cathay Pacific full marks for Air Travel, the wooden spoon going to Virgin (along with the trains), and cannot thank our good friends Ursula and Judy enough for the effort they put in, making our stay with them so memorable.

UNDER NEW MANAGEMENT

Douglas Dew retired in 1980 and this is when David Woodcraft assumed responsibility for the Battersea site in his capacity as director on the main board. He appointed Bob Banfield to take over from Douglas as Managing Director and this certainly met with my full approval as he had supported me fully, ever since I joined the company. In any event by then his time was mainly devoted to overseeing the remainder of our business as I was still fully in charge of the Leather Department, but obviously had to work under his aegis on matters affecting everyone in the company. We also met Ray Way who had been appointed Group Chief Executive, an earnest man who was yet another of the Professor's protégées, as was David Woodcraft. David very soon established a fairly rigid procedure requiring the production of a small booklet for the monthly board meeting which was a very time consuming activity. Ray would at some time during the course of the meeting ask various individuals what was their "gut feeling" and in time it really developed mostly into rubber stamping what had already been discussed individually earlier. From my point of view I suppose the single most useful contribution he made was to propose that my department should be made into a separate company called "Barrow Hepburn Seals & Packings" thus telling the customer what we actually produced, which had not been obvious before when we operated under the blanket cover of Barrow Hepburn Industries. In other areas he tried to diversify the non-leather sections of the company into products relating to the British Oxygen Company by whom he had previously been employed.

This entailed purchase of considerable stocks and all the sales staff being diverted on courses lasting several days. The net result was that in taking their eye off the regular "bread & butter" items there was an immediate loss of sales and the new lines ultimately proved disastrous and the stocks were sold back at a massive loss in value. Fortunately when he then alighted on "Janitorial Products" – toilet rolls and the like to you – we managed to knock this on the head. In a short while we became associated with Goodyear and had one of their American employees on our board – a very amiable chap. After a while it was agreed that we would acquire from them a machine which they used at Wolverhampton to swage the fittings on hoses used in filling stations which passed quite a large volume of business in our direction. This sounds quite simple but unfortunately this was far from being the case. Hindsight showed that whoever had been doing this job in the past had attained a certain level of skill which we had yet to achieve, and possibly the mere fact of moving a machine which had been static for many years had created problems which were initially too much for us to cope with. There came in reports that there had been a number of cases of leakage on the forecourts in London, and at one stage there was talk of the Fire Brigade taking action to prevent any possible disasters, involving closure of the sites in question, although fortunately it never came to this. I well recall the very next board meeting when David Woodcraft uttered the immortal words "We are just a fag-end away from the nine-o-clock news!" Fortunately after several hurried meetings, a new system was adopted, using my own foreman on overtime as the final independent arbiter, and this, combined with some attention to the machine in question finally solved the problems.

David once commented that there are three basic falsehoods although I cannot quite recall in which context he delivered them.

First came "Of course I'll still love you in the morning!" Secondly "The cheque is in the post!"

Finally "I'm from Head Office – I'm here to help you!" Naturally we understood what he meant on the last one.

Ever since we arrived at Battersea we had had only one switchboard for our company and Barrow Hepburn Equipment, operated by Joyce Green, and for a long time it was her hand written records which decided how the bills should be split, and this was an obvious bone of contention from both sides. Came the opportunity to buy a new switchboard we opted for an all singing affair which gave a direct read out on demand and stopped all arguments. Not only this but when the Equipment company suspected that someone in their organisation was giving information to a competitor we were able to provide print outs of all outgoing calls of various individuals and they very soon found, and got rid of the culprit.

This was a very difficult period, in particular for Barrow Hepburn Industries and as things did not improve Bob Banfield, my mentor and chief ally, was given early retirement in 1984. In his place they appointed the young Paul Alliston as his successor and although he knew nothing about Leather I was in the same position with him as I had been with Bob – excepting that Bob at least had some idea of leather – and me!

I have never known any one quite like him and for example he thought nothing of criticising people in front of anyone who might be around, not discreetly in a private office. Mind you he would do the same to all his suppliers and in this respect I suppose you could say he was consistent. Although there were very few reasons for us to get involved together there were three occasions when he tried it out with me. In each case, after a few moments I told him I was not prepared to be spoken to in that manner and just walked away from him. Of course I was in a strong enough position to do so and I did have a lot of sympathy for almost everyone else in the office and you can imagine how little this attitude did for staff morale.

The most significant development that followed came the day after the announcement that there was to be a Channel Tunnel. I happened to be talking to Joyce Green in our reception area when two men came in and asked who owned the freehold of the property. I very quickly escorted them to my office upstairs where we soon found out that they were acting on behalf of British Rail. Their interest in our site stemmed from the fact that we had one line on ground level at one side of the site, and another on railway arches at 90 degrees to each other, and the site was destined to become the right turn leading to the terminus at Waterloo. This was of far greater value to the group than anything we were likely to achieve purely by manufacturing and from that moment on our days were numbered. Some years later after I had retired I was called upon to sign an affidavit that the wire enclosed area immediately in front of our main entrance had always been used by us as a car park as apparently this had been omitted from the drawings covering the transfer of the property.

As far as production was concerned, by this time many of our former competitors had fallen by the wayside which left us in a much stronger position than we had been many years ago. In the early days there were those who would use quite inferior leather for their seals which meant that apart from undercutting us they also gave leather a bad reputation. The beauty of the new situation was that apart from getting their business we sometimes acquired work that could be cut from the centres of material which had already been used once. We were careful to maintain sacks of useable material in the form of circles and as it was already trimmed to a degree I often felt that the value was greater this way than in the original piece.

Paul Alliston decided that we needed a computer system, mainly for the non leather side of the business, and at the start he tried to rope the leather department in, not just for basic invoicing and such, but he thought it could be applied to our stocks. Fortunately I dug my heels in and he eventually gave way. Nevertheless the job of inputting all the necessary data was a mammoth one entailing considerable overtime and I had no option but to show willing and stay late with the others, unpaid of course. This went on for something like 2 years and, would you believe, as soon as it was completed, he decided it was not really what he wanted.

We then became a takeover target and several bids were made for the company causing the shares to rise considerably. As I had entered into two SAYE schemes this was another occasion when luck was on my side. Finally the day arrived when we learnt that B.T.P. had been successful and would become our new masters, Amazingly we had already made arrangements for a double retirement party, for Joyce Green and her husband George, in charge of our accounts department, to be held on board the "Hispaniola" moored on the Thames near Charing Cross, that very evening. George and Joyce had been originally at the old Head Office at Bermondsey for many years and everything had been arranged including transport home for all – which was just as well in the circumstances. I vaguely remember ending up on the piano at one stage, but I have to say I was completely nonplussed when asked on the following Monday whether I thought my photographs would be any good. I had absolutely no recollection of taking any! The changeover to B.T.P. was very smooth indeed from my department's point of view and we were virtually left to our own devices. It was not long however before Barrow Hepburn Industries was taken over by C.M.T. Industrial Supplies (UK) Ltd of Cradley Heath and this included my department. As this new company also had no interest in leather this was a rather worrying development, particularly as I was approaching retirement within a few years and I had reservations about my position in the circumstances. 1988 would signal the completion of 40 years under the same pension scheme and all that that signified. To enable me to complete my service I managed to persuade B.T.P. to retain me and bill C.M.T. which to say the least was fortunate. As it turned out I am sure they were quite happy with the outcome. By this time I was already giving quite some time towards assisting in debt collection for the whole of Barrow Hepburn Industries whilst encouraging my assistant to take over more of the day to day matters. What happened was that on the one hand C.M.T. were asking me to lay off the debt collection to give them some leverage in the final negotiations whereas I was still in contact with David Woodcraft, still employed by B.T.P., who urged me to get as much as possible. As B.T.P. were holding my purse strings I had no hesitation in getting hold of every penny I could. As a result I ended up being carpeted by the Managing Director on more than one occasion when he said "You're not listening Mr. Cook!" and of course he was quite right! I then made representations for early retirement and to my intense delight it was eventually agreed that I could leave in December 1988 at the age of 62 ½ on the full pension normally due at 65. I have to say that this was an ambition I had worked on for many years – to get my maximum pension from one company. Admittedly there were times when I had doubts and felt that some friends and acquaintances had really passed me by, changing jobs on more than one occasion, but so many ended up with fragmented pensions, some of which had been frozen for many years. I also had the satisfaction of doing a job I liked which suited my lifestyle.

My reservations about joining C.M.T. were soon justified after they had secured control of the phone system covering the whole Battersea site whilst there were certain contentious matters concerning the takeover still outstanding. In essence we then received no direct calls but were phoned internally by the employees of Barrow Hepburn Equipment when a call came through and had to race 100 yards or so across the courtyard to take the call in their offices. I made strenuous appeals for this to be sorted quickly and after a few days things returned to normal, but this was enough to justify my earlier doubts and I dread to think what might have happened if I had joined them.

You would think that having worked for the same company for so long two takeovers in my last two years would have been enough, but no! On Monday 5th December 1988 Barrow Hepburn Seals & Packings Ltd. became a wholly owned subsidiary of Pioneer Weston Ltd. Of Salford who were themselves fluid seal manufacturers, just three weeks before my official retirement.

Once more I had to give chapter and verse to another group of strangers, all of whom were highly suspicious of my possible motives. It reminds you of the old saying about waiting ages for a bus only for three to arrive in quick succession. To ensure I did not start up on my own right away I was given a consultancy for 12 months although in practice it was obvious they wanted me out of the way with a few notable exceptions.

Thus ended for me a most satisfying working life in which I

enjoyed considerable autonomy running a small virtually independent company, without the constraints of having to finance it myself. I call it luck!

Apart from this I now realise that the pension I had achieved was one of the very best available and for this I believe my thanks are due to George Odey!

MOVING HOUSE

I finished my working life on Xmas Eve 1988, and Jean followed me a month later on 31st January, her birthday. As it happens, and we were soon to find out, this was not a good time to try selling a house. We put 8 Queensville in the hands of 3 separate estate agents to start with, one in Streatham Hill, one in Streatham proper, and the other near Clapham South. The starting price was £134,500, which was in line with what had been considered reasonable previously, but by then the market had changed. Because we were desperate not to miss any opportunity, we invested in an ansafone, so that we could at least go for a walk every day, but for a long time absolutely nothing happened. Our area of Clapham Park had always been considered quite desirable despite the fact that a lot of the modifications that had been carried out to many of the houses did anything but enhance the neighbourhood. Every now and then we would go into Surrey to check on the market there, but we soon realised we had to get someone interested in us first. Eventually one of the agents recommended that we should reduce the price to around £128,000. which we did and still with no result. A little later when a further drop to £124,000 did not work the agent in Clapham South suggested we should widen the scope and give the sale to several more estate agents, which we did.

In the course of so doing we found one estate agent who would only accept us on a sole agency basis for which they were asking 3.25% which I told them was outrageous. They were quite confident of their position and were part of a well known insurance group. Funnily within 12 months they had shut up shop and sold out – to my intense satisfaction! From then on we were besieged with people from these agencies taking details of our property.

In one case two young girls were sent to measure up using an electronic device which, when placed on one wall, gave a direct read out of the width or length across the room. When I heard some of the figures they were calling out I had to intervene as I could not imagine any reading as low as they were producing. When I produced a tape measure it was obvious they had no idea how to use it and I asked for someone else to be sent to do the job.

One of the offices in Streatham Hill had a separate branch in the Abbeville Road area and I asked whether it would be a good idea if I gave them the details as well. I was told that because of their internal arrangements they would already be in possession of this information. Somehow I had a funny feeling about this and I phoned them to ask whether they had a property in Queensville on their books. The answer of course was in the negative! Obviously the internal commission arrangements did not encourage such a helpful attitude. For several months there was absolutely no response as the market was really in trouble at the time. As a result we were recommended to reduce the price by the agent in Clapham South on several occasions. When this course of action had been decided upon I phoned every agent at once. The following day we would get our exercise by taking a walk to all of these offices and on some occasions not one of them had yet adjusted the price in the window. The most that managed to act were two on one day. Considering the lack of interest at the time I felt that they were perhaps trying to justify their reputation for being parasites. The stalemate continued for the best part of 10 months before, at a figure of around £112,500, we at last got some enquiries and perhaps I should emphasise that the price alone was not the problem – the market as a whole was dead. Now we found we had problems from the intending buyers, the worst of which was a Jazz Ballet dancer and her mother, who seemed to be working on the lines of the tough policeman and his easier counterpart. The dancer would tentatively agree a price and then suddenly come back with all sorts of nebulous reasons for a further drop in price. Then she would disappear, we were told once to dance in America for a couple of weeks, leaving us to complain to her mother who would be terribly sympathetic. But, when the daughter eventually returned she always had some other angle to explore. After a time we found out that the mother's husband had thrown them out and we had a lot of sympathy for him. The last straw came when the daughter said she would like her surveyor to inspect the property, after which she said we needed new windows and a new roof with a further £10,000 off the price. At this I approached the agent in Clapham South for advice and he freely volunteered to look at the house, without charge, after which he confirmed that there was absolutely no substance to these claims. I had great pleasure in telling them both to get lost.

Then we had a group of young people from Hong Kong who arrived at the door complete with a contract ready to sign! You have to remember that there was no steady influx of potential buyers and we were extremely tempted by each individual approach. As it happens they managed to get someone at the other end of the road to accept their offer. We had friends living next door and after we moved we realised we had had a lucky escape. There was virtually no front garden in Queensville and yet when they moved in they built a six foot high brick wall in front to contain two large dogs which they usually left at home all day in the back garden barking continuously whilst they were all out. It was not too long before they did a moonlight flit owing money for a very expensive car and many other people chasing them for outstanding monies. Eventually, after a further reduction in price we found a buyer who had happened to see our details in the window of the most remote of our seven agents, not too far from Clapham North. He turned out to be a producer of a well known T.V. show and we at last agreed to sell for £107,500, nearly a year after we began. No sooner had we agreed the price than one of the previous buyers who had turned us down originally came back and offered more money. And there were a couple more who suddenly came alive, but I am very pleased that we resisted temptation and got ourselves an honourable buyer.

Now we had to look in earnest for a place for us to move to. When we started entering some possible houses we came across quite a number where there were rooms on the ground floor with steps up and down, and with an eye to old age these were quickly ruled out. Early on we were favouring a bungalow in Walton-on-Thames, close to the bridge. The garage was full of caged birds and apparently the radio was left on all day as this soothed the birds. I wonder what program would do that for me? As time goes on we were very grateful not to have settled there. The shops have deteriorated badly in the time we have been here and the council only last year decided that a new modern shopping centre is required and the work has now started. In addition the original (temporary) Bailey bridge) needed replacing and after much deliberation they have built – another temporary structure!! It would have been like living on a building site. Finally we came to Groveside, which we had inspected before and decided this was the best for our needs. Then it was our turn to do some bargaining and as this was in the hands of Executors we were at the end of the chain and in a good position. Here again my luck stood me well as Bookham is now one of the best equipped places for shopping in the area. We have three butchers, a wet fish and a fried fish shop, two small supermarkets open every day of the week, two green grocers, three bakers, a dry cleaners, post office, shoe shop, and I can almost say, you name it and we have it, I tell a lie – there is no betting shop – shame! Try finding an individual butcher in Guildford and you end up at Sainsbury's. We can walk to Bookham in ten minutes, parking is now free in parts, and we have a real village feel wherever you go. Oh! And a couple of banks including our own. Driving is a pleasure and the countryside very close to hand.

Once everything had been agreed we commenced clearing out many years of accumulated dross and waited for the legal proceedings to reach completion. Finally, on January 19th 1990, we were watching our treasured possessions being loaded into the removal vans when we had a phone call to say that we had become grandparents overnight with the birth of Emily in hospital in Gosport. As I commented at the time this really was a very moving day for us both!

Finally I should mention that although we did not achieve the sale through the agent in Clapham South I did give him a large bottle of whisky for being so helpful – and proving that they are not all parasites – just a large majority of them!

After all this, when we arrived at our new house I left Jean outside in her car with the cat, and went to the Estate Agents for the key, only to find that despite clear instructions from our Solicitors the banks had not confirmed receipt of our cheque in settlement. It was at least an hour and a half, and umpteen phone calls later that we were able to gain access. I would like to think that ours was an unusual case but it is acknowledged that moving house is one of the most stressful events and it seems it was just par for the course.

RETIREMENT

I have already dealt with the first year of our retirement under the heading – Moving House and this concerns life in our new abode. The house itself is of quite unusual construction having been extended some 19 years ago on a basic much smaller property dating back to the mid twenties, by the then owner of Bookham Coaches. It is a chalet bungalow on a site covering roughly 1/5th of an acre. The garage is approximately 33ft long, having been built with the intention of servicing the coaches. It has a pit but the council refused permission to build it high enough to take the coaches. We are on the last road out of Bookham on the way to Guildford and although the last but one owner sold off a large part of the original garden, which was massive by any standards, so far this has not been developed. As a result we frequently have some splendid sunsets which do not quite match up to those I remember in Palestine but are nevertheless quite spectacular. On the day of our arrival Gary astonished us by proclaiming the apple tree just outside our lounge to be a Bramley. As the trunk is nearly two foot in diameter we wondered how could be so sure, until he showed us the metal name tag still attached after all those years. We put out nuts for the birds on the tree and they came flocking both in numbers and types and as I have previously mentioned, once, whilst having a sandwich lunch, I made a note of all the birds I had seen during a period of one hour. The total was nineteen and there were others that came to see us on a more irregular basis, another nine or ten types. As keen birdwatchers, dating back to the time when Jean went to college as a mature student, this was sheer bliss. I recall one holiday spent in the Morecambe area when we deliberately broke our journey to visit a bird reserve in Staffordshire, famous for being the home of the dipper – and having walked miles after parking all we could see was a few very common birds indeed.

The garden is built on chalk and as such impossible for Rhododendrons and Camellias. On the other hand I have found that Daphnes and Viburnums thrive in this soil. I have a photo of a Daphne Burkwood on its own in a bed two foot across in the middle of the front lawn taken the day before we took possession. Today this plant is nearly twelve feet across. From this and one or two other plants already in the garden I have taken a special interest in the many varieties of these which are available and in many cases the scents when in flower are discernable from as much as twelve feet away. Over the years I have made many new beds and to give Jean an area of her own we had a raised L shaped bed built on one corner of the back lawn, specifically for growing alpine plants. This is twelve feet long by eight feet and has two feet of soil between the walls. When it was built we went to the Hampton Court flower show and saw all the specialists, ordering some from each one, and arranging to collect them when we left. At this point we found we had taken possession of no less than 54 plants. Small they may have been but the overall weight of the earth surrounding them nearly pulled our arms from their sockets. Amazingly, and by sheer luck, most of the originals have flourished and survived to this day without becoming overcrowded and the bed is a constant source of pleasure.

Shortly after our arrival we held a house warming party, musical of course, and since then we have had celebrations for our 40th Wedding Anniversary in 1992, and my 70th and 75th birthdays and this year (2001). We were already visiting Shepperton Jazz Club prior to moving here and were now able to widen the circle of friends we had previously as I have pointed out in a previous chapter. For many years now Jean and I have distributed literature for the club around the area, and it now enjoys a fine reputation. On one occasion I called on Sheargold's Piano Showrooms in Cobham with some literature for the club and the salesman just inside the door was showing several people a grand piano. As soon as he caught my eye he asked if I would mind demonstrating it for him which I gladly did. Now to my amazement as I finished I heard a familiar voice coming from behind my audience which turned out to be the wife of a very close friend who was a drummer. They had been upstairs trying out another grand piano and had just told the salesman that they would like me to vet it before purchasing when she recognised my style and I was able to approve it on the spot. As I am usually there for a matter of just a few moments every month this was an incredible piece of fortune.

In the chapter on "Moving House" I briefly mentioned hearing of the birth of Emily whilst awaiting the removal van. Later we learnt that she was born in hospital in Gosport during a very violent storm, which caused severe damage to a nearby garage and other buildings nearby, and as a result it was several days before Linda was allowed to go home. Some years later Colin was posted back to Bath and they moved there soon after and were able to renew the friendships they had built up earlier.

In 1993 Jean had an operation for removal of the gall bladder and this affected her very badly indeed and I think it is fair to say that she has never been quite the same since then. We tended to put this down to the effects of the anaesthetic without, of course, having any firm basis for such a theory.

In 1995 Thomas was born in January, which seems a favourite month in the family as Emily, my mother and Jean were all born then.

One of my ambitions for retirement was to become a member of a golf club and I applied to The Drift Club at East Horsley and was eventually accepted. My success here was I am certain due to the fact that I discovered the club secretary's wife was a singer and I gave him a tape of Annie Noel and myself, just to smooth the way – so to speak! Having never been a member of any club previously I was delighted to find that the membership covered a very wide spectrum of humanity. Furthermore the Seniors Section had regular sessions where you would be matched with anyone else in the section, something which does not always happen elsewhere I understand.

We attended the funeral of Norman George in the early days of our retirement together with Pete Towndrow and several other musician friends from years gone by. Susan made an eloquent reading about her "Mr. Wonderful" as she used to call him but unfortunately she charged the organist with playing the tune during the service. "Wonderful" it was not, and it showed up quite vividly how difficult many classical trained musicians find it to interpret popular music. Talking of Norman reminds me of the time when Susan was still with Jack Jones and they decided to go to Ronnie's with Norman and Billie. Susan and Jack entered the club ahead of Norman and his wife and Ronnie came out to greet them, walking straight past Susan and giving her parents a very warm welcome indeed. Not the usual reception for the famous, but a typical Ronnie Scott reaction!

One of my biggest disappointments was being invited to Billie's 80th Birthday party and having to refuse as we had already arranged to go on a Centreparc's holiday with Colin and Linda and the family. I heard it was rather special including a mock "This is your life" on video with some participants arriving in person including a singer I had not seen since my teens. If I had been able to go I would have played a beautiful melody taken down by Rex Cull from the sound track of the film "The Fabulous Baker Brothers". It is almost unknown outside this film but I would have hoped that Susan might have asked what it was called. It was given the title "Susie & Jack". Mind you by this time she was married to Simon McCorkindale so perhaps it was just as well I couldn't make it.

In the chapter describing our "Round the World Holiday" there was one significant and deliberate omission. During one stage of our stay in New Zealand there were several occasions when Jean showed uncharacteristic tetchiness with our hosts Ursula & Judy which frankly astonished me in the light of all that had gone before. When it even extended to making a scene in front of a visiting tradesman I was absolutely perplexed as during our whole married life nothing like it had ever happened. I of course had to apologise to them and put it down to the fact that she had not enjoyed some of the long plane journeys, nor sleeping with air conditioning. As it happened, almost immediately after our return, she had to have an operation to deal with polyps in the nose and grommets in the ears, so there was some foundation for my explanation. However even after the operation she was not quite herself and I eventually persuaded her to see our doctor who arranged for her to see a specialist and after numerous tests over quite a lengthy period we were told, in April 1996 that Jean had Alzheimer's. This was a devastating blow, although thankfully it was diagnosed at a fairly early stage. It was over a year later that we were referred to Epsom Hospital by our own doctor who advised us that they were now in a position to authorise limited prescriptions for a newly approved drug. I enquired about this treatment, involving tablets called "Aricept", and was told that because of the cost this was not available on the N.H.S. but they would give me prescriptions if we were prepared to pay. I was told that I should try several sources before handing over the prescription as I would find considerable variations in the market place – how true that was! I used "Yellow Pages" and was quoted a very wide range of figures – from £95 to £120 for a 28 day's supply for the 5mg size. There were two exceptions, one from a large chain of chemists offering £180 and refusing to accept that this was way out of line. I later found out that they could have been offering the 10 mg size, of which I was not aware at the time – but even so!! More interestingly, I arranged for my daughter in Bath to phone around locally and she unearthed one who quoted £67.59 which was quite an eye opener. I got in touch with him to confirm the price, which he did, but when I went back to him shortly afterwards to finalise matters, he back pedalled like mad, and claimed he had misread from his computer, and immediately quoted £97.50 or thereabouts. What he had done of course was to quote the figure then applicable for the purchases made under N.H.S prescriptions which were issued in a very limited number of Trusts at the time. We paid for a few months at the start but when we saw the specialist for a repeat supply he advised that one of his patients had discovered a chemist in the West Country who would give a much more competitive figure – i.e. £72.50. This was quite a relief but still cost over £940 a year. I feel that this helps to confirm my assumption regarding the price differences. When it came to a further prescription I phoned the chemist who advised me that he been had warned about his "aggressive" sales policy by the Pharmaceutical Society. He responded by telling them that was his business, whereupon they argued, successfully, that he should not send them by post, and this, he said, was a definite stumbling block. Fortunately for us I had an old Army colleague living some fifty miles away and we obtained the next supplies through him by post. When it was time for the next check up they advised that there was a new tablet called "Exalon" which was cheaper and could be offered under the N.H.S. – free of charge. These required a short period on 1.5 mg., another period at 3 mg., finally settling at the rate of 6 mg. The very first tablet affected Jean so badly that she had to go to bed almost immediately. Nevertheless she persevered but after starting on the 3 mg. Tablets it became obvious that she would be far better without them. When we went back to the clinic I asked if it would be possible to have the Aricept through the N.H.S. and after making a few phone calls they discovered that someone had come off the register and we were taken on in his place. This was in Epsom and I later learned that they had only 20 patients on Aricept and a further 20 on Exalon – and Epsom is a very large area with surely many, many more sufferers. After some time on the 5 mg. Tablets she was put on the 10 mg. size and since then, although the memory has continued to decline, we have managed to survive without too many problems.

In most situations an increase in output usually facilitates a reduction in price, but this does not seem to apply to medicines as a general rule. I would have thought that making much larger supplies available at a considerably lower price would enable them to treat many more people, whilst still making a profit, and allow them to remain with their families a lot longer. Being classed as an incurable complaint with inevitable, but prolonged consequences, should surely qualify these tablets for priority access. Certainly if one assumes that there is some profit at the N.H.S. price level there can be no excuse for these highly inflated prices. It is not as if it can be argued that they need the money for research as it appears to be the chemist who gains here, or does Big Brother get to collect them on his behalf? I believe Jean has been on these tablets for almost as long as they have been available and as such is a very good advertisement for them. I am told that some people find them ineffective after only 2 ½ years. However, in my opinion, they do nothing for the memory, but most certainly improve the demeanour of the patient and I consider myself very fortunate in this respect. Certainly not lucky that she has the problem – but at least I am able to cope much better than would otherwise be the case. Many people have told me this.

In the early years I could leave Jean at home so that I could have a break and play golf 2 or 3 times a week in order to preserve my sanity. However with time taken getting there and back and playing this can take 6 hours and this proved too long after a time. I was put in touch with the Alzheimer's Society who have a service "Share the Care". They arranged for someone to visit Jean for a couple of hours in the middle of my absence and this worked quite well for some time. I have to say that these people do a wonderful job as it is far from easy to have a conversation with someone like Jean, who seems to have almost reverted to childhood, possibly being influenced by her earlier devotion to the welfare of young children. Unfortunately I was playing golf when one my fellow golfers who was not playing that day fetched me from the course as he had seen Jean walking to Leatherhead in the pouring rain. We had ourselves already decided to leave the course after the next hole because of the conditions. We organised a search party and eventually found her near a church in the centre of the town, a good 2 miles from home, absolutely drenched. From that moment it was clear that she could never be left alone again. On the other hand I needed some time to myself and once again the Alzheimer's Society came to the rescue. Thanks to the efforts of Penny Weaver from Share the Care, Jean now attends an Alzheimer's clinic in Dorking twice a week where they look after her from 9am. until 4 pm. Not only that but they provide her with a mid-day meal, give her a hair-do, and once every 6 weeks or so a visiting chiropodist attends to her needs, for a very reasonable fee. The worst feature of this illness is the ever decreasing memory. Jean has been an avid reader since childhood and as time has progressed she has gradually ceased to read as she has literally lost the plot almost as soon as she turns the page – sometimes even sooner than that. Likewise television plays are of no use to her and what we really want is a succession of one liners from the likes of Jasper Carrot and company. Here again the modern so called humour does neither of us any good and if I am honest such plays as are shown seem to be lacking the spark that used to be there. On the other hand perhaps this is what it is like to be old – although I certainly do not feel completely out of touch – yet! Unfortunately for me Jean has always had a very orderly mind and, without being too fussy about it, she would make sure that things were tidied away before getting out of hand. The good news is that she will still do this – the bad news – anything can end up anywhere, not necessarily in the same room. The wooden board we use for preparing vegetables has disappeared at least four times in the past six weeks and it took four days to find it on one occasion. I have at last dissuaded her from carrying a handbag as she insisted on taking a very large one around originally stuffed with all manner of items. Not the usual contents by any means, and we had to collect it from so many different restaurants that I had to insist we could do better without it. She still uses it for storage and every now and then I sort it out. Once I retrieved 20 pencils, 6 combs (three of mine that I had lent to her), several pairs of scissors, loads of tissue paper, a bedside clock and I could almost say – you name it and it would be there.

Over the period since first diagnosed, i.e. April 1996 her concentration has gradually waned to the point when there is very little she can do to help. She does try from time to time but in most cases forgets what she is doing and walks off. In spite of everything there is always a lighter side to things and one evening when I was busy cooking the meal there was a knock on the front door. When I opened it there was a well dressed young man holding a file and asking if I could spare a few moments. From the look of him I felt that had he been wearing a cap on his head he could have come straight from the Wailing Wall. Without further ado I said "Look – I'm cooking the dinner – I was in Palestine in 1945 and they have not sorted it yet, the Irish still have endless problems, so it's quite useless you coming here to talk to me about religion!" There was a slight pause and he said "Well, actually I was trying to drum up some business for a new Italian restaurant in Dorking!" ------- Collapse of stout party. I used to be so good at spotting the Witnesses – must be more careful in future.

Reverting to Jean, she will talk to almost anyone given a chance but if I am not right there and in a position to intervene you will suddenly see the other person's eyes glaze over as the conversation suddenly gets out of hand. As time passed I have thought it necessary to make certain people aware of her problem and sometimes I am quite surprised to find they had not realised until then.

She is happiest when we are going out and I endeavour to find a reason to visit all manner of places. Obviously winter is the worst time as most of the stately homes and gardens are closed. Nevertheless with the help of Jean's cousin Eileen, my cousin Kath and her husband, and Sylvia, and more recently Harriet, from the Jazz Club, we have had some wonderful days out in the last few years. The addition of just one extra person is so important and I will be eternally grateful for all the help and support they have given me. The downside to all this is that no sooner are you back indoors than she has forgotten ever going

250

out and will sometimes appear wearing her outdoor coat and wanting to know where we are going next!!

Having reached the age of 75 I decided to apply for the free medical check up to which you are entitled. Not that I felt there was a problem, but in the hopes of catching anything that might have been brewing, in its infancy, leaving me in a position to look after Jean as long as possible. I passed all the tests with no problem except to be told my cholesterol; was high. Now to be honest I had never been tested for this and was not aware of what it should be anyway. I was told to discuss this with the doctor and in answer to my query he told me the correct reading was about 5.0 and that I was 7.1, but he said even if it had been 9.1 he would not have prescribed any treatment as I had the blood pressure of a 30 year old.

You will be aware by now that my underlying theme for this book is how lucky I have been throughout my life and this is just another example.

In a slightly different vein, we were on our way home from attending a Jazz Dinner at Haslemere and it was rather misty and I took the road between Ripley and Clandon and had a puncture just after midnight in an area where everyone had gone to bed. There was not a glimmer of light from the few houses where I had come to a halt. I was quite certain that the arthritis in my left thumb would not help me in getting the wheel off and became rather worried to say the least. A small number of cars passed without stopping and just as desperation was setting in one car stopped just up the road. I dashed up, opened the door and said "Would you be good enough to phone the R.A.C. for me?" and a voice said "Hello Roy – what are you doing in this part of the world?" It was another pianist – Mark Bellamy, father of a now very famous Jazz Saxophonist Ian Bellamy, and it must have been the first time we had met for possibly 6 years. He not only stopped but actually changed the wheel for me which I thought was quite wonderful. Oh! And yes I now possess a mobile phone, something I had fiercely resisted up until then. I have to be honest and say I was always scared of losing it, or having it misplaced for me! Anyway it stays in the car purely for emergencies.

I briefly mentioned going to see Benny Green when he was starting to write a book about Ronnie Scott, after his death. When I phoned him at the instigation of Roy Babbington and mentioned my early experiences with Ronnie in the East End of London and at the Orchard Club he was most interested. I was with Ronnie when he was 16 & 17 years old. He was born in January 1927 whereas Benny did not arrive until December of that year and Benny was quick to point out that until I spoke to him he had very little information about Ronnie's earliest activities, being too young at the time. Jean and I were given a warm welcome and it was nice to see that he was exactly as you would have expected having listened to him for so long, particularly on Sunday afternoons, Sundays which have never been the same since. On the other hand it was fairly obvious that he was not in the best of health but we spent nearly 90 minutes chatting during which time he was making copious notes – by hand. When I commented on this he said he could not write any other way. After he had all the information he needed I asked if he could help me prove that a certain melody I always member from childhood actually existed. I played it for him on his piano and challenged him to name it, as I have done to countless people over the years, and always ended up saying "you're wrong" – which happens to be the title of the song. He then took us upstairs to a large room with a centre table, lot of c.d. s and books and not much else around. He picked up a book full of titles against each of which was a number, and in a separate book this number confirmed who had written and performed it and there it was. Up till that date I had found nobody who knew it, although a couple of years later I asked Rosemary Squires who immediately sang the melody – and not a lot of people knew that! We had a couple of phone discussions later, but when I next called his wife told me he had been very ill and it was not long before he died. I waited several weeks before phoning her and after commiserating I enquired just how far he had got with the book, only to be told that it was a virtual non-starter because of the seriousness of his health. She told me that Ronnie's partner Mary Scott was proposing to write a book with their daughter, and at her suggestion I contacted Mary in America and passed on the information I had originally given to Benny.

When the book was published we were invited to the launch which took place upstairs at the club and Mary came over and introduced herself and her daughter, and we had a reunion with quite a number of people from the past, and we met Spike Milligan who was looking quite frail. Also there were Dave Green, Allan Ganley and June, Vic Ash, Pete King to whom I had never spoken before, Harry Pitch, Barbara Jay, Lennie Bush, and John Critchenson, his last pianist. Also a name from the very early days, Alf Summers, who like Harry Pitch goes back to the Stepney Boys Club days. Jean and I had never been to a book launch before but a couple of weeks earlier I read an account of another similar event which was quite hilarious. Unfortunately absolutely nothing happened apart from individual conversations after being introduced by Mary and having purchased the book. Considering Ronnie's reputation as a story teller, I was expecting someone to get up and say something but no such luck.

As to the book itself I found it interesting if quite tragic, and couldn't help thinking that if Benny had been able to complete his version it would probably have been totally different.

Seeing Spike Milligan reminded me that the husband of one of Jean's cousins once visited the Milligan household when he was running a T.V. business in the Harrow area. Apparently, at this time, he was not talking to his wife, and he offered Derek a cup of tea and then sent her a telegram asking for it!

I am convinced that becoming involved with the Ronnie Scott book made me think about writing one myself. As Jean tends to go to bed around 10.0 pm. I frequently stay up until midnight working (or cursing) the computer and it helps me to take my mind on to other matters. Apart from this some of the research has taken us to various libraries and buildings which all helps to keep Jean interested. Unfortunately there is no possibility that she could ever read the finished book which is why I now feel free to talk frankly about her problems.

Jean, Benny Green & Roy

SUMMING UP

In the middle of writing this book it suddenly occurred to me to check whether my preferred title of "I should be so lucky" was already in use and to my amazement the nearest similar title was "We should be so lucky" subtitled "Love, sex, food & fun after 40". So you see my luck holds, at least for the moment. --- well I can still think about it! I was so fortunate in meeting someone like Jean, who must be one of the few women who required persuading to have a new kitchen, and was never particularly concerned with material possessions, and for the most part having decided on a particular item of furniture or whatever, was never craving for something different a year or two later. I have come across so many people who must have spent a small fortune this way. This, and of course spending far too much time – and money – in the pub. Even though Jean's affliction is presently changing our way of life we both agree that not too many people have enjoyed the satisfaction that we have had until recently.

We have two wonderful children in Linda and Gary both of whom are very level headed indeed, and both are concerned more about other people than anything else. Linda's husband Colin is a wonderful man and of course, their children, our grandchildren, are a joy to behold.

On the music scene a large number of the Jazz Greats have died in recent times and I am sometimes surprised to find that many of them were younger than me. However all is not lost, as I have already mentioned, and there are quite a number of youngsters and relative youngsters who are still capable of putting up astonishing displays. Mind you for me it has to be melodic and I really cannot stand the modern tendency of some players to take a theme, worry it to death, then start on something entirely different and carry on relentlessly. I feel it is like being unable to construct joined up sentences. I have very strong views about the so called Jazz F.M. radio program When it first emerged there was a period when it had to change the name because of the low Jazz content. Eventually it changed back but then I used to listen more in the afternoons and after a while I realised that they were concentrating on around 30 C.D. s and only one track on each. Now for me the whole point of jazz, apart from it having to swing, is the joy of listening to as many different tunes as possible played in different styles and this constant repetition drove me to complain. To my amazement I was told that this was being done deliberately, presumably on the basis that if the new audience they were aiming for heard it enough times they would think they understood it. On the other hand genuine fans were absolutely bored to death by this constant repetition. Since then they have tried to re-invent the wheel and every afternoon we are subjected to what I can only call thinly disguised pop. It is obviously intended for the youngsters of today and the background beat is identical to today's pop music. Then on top of this we have the almost inevitable soprano saxophone, never my favourite instrument, often sounding a bit like paper and comb, playing mostly banal riffs with so little improvisation that the word jazz hardly enters the equation. This to me is a form of rationalisation by the back door and soon these youngsters will really believe they are listening to jazz. All this would not be so bad if at the same time nearly all the newspapers had not consistently reduced any reference to Jazz to an absolute minimum. Even worse they are beginning to refer to some of the so called Smooth Jazz albums on their own, as though the real Jazz no longer exists. Some have ceased to give reviews to Jazz C.D.s but what really gets me is the pretentious language used to review Pop music, in many cases glorifying violence and bad language at the same time. I do not read these all the time but I have on occasion read at a later date that such and such a group were not that good after all! They say anything to fill a page, which brings me to a very sore point indeed.

The older I get the more cynical I become of what is put into print. For example a relative of mine used to be a photographer for a fairly large local paper and one Saturday many years back he was asked to go into town and take pictures of supporters of the local football club and Spurs fighting in the streets before the match. When he went back to the office and told them nothing was taking place he was ordered back to get pictures without fail. He is an honest man and in the end did not oblige but this incident went down in the book against his record.

More recently we acquired our own policeman in Bookham for the first time in the 12 years we have lived there. I took the opportunity to make his acquaintance the other day asking if there were any regulations about the use of fireworks of which we have had quite a basinful recently, not just for Guy Fawkes Night, and usually starting just before midnight. Apparently this is not too well covered by legislation at the moment.

I then said that I was disturbed to read in the local paper that there had been a fight near a pub in the town centre when a gang of young lads attacked another lad just after 6 o'clock in the evening. According to the officer they were all part of the same group who had been drinking together in the pub and this of course puts an entirely different slant on the matter – but makes more of a story.

On another occasion a local resident complained of the activities of some youths outside her house.

After investigating he discovered that the woman in question happened to be the mother of the reporter dealing with the article.

I appreciate that in recent times there has been a spate of revelations regarding mistakes made by doctors and surgeons and in many cases there have been good grounds for complaint. The problem is that when any other doctor makes a mistake the media, with the help of the new breed of litigants of the "No win – No fee" variety, amplify the matter out of all proportion. In any other profession including those of the complainants I guarantee that hardly a week goes by without them making an error. It is merely the fact that it is not life threatening in their cases that saves them from being exposed, and doctors are just like everyone else – they are human beings, and I believe most of them do the best they can, often under great pressure.

I also object to the way the volume is increased for radio commercials and to the repetition, ad nauseam, of people yelling at the top of their voices. In desperation I often turn to Classic F.M. only to hear the selfsame commercials, and I usually end up listening to some of my own cassettes. I also find the slogan "You are listening in colour" most irritating and the only person who qualifies here would be a blind man with a colour T.V. for which he is allowed a couple of pounds reduction on the annual licence! O.K., I am being a bit churlish here but advertising seems to have gone completely out of hand in recent years. Possibly it is my age, but if it is meant to instil an image of the end product it fails miserably as I really cannot recall too many even if I remember some of the preceding action in the ad.

As for television will someone please tell me why it should be compulsory for everyone to wave at the screen. Is it to prove that they are alive, and when it comes to the lottery why does everyone cheer as the balls come down – I notice we never see a sign of the audience these days. Now I am well aware that I am out of step with modern T.V. comedy which to me often seems steeped in childish smut, but when it comes to strip cartoons I am absolutely amazed what is put forward in the name of humour. My best source, apart from other musicians, comes from the Guardian apology column. To keep a balance we take this during the week and have the Telegraph on Saturday, and the Independent on Sunday. Recently the Guardian apology column referred to an article on "Misspelling" in which they had misspelled "misspelled"!!! – and only one reader commented.

The best was a write up on the play "The Blue Room" starring Nicole Kidman in which the reviewer commented to the effect that the sight of Miss Kidman walking across stage "hand in knickers" was one of his most erotic experiences. The next day they re-arranged the words in the apology to "knickers in hand" – whatever turns you on!!

I firmly believe that all the newspapers should be compelled to have an apologies column at the top of the right hand side of the front page so they can be read by everyone at first glance and not be secreted away out of sight. Reverting to the story of Nicole Kidman I am reminded of my early youth when Walls Ice Cream was sold from special tricycles roaming the streets with the slogan "Stop me and buy one". I was told that they sometimes sold condoms at the same time and I often thought the slogan could be reversed to produce "Buy me and stop one!" Here I must emphasise I am unable to vouch for these comments – it is all hearsay!

One of my greatest regrets is the virtual disappearance of

the small specialist shop. None of these can afford to operate in the West End as they used to when I was young and in my early days with Barrow Hepburn I was on record as saying that if companies continued to expand by acquisition then there would be no room for the individualist. Events seem to have proven me correct although this gives me absolutely no satisfaction. Ironically we now live in the age of the car, when distance is no problem, but if you go from one town to another in this country you will generally find the same shops everywhere, with few exceptions, so why bother?

On the other hand, instead of going to Southend on Sea for the weekend people fly off to the Continent. Recently Gary, together with 16 other members of his cycling club flew to Trieste to celebrate a double 40th birthday, just for a long weekend.

Against this you are very lucky if you have anything approaching a decent bus service if you live in Surrey. Since we moved here the service which came from Sutton past the bottom of our road, terminating at Guildford has been firstly re-routed well out of our walking range, and then replaced with a service ending less than a mile along the road at Effingham. If you had to go to Guildford by bus a separate route circled the village coming back to the main road well past our road and not even stopping so a transfer could be made at Effingham. As Jean's cousin Eileen had previously been able to come here direct we were most upset and apart from writing direct to the bus company concerned we also took this matter up with our local councillor – all to no avail I fear. Subsequent journeys requiring changing buses were so horrendous that believe it or not she now comes by train to Bookham in less than half the time, but of course I have to meet her at the station by car. We seem to have one of the worst services and the other day we were behind a double decker bus which was so filthy as to be almost unrecognisable as such. It was late afternoon and the sun was very low and as we arrived at a slight uphill gradient only then was it possible to read the lettering on the back window reading "Would you like to drive this bus ---- if so phone -----!" The actual phone number was quite impossible to make out, but I didn't fancy it anyway. It reminds me of that old song "Arriva dirty" or whatever!

For the life of me I do not understand why the use of mobile phones should not be banned when driving a vehicle. Every day without exception I see drivers turning corners and negotiating roundabouts when they cannot possibly be in full control and there can be no excuse for this.

As for the latest fad of sending text messages, I thought there was enough ignorance of the English language without causing absolute mayhem. It seems a bit like learning Welsh. I used to go to Cwmbran to Girling's factory and seven letters with only one vowel seems rather in keeping with the new fashion.

I firmly believe that my generation have possibly enjoyed one of the best periods in the last century. At the start the war in 1939 created a camaraderie which has long since disappeared. In addition a large percentage of the population were able to work throughout the period with minimal interruption and there was a certain pride in many occupations which were regarded as rock solid jobs for life such as my grandfather on the Railways and Banking.

Buying a house proved one of the best investments and it is ironical that as I write this the mortgage rate has at last reduced to within ½% of our starting rate – but prices just do not compare. This is one area where I feel some sort of control would make sense although I have to concede that we have done very well as it stands. At the moment two of the largest companies are cutting down on the percentage they will allow on the value of the house, quite reasonably, if one takes into account the number of people who suffered negative equity around 10 years ago. The remainder are upset as they feel this may stop further price increases and this is where greed takes over. Most other businesses have some form of constraint but why, for example, a landlord can pick a figure out of the air and increase the rent by so much above inflation is an eternal mystery to me, and some control over house prices would surely benefit us all in the long run.

In my opening chapter I made reference to one of my forebears on my mother's side, one Reginald Vincent Shimell, who started the family tree and whose son, Ron, has now completed the job after painstaking research. At one stage we were sent his account of life as he saw it and having re-read it recently I have asked permission to publish it as a final chapter in the book.

I feel there is quite a parallel in that Reginald was born in December 1899 and would have been 14 on the outbreak of the Great War and I myself was 13 when World War Two started. We both ended up working for the one company, in his case J. Lyons & Co., for the majority of our working lives, and there are one or two interesting price comparisons to be made. It is a pity he never managed to complete his tale but I found a lot of his stories fascinating. For me the item about the "Chain Horse" helping others up Balham Hill from outside the old "Hippodrome" was most interesting.

If and when I succeed in publishing this book it is my intention that all profits shall be given to the Alzheimer's Society to help them to carry out the good work until such time as someone, somewhere, comes up with a cure.

It seems a pity to me that a proportion of the lottery money is not allocated to the major charities, which have undoubtedly suffered since it came into being. I have been told that some money has actually been given to Golf Clubs from the lottery and surely this cannot be right. I suppose if I was asked to give my own personal philosophy in a nutshell, it would have to be "Do what you enjoy and enjoy what you do – and try to see both side of an argument". I hope I've convinced you that for me at any rate – it worked – or was it just luck! See you at the book-signing!!!

A CHRONICLE OF THINGS THAT I REMEMBER

By Reginald Vincent Shimell (1899-1979)

In trying to tell the story of my life and times I shall endeavour to keep the dates of all the happenings in order. I cannot of course remember the day I was born but it was on the 5th day of December 1899 and I was the fourteenth child. When I was 18 months old my mother, Harriet Louise died. She, as I was to learn later, had given birth to my younger brother, her fifteenth child and this had caused her death.

My first memory came at the age of 2 years when I recall most vividly having my photograph taken standing on the coping stone at the front of our house 18, Graveney Road, Tooting, SW17, with my hands clasped behind me holding on to the railings. I was dressed in my best frock which my sister Miriam had taken from the wardrobe in which to dress me for this special occasion. It was customary for boys to wear frocks, long stockings and buckled shoes up until the age when they were ready to start school. I also remember when I was three that my eldest brother Charles was invalided home from the Boer War having been serving in the 2nd Devonshire Regiment. Then when I was four years old my father re-married and so from now on I shall refer through these pages to my step-mother Susan as mother to avoid confusion.

School began in the Infants Department at the age of five years and had mixed classes. The first books I had to read were of animals and objects. The first letter 'A' was for Apple and so-on through the book. Learning to count, apart from using the fingers and toes was done by moving beads on wires attached to a small frame or rack. There were boxes of bricks with parts of pictures on each side of every brick and we had to try and put the bricks in the right places to complete the whole picture. This meant that you had six different pictures on each set of bricks. One of the highlights of the school year was Prize Giving Day. If you attended regularly and did not stay away from school, the Headmaster would hand you a medal and a prize.

At this part of the century, 1904, deaths in childbirth for mother and/or baby and also from consumption were rife and London in particular was a black spot. At the age of five years and six months I had a large lump appear on the right side of my neck. This meant that I had to be admitted to St. Thomas' Hospital for an operation to have it removed. Subsequently, this had repercussions right through my life and to which I will refer later on. It was thought at that time that my life span would not be very long and according to the experts of that day, would not last beyond fourteen years of age. This lump or growth was diagnosed as a 'Tuberculin Gland'. I spent three weeks in hospital and it was then suggested that I went to the seaside for convalescence. A lady from the hospital almoner's office called at the house to see what the conditions were like. She was invited into the front room. To digress slightly, it was only permitted in these times to enter what was considered the 'best room' by invitation. To return, when the lady form the hospital was invited into the front room she noticed that we had a piano. A piano was a partial sign of affluence and because of this no assistance could be given with the expenses for my convalescence trip to the seaside. To give you some idea of our social standing, it will be proper for me to tell you something about my father's line of work. He served his apprenticeship as a carpenter joiner and upon completion of his indentures he received his certificate into the Guild. He became the pattern maker for a company which still exists today 'Pottertons' the boiler and central heating manufacturers. My father's' job was to produce a working model right down to the smallest screw, and all this in timber. His place of work was a yard workshop situated on the corner of Ravenswood Road and Cavendish Road, Balham. He worked there until he retired at the age of 70 years. The skills that my father possessed were such that a prospective employer requiring to employ such a man, would enquire as to how much wages he the tradesman wanted. To give you some idea of the sort of wages being paid at this time if you earned an amount between 15 shillings and one pound, this was considered reasonable and families could be brought up on this amount. At the time there were no £1 or 10/- (ten shillings) notes, these amounts were in coinage, made in gold and there were 240 pence to the golden sovereign.

To give you an impression of the prices of things relative to the wages paid about this time I will quote some of them. Gas and electricity did not exist and therefore lighting was by candle or oil. Paraffin oil was three pence (3d) per gallon, candles one or one and a half pence per pound weight according to their size. At Easter time chicken eggs 24 for one shilling (one shilling equalled twelve pence). Butter 10 pence a pound (lb), a two pound loaf of bread cost two pence (2d) and if the load was under weight the baker would cut a piece from another loaf to correct this, (a make-weight). Household blend of tea was four pence per quarter pound. Tea dust would cost one shilling for a pound in weight. The poor and the large families would wait for their food as late as possible on Saturday night because as there was no refrigeration as we know it today, this meant that meat and fish would be sold off at a cheaper price. A large shoulder of mutton together with two breasts would cost altogether two shillings. A pair of solid leather working men's boots in 1912 would cost one shilling and eleven pence half-penny and they were called 'Hob-nailed' boots. These boots had an iron plate around the sole and heel and iron studs over the sole. The shop assistant would ask you to take an extra pair of laces for the half-penny change from a florin (two shillings). The very best hand sewn boots would cost three shillings and six-pence per pair. Rents for houses were low, for instance, the rent for our house at Graveney Road was seven shillings and six-pence per week which went up to nine shillings later.

The house comprised three bedrooms, bathroom and toilet upstairs, three rooms on the ground floor plus a large scullery, as it was called. A scullery is a place for the dishes and the kitchen utensils and in there also was a large copper (a deep curved bottomed vessel). This usually had a fire hole underneath so that the water in the copper could be heated for the purpose of washing clothes etc. There was also a rubbish pit at the side in which all stuff that would burn was kept to help fuel the fire. We had a medium sized garden at the back of the house and a small one to the front. In the house we also had a large cellar reached by a ten tread stairway from inside the house. We used to have delivered about three tons of coal at a time to be kept in months when they charged about 18 shillings a ton. Winter prices were about one pound (£1) per ton.

My mother (Susan) had six children. The first three died at very early ages and the last of these three Nora lived to be about one and a half years old and died of convulsions and water on the brain during a teething period. The other three children survived and were Doris, Henry and Leonard. As I was the youngest of the first family many of the household chores fell upon my shoulders and this included doing many things and giving attention to these three younger members of the family. Many of my elder brothers and sisters were working and some of the boys had joined the Armed Forces.

The school leaving age was at fourteen years and when my turn came the normal thing to do was to try and find a suitable job which, with my health situation in mind had to be in the open air and of not too strenuous a nature. I actually stayed at school for three months after my fourteenth birthday. During this time, I heard that a job was going as a van boy at a warehouse on the very corner of the road where we lived. A young friend of mine, although I cannot now remember his name, was leaving and with the rest of his family was emigrating to Australia. It had been his job that I made application for and I was successful in getting this employment. This was a milestone in my life and I was introduced to the world of commerce.

Also, at this particular time of my life, I was friendly with a certain young lady by the name of Lydia Evans. Her father was related to a comedian of that time named Mr. Williams. Lydia had a talent for playing the piano which she played for her father who, although a train driver, used to sing comic songs and ballads such as 'Burlington Bertie from Bow'. My association with Lydia did not last very long.

Back now to my commercial beginnings. It was May 1914 that I got the job in the warehouse and it was with a company that, even at that time, was a household name and that name was J. Lyons and Company Limited. I was to work in the wholesale side of the Tea and Coffee Department. I made up my mind that I would remain with this company for the whole of my working life and as good fortune had it I am very happy to say I accomplished my aim and ambition. I will tell you why I made up my mind on the spot like this, especially at such a young age.

The things I saw happening around me at this time such as

269

children going to school with the seat of their pants missing, no shoes or socks on their feet, and a slice of bread and jam for their mid-day meal etc. If the parents of some of these children were unable to pay the rent then the Landlord would put their goods and chattels out on to the street and they would be marched off to the 'Workhouse' institution and the children would be taken into care. My whole family considered it to be most fortunate that our father had a good job and he knew how to look after it. A man with a job was a prince among his fellows and a man without, he struggled to survive. Many was the time when a man that I knew who drove horses and vans for a living would bring the harness home at the end of the day to ensure that nobody else took their van out before they themselves arrived the next day. This was a time when there would be more than ten men looking for one job, so it can be understood that a job attained was jealously guarded. In work, the boss was the boss and what he said went. Whatever he wanted you to do, that is what you did. He always expected a good day's work and that is what you gave, with no argument.

When I arrived at work for my first day at 8 o'clock a.m. I saw that the salesmen all arrived in their best clothes, straw boaters and some were wearing 'spats' (these were worn over the boots as protection). Most of them were also smoking cigars. It was obvious that a certain high standard was kept by the employees and that this was also expected by the Company that I had joined. Smoking was not allowed by the staff on the vans and this ruling was strictly kept. Break this rule and it was instant dismissal. Cigars by the way cost 2 pence each or seven for a shilling and these were called 'Black Treats'. All this greatly impressed me and I knew that I would have to work hard to become like these salesmen. There were no £1 a week jobs for someone of my age in those days and my wages were to be seven shillings per week. If I gave good assistance to the salesman then I got sixpence from him.

My duty was to make sure that the van was loaded with the goods which we had to sell and the other important part was taking care of the horses making sure that its nosebag was full and hung under the van. I also had to put a spare sack of fodder in the 'Boot'. The boot was in fact the driving seat. With the food, I also had to make sure that there was a clean bucket for water for the horse. It was a company rule that we had to draw water for the horse and not allow any of our horses to drink from a horse or cattle trough. The salesman was paid two pence a day for this which he in turn gave to the van-boy, usually at lunch time with which to get a mug of tea and a piece of suet pudding with jam on it.

With my work I learned a lot about figures because we took a van stock check at the end of each day. The salesman had to have either stock or a money balance against the starting stock of that day and any discrepancy had to be accounted for with the Depot Manager. I also kept my eyes and ears open busily taking in the wholesale and retail prices of the various lines we carried and watched the methods used by the salesman in dealing with customers.

Some of the prices I can well remember. Teas for instance were identified by their colour packet label and Blue was one shilling and four pence (1/4d) per pound and cost one shilling and 2pence (1/2d), Silver one shilling and sixpence (1/6d) cost (1/4d) per pound, quarter lb tins of Grade 'A' Cocoa at one shilling and four pence (1/4d) cost 1/1d per tin.

The period about which I speak is about the years 1913/1914 and horses were used to pull many things. For instance, Public Transport, both buses and trams, were drawn by horses and the cost of a fare for about a half mile journey was cheap at about a half penny. I can also recall another use to which a horse was put. There was a very large Dray-horse which stood at the bottom of Balham Hill and it was known as 'The Chain Horse'. Any cart with a load unable to get up the hill would be hitched to the Chain-Horse for extra pulling power. It would cost the Car-man two pence for the trip.

I now get to a time in my life which also changed the outlook of so many families. It was getting nearer to August 1914 and there was much talk of War. Most of my elder brothers were in the Forces already. My eldest brother Charlie was not called up because he had been invalided home from the South African Boer War which I mentioned earlier. Norman the second eldest, was serving in India in Rangoon when the 1914/18 War started and as far as I can remember his Regiment was the East Surrey's. The Regiment was returned to this country and then on to France. Whilst there, he (Norman) suffered frostbite to his feet because it was one of the worst winters we had ever had. So much so he was invalided home to a hospital in the St. Johns district. I can recall that whilst he was there that the local Gentry used to send round their cars and Broughams to the Military Hospital just to give the wounded Tommies an outing.

During one of these outings, Norman met his wife-to-be and her name was Gertrude, then, when Norman had recovered well enough he was supplied with surgical boots and he was put back on duty. He was also made up to Company Sergeant-Major and put in charge of a Recruiting Office. After Norman and Gertrude were married they lived for a time at our house in Graveney Road.

Brother Harold being on the Reserve was called up immediately into the Horse Transport (Army Service Corps). Percy was already serving in Norhern Ireland – Royal Field Artillery and Leslie served in the Royal Navy. I recall that his ship sailed from Irish Waters to the Dardanelles. Brother Roland also joined the Royal Navy and his ship was HMS Raglan which was unfortunately sunk during the War and Roland was killed. My other brother Cecil joined up in the Motor Transport section of the Army Service Corps. I at this time was too young to join up but I went in the Army later on.

More on my brothers later.

My father and his brother, my Uncle Bill had so many of their male children serving in one or other of the fighting forces that King George V wrote to both of them through his Privy Purse Office, Buckingham Palace. The letter was dated 20th August 1915 and the one to my father said:-

Sir,

I am commanded by the King to convey to you an expression of His Majesty's appreciation of the Patriotic spirit which has prompted your six sons and one son-in-law to give their service at this present time to the Army and Navy.

The King was much gratified to hear of the manner in which they have so readily responded to the call of their Sovereign and their Country and I am to express to you and to them His Majesty's many congratulations on having contributed in so full a measure to the great cause for which all the People of the British Empire are so bravely fighting.

I have the honour to be,

Sir

Your obedient servant

F.M.Ponsonby

Keeper of the Privy Purse

Mr. C. Shimell

A picture of my own mother (Harriet) and my father together with my six brothers appeared on page 4 in the Daily Sketch dated Wednesday 1st September 1915 and copies of this can be obtained from the British Museum Paper Library at Colindale. The picture also shows my Uncle William and his sons who also received a similar letter from the King.

It is now 1916 and the War has been going for about two years. More and more able bodied men were being called up for active service which left fewer men to run the depot. I then got promoted to Warehouse Foreman which I ran with the help of two female assistants. My wages had risen to eleven shillings and sixpence per week with 4d being deducted for an Insurance Stamp. This Insurance Stamp was started by Lloyd George and came to be called 'The nine pence for four pence scheme'. It only covered the male members of the family who were working. A Doctor Powell of Tooting started a scheme of his own and for 3d per week subscription, it covered the wife and children for medical visits. I know that this was a fact because I had the job of going round to collect these subs from those who had agreed to join.

Because so many were away at War, work was plentiful of course. Many who were able, worked in munitions factories and earned good wages, which meant that more money was coming to some households. One of the first things people would buy was a piano because having one was a sign of a certain level of affluence. It was common practice to gather round the piano and have a sing-song. The most popular song at this time was 'Keep the home fires burning' which was a way of saying that a warm welcome was waiting the Soldiers and Sailors when they came home from the battle fronts and the War at Sea.

I decided I should be earning more money and on seeing an advert in the paper that J. Lyons & Co.Ltd. produced, that they required Porters, I applied and got accepted. By getting this job, it meant that I was transferred to what was known as 'The Tea Shop Department', but just prior to my starting my new job at Tea Shops my brother Harold had returned from Salonica and was stationed at Park Royal, near Ealing. So I decided that I would walk there in the hope of seeing him. I started off at about 3.30am. on a Sunday morning and as I was crossing over Hammersmith Bridge I met a man who walked along with me. It turned out that he was a Foreman at a Munitions Factory which was also at Park Royal. Nearing our destination this chap had to hurry on because he had to blow his whistle for the workmen to start at 8 am. and could not be late. Unfortunately, my brother had had a slight accident the previous night and was in the sick bay so I was unable to see him. I therefore had to start walking back. I had one penny in my pocket which I had saved so that I could pay my fare from Earlsfield Station back home, but before doing I called in to see my brother's wife Fan to let her know of my intention to visit Harold, but I could not stay long as it was necessary for me to be home by 2.30 pm.

At this time I was very friendly with a young lady who lived in a turning off Garratt Lane. Her name was Isabella. However, after I started my new job on the Tea Shops she and I drifted apart, but she stayed very friendly with our family and eventually married my brother Cecil. His family and mine used to visit at times and eventually his youngest daughter Eileen was bridesmaid to my daughter Irene at her wedding.

Now back to the Tea Shop story. I had word brought to me by the stable boy at Tooting Depot that I was to report to 213 Piccadilly. I hadn't the remotest idea where it was so on the Sunday morning I started walking the journey,

276

that is after I had made some enquiries as to the direction that I had to go. I eventually found it and from Swan & Edgar's I could see the lights of 213. There was also a big sized brass plate running the length of each window. The lettering on these plates said 'J Lyons & Co Ltd., High Class Refreshments, Popular Prices, Ladies Room, Smoking Room'. The thought that went through my mind said "here's to tomorrow". I also found that the fare on the tram before 7.30 am. to any of the bridges was 2d Return Workmans.

On the Monday morning, I duly arrived at 213 for my first days work with my mind set on the job of cleaning glass and brass. Imagine my amazement when I was confronted by another porter with these remarks. "Oh hello you must be Shimell and you have come to clean and stoke the boilers". Well the only boiler I had seen was under my mother's copper. So we went down to the porter's dressing room so that I could get fixed up with a boilersuit. In this room were a number of uniforms. They were colured brown with yellow piping and brass buttons, but more about them later on. We then proceeded to the kitchen to collect the skips for filling with coke for the boiler. There were eight of these skips in all and this amount of coke would last all day. The refuse bins from the kitchens also had to be put out on the pavement for collection and after emptying they had to be returned back inside away from the eyes of the public by not later than 8 o'clock am. We then started work on stoking the boiler to get sufficient steam up to drive all the appliances. Everything was driven by steam and included three tea boilers, egg poachers, bain maries, a very large water tank for the kitchen and a potato steamer.

I had been under instruction for about three days but was making very little progress and was not enjoying what I was doing so when another porter arrived he took over

277

the boiler work and I went on to cleaning 'fronts'. I recognised this new porter as being a van boy previously at Tooting Depot, his name was Herbert Simpson. I still had to learn about the boiler work so at lunch times I had further instruction from Herbert and learned more in three lunchtimes than I had in the three previous days. Because of this I became quite proficient.

At 213 Piccadilly, I became very friendly with one of the waitresses, her name was Grace Willis who lived at 33 Dartrey Road, Worlds End, Chelsea. We were getting on fine, until one day, when her father appeared outside the shop where I had arranged to meet her and he said he would be taking her home. He thought that we were too young to be serious, and so ended the romance.

The brown uniforms I mentioned before were issued for when you had to appear in public and in all areas. They consisted of reefer jacket and trousers, white gloves and a peaked cap to match. Part of the public duty comprised having to stand just inside the door to the shop and close to the cash desk. Should a customer pass the desk without tendering a bill you asked he or she if they had been served. If the answer was 'no', you had to try and persuade the customer to return to the table and then get a waitress to serve them.

I worked in quite a number of Tea Shops, 213 Piccadilly of course, 9 Regents Street, 37 Piccadilly, St James's Street and Leicester Square, to name but a few. Time went on and I was nearing my 17th birthday and the War was still going on. Lord Derby started a scheme of Reserve Volunteers for the Services whereby you could attest and receive the King's Shilling. This put you on the Reserve for call-up. However, if one attested and had not waited to be called up on your 18th birthday then you got an extra month before having to report. So instead of me joining up on 5th December 1917 I actually went into the Army on 5th January 1918, so I had both my birthday and Christmas at home.

I reported for my medical examination on that January day at 9 am. and as it happened it appeared that a general call had gone out to all Medical Units that 'anybody who could stand up' was to go into the Army. So even though I was so deformed in my right shoulder and there was no hope of me handling a rifle, I still went into the Army. So, on 5th January 1918 I became Private Shimell R.V. 461316 Home Service Employment Company.

I cannot recall the full address at this time but for the time being we were being sent to Maidstone in Kent where we arrived at the Tythe Barn at about 1 o'clock pm. and where the Sergeant managed to rustle up some food. The next night we spent in Maidstone slaughterhouse and it was very cold. This was January remember and there were no home comforts. Altogether, we spent about a fortnight there before being posted to Blenheim Hutments, Stanhope Lines Aldershot.

The next day we were kitted out with our uniforms, all except for puttees. All our civilian clothes were parcelled up and we had to send them home by rail. On our way to the railway station we were however, accosted more than once by the Military Police for being improperly dressed. There were always plenty of M.P.s in Aldershot Town so we had to keep on explaining to them the reason we had no puttees. We were allowed to proceed but they kept a watch on us for our immediate return to Barracks. In February we were drafted to the 'Aldershot Command Officers & "C" Company of NCOs " School of Instruction, for duty. Both the Officers and the NCOs were learning Swahili and other languages for Service in British East Africa. This unit I was in was made up of Low

Category Personnel and we were known as 'Details'! I became the Camp Postman and also Orderly-Room 'Runner'. I sometimes had to visit another Camp which was opposite ours, to deliver mail and on one day I saw a chap over there going about picking up paper with a nail on the end of a stick. We got chatting and found out that he had joined up on the same day as me. It was certainly seen that the Medical Instructions had been fully implemented because this chap had a 'wooden' leg. Naturally his nickname was 'Peggy'. However, he did tell me at this time that he was due to be discharged in a few weeks time, we then had a change of Commandant and the new Colonel said that the Camp Postman should have the protection of the stripes of at least a Corporal. I was however, reluctant to receive these for reasons I put forward at the time, and these the Officer accepted, so I became an Officers' Servant. The details of my new job were as follows:- I was responsible for keeping their Quarters spick and span, attending to the laundry, making sure that their uniforms were in good order and being as useful as possible to them for all manner of kindred requirements.

After the end of each five week course when the Officers had gone and after we had cleared up everything we were granted a long weekend pass from 12 o'clock noon Friday until 2400 hours the following Tuesday. This routine went on until about September 1918 when all the detachments of 'Detail' were then sent to the NRA School of Musketry. I was drafted into the Orderly Room because of my shoulder and I also used to help the chap in preparing the firing range for rifle practice. During this period we were to come across a Medical Officer named Dr Worgman who was a most extraordinary character. His prowess with two Smith & Western revolvers was so remarkable we named him Buffalo Bill. He used to carry his guns in holsters tied down his legs just like in the Wild West in America.

The War was now coming to an end and when one of our number on his return from leave on Sunday 10th November said that it would be announced officially on the following day we of course could not believe it, but as it turned out, this was so. There was a big parade for all ranks, that is except for us 'Details', where it was made known to everyone.

We 'Details' were mustered after the parade, all fifteen of us, and I remember that Dr. Worgman came along our little line and gave each one of us a £1 and an invitation to the Canteen., Now the fighting was over the next move was to find ways to get back to work. The first men to be released were those who were the Employers of Labour. They were referred to as 'Pivotal' men. Then those like me who had a job waiting for them to return to came next. So in February 1919 I was discharged as medically unfit for further service.

I was sent to Telavera Barracks to get kitted out in civilian clothes which I must admit were very good. When that was all completed I then arrived home. Once there I went off to see my boss who advised me to see the month out and he then instructed me to report for work on the first Monday of March 1919.

The first Shop I was sent to was number 15 Whitehall, Code Z3 and it was at this branch that I first came into contact with a young lady who was to become my wife, but more about this later! The Company had decided to branch out into a new direction of a Sales Service called 'Front Shop Service', where it was possible to purchase pre-packed luncheon boxes ready to serve. This service was used by all Domestic servants before the War. There was now a shortage of this type of employee because many of the girls had found more lucrative employment.

Also, about this time, a gentleman from the USA came over bringing with him his ideas about 'Ice-cream Soda Fountains, - so the 'Ice-Cream Soda Bar' was born. I took on the training and eventually became proficient to such an extent that I trained many staff to operate these Soda Bars. I also drove the passenger lifts both by 'lever' and/or 'rope'.

I lost count of the actual number of Tea Shops I worked in, but it is safe to say at least a hundred. Part of my work was cleaning and polishing glass ceilings. Some of these had to be done on Saturday nights and me leaving in the small hours of Sunday morning and walking home. Of course, there was extra wages for this. It was also a job which could be left at any time, which often was the case should one of the porters fail to report for duty. I would then carry on his duties until his return. Most of my time was spent in the West End of London branches.

Another memory of 1919 comes to mind and it concerns the J. Lyons & Company Sports Ground at Sudbury, where I used to go on a Saturday morning to prepare for the sporting events. There was a small boiler to stoke to supply hot water for the kitchen and the showers. There was a cafeteria where they had dancing in the evening which meant having to move all the tables and chairs, French chalk the floor and set them all out again. All these jobs I had to do were in the very beginning but eventually this was to become I should think one of the finest Sports Centres in the country. This Sudbury Sports Centre was bought by the Company as a Memorial to all the 'boys' they had lost in the War.

To give you some idea how remote Sudbury Hill was, I went down there on Mondays and Tuesdays to clear up, and to get there I had to travel by Underground. There was no station so I had to get the guard to stop the train to get off and on my return journey had to flag the train down. Later there was a special exit from the Underground to the Sports Ground and also at a later date the drive from the gate down to the Pavilion was widened to take coaches.

A Children's Corner was made with a person put in charge, there was also a theatre and dance hall, swimming pool, football & cricket pitches, bowling greens which were laid with Cumberland Turf and tennis courts. All these facilities were added over a number of years.

I am now going to continue to refer to the years 1919-1921 and during these 2 to 3 years I studied many of the girls with whom I had been working and I spotted one particular young lady who I had been watching for some time. I decided that she was the girl for me and hopefully she would say 'yes'.

Well we went out for several walking trips together picnicking on Epsom Downs and Riddlesdown to name but two. We got on fine and decided that this was it. Of course, we could not proclaim this at the Shop because this would have meant a separation, so we staged many rows and off-handed episodes for the benefit of the staff and the manageress and it was not until after we became engaged did it leak out.

Our engagement took place on Flo's birthday 17th May 1921. We went for a drink to celebrate to 'The Feathers' in Whitehall. The first person to know about us was a Mrs. Gertrude Corker who had lost her husband, killed in the 14/18 War. She had a daughter also called Gertrude and I am still in touch with her to this day. Gertrude the mother passed away some years ago.

The next thing to think about was finding somewhere to

live and set up home. We were lucky enough to find two rooms right at the top of a three storey and basement house at the address of 27, Ackerman Road, Brixton. The rent being fourteen shillings per week which we could just about manage, we took it in the July of that year and then set about furnishing it.

The rooms consisted of a very large front room/bedroom and next to it was a kitchen of sorts. The gas cooker was on the landing outside the rooms. We had to fetch up water from the bathroom down on the next floor and the toilet was on the ground floor. We worked hard and saved hard and slowly it began to take shape and by the end of August it was ready. Of course, we had been paying rent all this time.

We were now all set for our wedding which took place at All Saints Church at the top of Lyham Road on Saturday 22nd October 1921. We could not afford a Honeymoon but went straight back to our small flat. My wife had always thought that her name was Florence Ada Neat as everybody called her 'Flo', when in fact it was Ada Florence so we had to return to the Registrar and get it altered. Also, I had said that I was 22 years of age until my father said that I would not be until December so that had to be corrected.

One other thing I must mention before I forget, because my wife and I had completed the correct number of years with the Company we each qualified for a Wedding Cake, but we asked if it would be possible to have one large cake instead of two small ones, which not only did the Company agree but they also supplied a large silver stand and knife together with lots of decorations. This was wonderful we thought. I returned to my old home on the Sunday morning to collect my working clothes. I also learned while I was there that my father was disappointed that I had not had my voice trained as he thought that I would have made a good baritone. I had sung two ballads at my wedding namely 'Navarna' and 'Thora' and he thought I did very well.

The wife had a week off and she spent quite a lot of time apart from making the flat nearer to our liking making up a list of the dry goods for the food cupboard. Flo returned to work for three months until she was convinced that there was going to be a new arrival to start our home. The three months wages she earned completed what she had set out to do in having a food store cupboard. From ten on she was preparing baby clothes for the new arrival making everything she knew that she would require.

During July of that year my brother Charles passed away in St James Hospital, Balham. Having been discharged from the Army in 1902 he worked as a porter at Tooting Grove Hospital and then as a Motorman on the trams run by the London County Council. The tale about the Benefit Show I'll tell you about later. One incident that I remember was when he was on the no. 34 route which ran from Camberwell to Beaufort Street, Chelsea. It had to negotiate a hill coming up from Wandsworth Road to Clapham Common, namely Cedars Road so of course there was no stopping until it reached the top. Halfway up a lady started to ring the bell for it to stop and kept on ringing. Charles swung back the door which divided the driver from the inside saying as he did so "Don't worry Lady it's quite alright we are just going round to your house".

About this time I was working at 450 The Strand and I remember very clearly on one morning a customer came to the front shop counter to purchase what first appeared to be a cake. Well she cross-examined the counter-hand taking her through the entire range of all types of cake, what were the ingredients in each one etc., etc. This went on for something like 15 minutes, by which time the face of the counter-hand was becoming redder and redder. Eventually the customer brought two penny buns. Collapse of counter-hand. The slogan of the shops was 'The Customer is always right' and no matter what happens staff had to keep as calm as possible in all circumstances.

Talking of slogans, another one was put up in the kitchens which said 'one plate worth1/-, 4 quarters worth nothing', this meant that the staff should handle the crockery carefully and not break any.

Well, the 23rd October duly arrived and the wife had a busy day washing. I arrived home about 5.30 pm and she was showing definite signs of the coming event. I took a hand to some extent before rushing off for the mid-wife who arrived in good time. I had lit the fire in the bedroom and got plenty of hot water on the go. Eight thirty arrived and the cry I had got used to hearing at Graveney Road at the birth of a baby was also heard. We had got our wish for a baby daughter whom we named Irene Margaret.

We had bought an orange crate which was divided into three compartments. The top of each was a half circle which I removed and tacked to the under part at each end and this formed a very good 'crib' and 'cradle'. We lined it with cotton wool and a large feather & flock pillow case for the base. 1922 was our family milestone.

Up till now I have only mentioned about my brother but I must not forget that I also had three sisters namely Miriam, Evelyn and Gladys. More about them later on.

Time does not stand still. 1923 was not very eventful

except for the progress of our daughter until later in that year when Flo and I were expecting the arrival of our second child into the family sometime in the early months of 1924. I was working at Marble Arch Tea Shop at the time and I well remember one day when we were very busy about mid-tea-time and I noticed a gentleman pushing his way to the front of the queue. It was none other than Flo's father. I naturally let him through and he told me that they had taken her to the Nursing Home at West Norwood and for me to ring them later for news. I did this when I was able and was informed that I had a son. After seeing mother we talked about giving him his name. Mother said that we could not want another Reginald in the family even though it was customary for the eldest son to be named after his father, so we gave him the names of Ronald David Charles. The last of the two names being each of his grandfather's names. He was born on Easter Sunday 20th April 1924. I cannot remember Easter Sunday ever falling again on that date right up to the present time. You were not allowed too much time off even at this sort of time so later that week I had to return to work, still mother and I were quite happy with our family even though our little flat was getting cramped.

I was working at Section Z3 Whitehall at the time and I can recall an amusing incident that took place during the week after I had returned to work. There was a bus stop just outside the shop. I was walking between 25 Whitehall and 15 Whitehall (Z3) and a bus had just pulled away from the stop when I saw a man running after it to get on. He sprang on but the case he was carrying swung around and hit the hand rail and in so doing the lid flew open and the contents were spread in a neat half circle pile on the pavement. Laid out in perfect order were his pyjamas, hair brushes, slippers, shaving gear and clothes brushes. Some bright spark passing by uttered in a loud voice, "What time does the sale start Mister?"

1924 saw the end of the 'waitress' as we knew her. Her uniform had been a long Alpaca dress with a long starched apron, white collar and cuffs with a white hat that fixed to her hair had to be done in a bun style. The new uniform was in the shape of a page-boy with red buttoned front, broad lace collar, a white lace-band cap and short starched apron. This was the birth of the 'Lyons Nippy'. Nippy in appearance and in service.

There also occurs at this time one of the greatest feats of all time in respect of Lyons Waitress service. The Grand Lodge of Masons in England held a lunch for 1000 people at Olympia in London and our waitresses and wine waiters had a fortnights training in the preparation for the event. I can assure you that the Brigade of Guards could not have held a candle to them. Mr. I.M. Glucstein was up on a platform in the rafters where he had a complete view of all that was going on. He held in his hand a bell-push. Mr Hunt who was manager of Maison Lyons of Oxford Street was in charge of the food arrangements, which was arriving from Cadby Hall in Kensington by many vans. The whole thing was being organised by using a system of colours. For instance, on arrival a gentleman guest with a white ticket left his hat and case at a cloakroom with a white card sign, he then proceeded through a curtain marked with a white card and sat at a table similarly marked which also had his ticket number on it. This system applied to all the other colours and it ensured that all the diners had a comfortable and easy way of arriving at their tables. The waitress service was also controlled in that the first waitress to enter went to the furthest table so that as the last one came in they arrived at their posts at precisely the same moment. Having placed her supplies on the table she would about turn and wait. Mr I.C. Glucstein looking on the scene would at the right second ring the bell. The waitresses would then all leave and as soon as they had left, the wine waiters moved in from the other side.

I am not certain if the following persons were on a raised dais but I have reason to believe that Earl Haigh and Earl Beatty were the Guests of Honour. To put the whole thing into a nutshell, the event went off like a piece of well oiled machinery with not the least sign of mishap and many remarks were passed to us in the various cloakrooms about the most wonderful service. Mr I.C. Glucstein summed it up in the following terms. 'The success of Olympia can only be attributed to the working of a wonderful staff'.

I cannot remember any specific things that happened during the next two years except that a Mr Clarke joined the Company and I had the job of teaching him his portering duties. I also had to get him measured for his uniform at 'Cleavers' in the Strand. Cleavers made all the uniforms for the staff of J. Lyons & Co. I returned also to the Ice-Cream Soda Fountain section to train more staff and instruct them in their duties.

At the beginning part of 1926, Flo and I were expecting another addition to our family which would come later in the year and it was at this time that I was moved from the Oxford Street section to Victoria. This meant that I lost my extra work and its pay, which was agreed as my pocket money. Mother had my wages and I had the extra, if any! There was only one thing left for me to do and that was to apply for a transfer so that I could earn more wages. This I did and obtained a move to the Wholesale Tea Department. On the date of my transfer I duly arrived at the Peckham Depot for training under a first class salesman by the name of Mr W. Willingham known affectionately as Bill. Of course, I had remembered quite an amount of the trade from my van-boy days. The salesman I was with then was a Mr George Hammaton who had also been introduced to this Department by Bill Willingham. I was on a six week trial period to see if I could make it. The answer to 'did you?' is yes, because I stayed with this department until I retired in 1962.

As we were expecting the third addition to our family we had to start looking for larger accommodation. As luck would have it, and at that time, the cottage next door to Flo's father became almost vacant. I say almost because there was an elderly couple occupying two back bedrooms upstairs, a Mr & Mrs Jennings by name. Anyway, I went along to be introduced to Mr Lawrence the Landlord and was accepted as a tenant. The rent was no more than I was paying at Ackerman Road for the whole cottage, so I reduced the rent for the Jennings from what they were paying and they remained at 147 Cornwall Road until they passed away. The cottage gave me the extra rooms we required and eventually three bedrooms. The arrival of our third child was on 24th October 1926 and was another boy. We christened him Malcolm Dudley.

My wages at this time were £3.15.0d per week and of course in my new job one was expected to dress smartly. One item was a must. This was a bowler hat and if for instance you entered a shop and a lady or ladies were present, you acknowledged them by raising your hat. This also applied at any time when greeting a member of the opposite sex. Mother and I went to Middlesex Street better known as Petticoat Lane Market and bought a three piece grey suit and a rough sort of fur-lined overcoat for a total of £3.0.0d to start my new job.

I became firmly established in the Tea Sales Department

learning by doing the job. My wages were increased by 10/- per week and this amount was paid as a commission on a monthly basis and I became what was called a 'Permanent Relief'. However, if I did a 'Journey then the commission went up from 10/- to 15/- or £3.0.0d per month. I rode with as many of the salesmen as possible as it became apparent to me that this was the best way to achieve greater experience. All the areas and different shop and business owners required handling in so many different ways. Sales methods changed to suit the occasion. Well in the January I was asked if I would go to Portsmouth canvassing on behalf of Black & Greens Tea. They were an associate company to J. Lyons and there were three different priced packets of tea to demonstrate. I was joined by another relief salesman named Gerald Jacobson and we duly arrived at Portsmouth with our first priority of finding 'digs'. We found them just around the corner from the station at Madelins Hotel. We stayed there just three days and nights as it was anything but a desirable place to stay. We reported for work to the Depot in Basing Street near what was known as Kingston Cross where there were four other salesmen. Our duties were to canvass all the private houses and also the shopkeepers in the area. All these journeys were now being served by motor-vans instead of horse-drawn vans and I must add that this canvass was very, very successful. We were there for about three to four months till about May 1927. Three of the other salesmen were Mick Crawley, Mac MacGrath and Jimmy Rolfe. I have kept in touch with the last named right up to the present day. During the time at Portsmouth, Flo's mother passed away.

My next canvass was in Haslemere. We had a job trying to find 'digs' so had to resort to calling into the local police station. We were just walking down a long carpeted corridor when a lady put her head out of a door demanding to know what we wanted. She escorted us back to the charge-room where a sergeant was sitting at a desk. After explaining what it was we were wanting he took us outside and pointed to the White Lion Hotel. Jacobson then told him to apologise to the charlady for the intrusion. When we had gone a few yards I turned to Jacobson and said that the lady could have been the sergeant's wife. We spent a week at Haslemere doing another successful canvass and then returned to Shepherds Bush Depot, Latimer Road.

Apart from the main journeys running from various depots in the London area there were some which were called 'unattached'. There were two at Kingston upon Thames, two at Crystal Palace, two at Croydon and one at Bromley in Kent. I covered most of these as a relief when the salesmen went on holidays, and I must admit that this was a very excellent way of gaining a wide and varied knowledge of different areas of operation. During this time nearly all us salesmen had been put through the Motor School at Park Royal as we were fast turning to motor vehicles to replace the horses.

Before continuing I must record here that in October of 1927, in fact, on my son Malcolm's first birthday, 24th October, my father died and his passing was very sudden. As far as I remember he was still working at 70 years of age and therefore had not been retired for very long.

In 1928, before we went over entirely to motor transport, the horse that I had to pull my van was called Bridget. She was one of two fine horses that I had and she had some quaint habits and characteristics. She was for instance a very clean horse in so far that although like all horses do, she would use anywhere in the street for her toilet, when out with the van, once she entered her stable in the evening the head horse-keeper had to put a bucket in one part of her stable because she would never foul her stall. On the journey she also had favourite ports of call. One was where she always got a jam doughnut and another always occurred on a Tuesday after lunch when on hearing our returning footsteps this was a signal for her to throw her nose-bag into the air for her two pieces of sugar. There was also a shop where she would not move until the shop-keeper came out with a little bar of chocolate and I remember on one occasion, Bridget putting her head round the door as if to say "Where's my treat?"! She also knew that if I were to drive home to Cornwall Road this meant a cup of tea for the van-boy and sugar for Bridget. I was one of the last salesmen to go for motor transport training at Park Royal and spent ten days learning on a Morris. On my last day I learnt that I had to return to Brixton Depot to take over a journey which was being done by a Ford van. I knew nothing about driving a Ford and they were so different to the Morris. However, after several attempts I managed to master it, which stood me in good stead because there were several of the journeys which used this type of vehicle. The management also at this time decided to bring the unattached journeys under one roof, Plaistow Depot moved en bloc to Mildmay, at Acre Lane, Brixton, which for myself I have to say as far as I was concerned was most convenient. I could walk from home to there in a little more than ten minutes.

Now it was time for Ron to go to proper school like Irene which was only a few minutes walk away from home called Lyham Road School. Malcolm the youngest wanted to know why he could not go to school like the others and because of this he was no problem to take to school when it became his turn. At work, I was always on stand-by in case any of the salesmen were away sick, which meant that I had to take over their journey. Apart from the tea and coffee and other lines that we normally had to sell, one or two extra items were added in the way of confectionary such as '1-penny Buz bars' and '1-penny Jack-O-Bars'. Then we used to get new sales items to try and sell to our customers. One of these was a very elaborately packed carton which contained sachets of custard powder each sufficient to make one pint at 1d per pint packet. The Company managed to get a machine which was able to pack the powder at half the cost previously charged. These single packets were in boxes of 5 dozen and the wholesale price was 1/10d half-penny, to be sold retail at 2/6d. The greatest selling point being that for every packet of custard powder would mean a pint of milk which the dairymen to whom we sold this particular item were very quick to grasp. This did very well for J. Lyons because all the competition firm's packets were for 3 pints. Ours could also be sold as single units to housewives, and it proved to be a winner.

I forgot to tell you what the confectionary items were like. The Buz bar was a honey-comb wafer covered with milk chocolate wrapped in foil with a yellow motif on the outside wrapper, and the Jack-O-Bar was a bar of toffee and nuts also covered in chocolate. Both these items sold like Hot Cross buns at Easter time and were very popular with the public, in fact there was no way to hold these sales in check.

At budget times there was always a chance that a tax would be put on tea. This was usually 4d per pound and meant that we had to take a complete van stock check, then stick labels on every single packet and after which we all had to give a hand to label up the whole of the Depot stock. At times like these, Flo came down with other salesmen's wives to lend a hand. Because we had our own bonded warehouse at Greenford, the Customs and Excise Officers collected the Tea Duty before any was allowed to be removed. Greenford, being built on a triangle of the waterway, the railway and the road meant

294

that we could transport our goods by any of these three methods to all parts of the country. In fact a large part of our tea supplies were transported directly down the Grand Union Canal.

Well for the next few years very little occurred to upset the normal running of the home, or my particular job. The three children were all settled at school and they all attended the church in which Mum and I were married, All Saints at the top of Lyham Road. Ron became solo soprano in the choir and he also became later on School Captain and a leading singer there in various school productions.

I still moved around with various salesmen in all parts of the London area until one day when the Area Manager suggested that I learn about glass-fixing for advertising purposes. I duly went with a Mr Myers who pushed a truck around and a Mr Early who drove the van. Their jobs were erecting very large enamel signs on outside walls with advertising matter on them and also doing the same in glass. The most interesting advertising I found was in the glass fixing. The pieces were in uniform sizes and could be cut to fit almost any design. They were 30 inches long by 11 inches deep with a blue background. The words 'LYONS TEA' were set in white with an orange and white border which was also incorporated on these panels. One particular sign which I was able to set was on the bottom of a café window on Brixton Hill. I had to wait and see the proprietor when he had returned from an appearance at The Grand Theatre, and this was at 1 o'clock am on an early Sunday morning. It seemed that his customers had complained about being overlooked when seated at the window tables and so he thought that if this could be covered then it could be advantageous and cure this small problem and keep his customers happy. I drew up a diagram of the said window spacing out the 'LYONS TEA' sign, then filling in the blank spaces with plain blue glass. I then ran this together with a complete border round the whole outside, which suited the café owner very well. This took me almost five hours to cut and then I proceeded to the site for fixing. After its completion and unbeknown to me Mr Harry Lavender our Sales Manager drove by and remarked to Mr H. Dicker the Area Manager who was with him at the time that he thought it was marvellous piece of advertising for the Company. Henceforth Shimell was to be given a spare van and a free hand to go on any salesman's journey and carry on with this type of work. This I did for the next eight or nine years and I also trained several young members of the staff in this particular field of advertising. It got them used to meeting shop-keepers, gave them an insight into salesmanship, so much so, that some of them became, later on, relief salesmen in their own right.

Time passed on at a fairly even pace, our children were all progressing well with schoolwork, Rene was at Central School, Ron got a scholarship to train as a chef at Westminster Technical School and Malcolm had taken the LCC examination for entry into the Grammar School but more about them later. 1938 had come and there was talk once more of war with Germany because of the Nazis under Hitler who were causing so much trouble in Europe.

In the July of 1939 saw the passing of Flo's father David Neat, who had lived as I said next door to us. Flo's sister Annie and her husband had taken over the tenancy of the house so they were our neighbours and this continued until both Annie and I moved out into the Old-People's Home in Clarence Avenue.

Back to 1939. Right opposite us there had always been a Barracks and Riding School which belonged to the Queens Own Regiment. Many's the time when they and the Territorials would gather there and go off on manoeuvres. Well it was decided that the old corrugated riding-school building would be pulled down and a proper brick built barracks would be built on the site to house the East Surrey Yeomanry. This was completed and officially opened by Her Majesty, Queen Mary as its Commander-in Chief. We got to know many of the soldiers who were stationed over there and as the threat of war became more and more imminent we saw many of them going off to fight when the actual conflict started in the September. These terrible events took my thoughts back to August 1914.

Many of our younger salesmen were joining up in the Armed Forces at that time and I was operating the Streatham journey. Then because of the staff shortages all the journeys were to be worked on a fortnightly basis and this was carried on until 1942 when it became difficult to operate the County and Provincial journeys. I found myself dashing from place to place trying to keep them in service.

1942 also saw Rene in the Women's Army and Ron although not having been long over a period in a number of hospitals he volunteered and saw service in the Royal Air Force. When it came turn for Malcolm he was rejected because he had a perforated eardrum. He joined a Shipping Company for a number of years and then eventually joined Lord Vesteys meat exporting concern.

During the years 1942-1946, I moved around the country on various journeys where we were short of staff. I started in Portsmouth for about three months then when a salesman who had been released form the military services took over I came back to London. Not for long however, because it was found that Witney & Banbury areas were not staffed and so I went there on the understanding that it would be for a short period of time only. This short period eventually extended to one whole year.

My son Ronald met his young lady in the Airforce and she was to become his wife after the war and they were stationed for a time at Brize Norton which was quite close to Witney so on one of their days off they visited me during my time there.

One of the conditions of my going on these various journeys round the country was that I was able to return home for weekends and whilst I was at Witney a Flying Bomb was dropped on to a piece of spare ground at the back of our house doing some considerable damage. When I arrived home I found the Navy boys putting cellophane covering right over the windows. After my year at Witney, I returned to London.

J. Lyons at this time decided that the store at Bungay, Suffolk was to be removed and set up again at Yarmouth, but before I was sent to do this job. I spent six weeks at Reading and three months at Weymouth, both of these places I found to be very interesting. I was then sent to Yarmouth to effect the change from Bungay and make the goods-yard into our Depot gain and re-establish the garage.

I was still there on V.J. Day in 1946 but after that I came back to London to take over the Kilburn district. Flo was convinced that she expected to hear that I was off to Scotland so to keep the pot boiling I got Rene to look up the train times for Edinburgh just for a joke. Mother was not amused when I said "No, I was not going to Scotland just to Shepherds Bush depot and the Kilburn journey". Not long after that the Depot Manager discovered that a salesman by the name of Wicks was doing the Battersea journey so he organised a swap between us. During my time on the Battersea run I met Mr Crown who owned a café which was on one of my regular ports of call. Mr Bill Crown, the son, was also in the business and he and I became very good friends and has continued right up to the present time. The café business was a customer of J. Lyons on my books and I regularly took my meals there as well. On one of these days when I was in the café, Mrs Crown who had just that week returned from the hospital bringing with her their new family, got Bill to invite me up to their flat to see them. To my surprise it turned out to be twin daughters. It so happened that I had in my possession two Commemorative Crown pieces of 1935 of King George and Queen Mary so I presented the Twin Crowns with the two Crowns which to my knowledge they still possess.

At this point, the notes by my father stopped and therefore nothing more can be added to this treatise. This he started in July 1978 and when he died on the 16th February 1979 there were so many references to his early times, about his brothers and sisters and about life in general which were unfortunately left out and unfinished, as he himself said:-

'More about that later'

The pity is that the 'later' was never to be.

So much has been lost of the facts which surrounded the earlier half of this century of the life and times of this 'common man' known to so many as 'Reg'.

AND FINALLY

Having re-read the book from the start I feel there is a need to write just one more chapter. So many of the people who were alive when I started, are no longer with us. On the family side my cousin Douglas from the Isle of Man died earlier this year and there has been a steady procession of musicians including Harry Hayes, Spike Robinson. Oliver Jones, Bill le Sage, and Lennie Best. Of these the only one I did not know personally at some time was Oliver Jones, a very fine pianist.

In the obituary on Harry Hayes the suggestion was made that most of his solos were written and presumably memorised prior to playing and this certainly seems probable bearing in mind how immaculate his performances were. I wonder whether he had a chart for "After you've gone" in the key of "B".

Spike Robinson was a wonderful character and in his obituary it mentioned that he was in England just after the war as an American soldier at which time there was little demand for the marching band he was in. He then became quite involved in the British Jazz scene which came to an abrupt end when his appearance in a Jazz Concert at the London Palladium came to the notice of the Musician's Union and as a result he was posted to Italy. After service he went back to America and after trying to make a living as a musician he worked on missiles at Cape Canaveral, and after for the Honeywell Corporation, but after a time the urge to play took over and he begun touring again. This was not easy and he related one time when he was waiting for an early morning train in North Germany, feeling very tired – slightly hungover, and then he thought, "If I were not here I could be attending a quality control meeting for Honeywell" –

and immediately felt a lot better! Amazingly he was a keen cricket supporter and attended many test matches and often played with John Barnes group before the start of the matches. He was seriously ill during the eighties and although he made a recovery he could never give up smoking. At his funeral Jack Parnell said a few words – including "What a way to give up smoking!!!" I must say from this point of view funerals have in general become a little less sombre these days – quite rightly so.

Mind you I am reminded of the story of the funeral of one of Count Basie's Band at which they played "April in Paris" – one of his most famous arrangements – just as the coffin started to disappear through the curtains. Then in keeping with the original a voice said "One more time" and the coffin emerged twice more!

I had known Bill le Sage from the time he and Allan Ganley were playing with the John Dankworth Big Band and they both called at Queensville Road during our first years of marriage on the way to a gig at Streatham Hill Theatre. In more recent times I had seen him at Shepperton and one or two other venues and when I discovered that his wife had the same problem as Jean, I used to tackle him on the subject. Very unfortunately Bill's wife eventually had to be taken into care and after some considerable time Bill himself was in hospital when she died and had to attend her funeral from his sick bed and within a week or so he himself died. During my discussions with him he stressed the need to maintain a sense of humour despite the circumstances and I can confirm that this has helped to keep him going on many an occasion. I found it very helpful to be able to relate to someone with first hand experience of the problems and of course, in this context, I cannot speak too highly of the support I have had from the Alzheimer's Society.

One point I should have mentioned before concerns one of Stephane Grappelly's annual concerts at the Royal Albert Hall which we attended. His guest on this occasion was Julian Bream, the classical guitarist, and after performing something from his own repertoire he then joined in a jazz version of "Sweet Georgia Brown". This was fine until he finished his solo whereupon Stephane egged him on to do a second chorus and of course all the poor chap could do was to repeat what he had already played as the part had been written for him specially – which rather gave the game away. I gather Stephane rather enjoyed wrong-footing people and in his autobiography Julian Bream revealed that he was rather upset by this incident.

Since I wrote about the avant-garde pianist John Law he has made a new C.D. which was reviewed by John Fordham in the Guardian, and his comments fully justified my feelings on his earlier performances when he stated that the record was dedicated to "Italian pianist/composer Antonio Zambrini, who the English pianist John Law credits with helping to change his jazz perspective in 1999".

Talking of Law and stretching a point somewhat, I wonder whether you have noticed that there are far more Jazz Duo's than Trio's and upwards playing in pubs and restaurants. The reason for this is an archaic law which decrees that any place offering music with more than two musicians has to comply with very strict rules covering fire regulations etc. This on the surface seems quite reasonable until the same place is hired for a private function when these rules do not apply. They can have a band as large as can be accommodated, a very large audience, and all these rules go out of the window which is grossly unfair and impossible to justify. The government made an attempt to rectify matters very recently with a bill that would require ALL establishments to have a licence irrespective of the numbers involved, which would probably stop for good a lot of the duo's at present in existence and cause great harm to entertainment in general. This rang alarm bells every where and the subsequent lobbying resulted in the Bill being defeated in the Lords initially, but I understand that is has since been approved to become effective some time in 2004. I fear this will prove to be a disaster and yet another ill-thought out initiative!!

I saw a couple of late night TV programs about the Piano, narrated by Jools Holland starting at Hatchlands National Trust Property, which houses a large number of pianos originally owned by some of the great composers. From there he went to archive shots of a lot of jazz pianists from Scott Joplin through to Meade Lux Lewis the boogie-woogie player, Ray Charles and beyond, with interviews with George Shearing and others. The whole was very interesting but what amazed me was that the producer was the chap who bought our original house in Clapham Park. I later phoned to congratulate him and took the opportunity to ask whether he had had to have the roof or windows replaced since we left, 13 years ago. He has very recently had just one of the windows replaced – so eat your heart out Gigi – wherever you are!

Early in 2003 I made a call to Jazz FM and was surprised to be told that unless they played pop music in the afternoons they would not be able to continue, which is quite a refreshing bit of honesty on their part. I still have concerns that the youngsters of today will think that this constitutes jazz, as it is rather like selling paste in place of diamonds, excepting there is at least some similarity there. Mind you they do seem to have picked up in other directions and stopped the endless advertising of Jazz Festivals the world over, months in advance which seemed rather mindless, and concentrated on playing more music.

Mind you they never miss an opportunity to sacrifice Dinner Jazz and recently, because of the fame achieved by Tony Blackburn in the "Survivor" program he was given a regular 2 hour slot from 6.00-8.00 pm every Saturday playing Soul Music. On one of these days I waited patiently until after 8 o'clock only to hear Tony Blackburn still playing his stuff which was very repetitive. I phoned the office number to complain and a recorded voice said that if urgent I should contact another number which I did. After waiting quite a long time a voice said "Hello", and I said "Why the hell are we listening to Tony Blackburn at this hour of the night?" The respondent said "There's no need to be rude – this is Tony Blackburn". He then told me that his program had been extended because of the death of Barry White – the soul singer – the day before. Now why on earth could it not have been included in the Soul program. I fear we were both a bit taken aback and the rest of the conversation deteriorated somewhat. If Campbell Burnap can manage to deal with all the obituaries in the Jazz World in 2 hours on Sundays, why this constant erosion?

A couple of weeks later, immediately after Campbell's program, I nearly hit the roof when Sarah Ward opened the program with a Rap artiste. Now this really was the pits and she spent quite a while chatting to him and in effect giving this idiom some status. I personally cannot stand listening to someone talking fast "In a Monotone" and whilst I respect other people's tastes this was not the place for it. I would prefer in any event to hear the records and not so much chat in between, which, before I switched off in disgust was pretty banal to say the least. I tried phoning the number again but this time no one replied!

Everything has to have a label these days and I once heard a B.B.C. trailer for a regular Monday broadcast by Humphrey Littleton which called it "Smooth Jazz" – since when? In addition there seems to be an obsession with popularity rankings, even on "Smooth Classics", and in every way people dash to make phone calls on every banal subject and in that context there was a phone poll to decide whether people thought that Saddam Hussein would or would not use chemical weapons. How mindless can you get? Ask these same people to vote for a government and I doubt whether they would even give it a thought.

Ken Livingstone must be grateful that his congestion charge for entry into central London is working quite well. Some time before this began we paid a visit to the National Portrait Gallery – highly recommendable – and on the way back I took 3 photos covering the whole of Trafalgar Square, where he had banned feeding pigeons. It was around 11 am on a Wednesday and you could almost count the people on both hands whereas you could hardly see the ground for pigeons – that idea seems to have failed miserably. During our dealings with Sudan I once had to attend a meeting with our agents, in Central London, and as we were then at Bermondsey I took the tube from Elephant & Castle and came across a poster covering 3 films of the day reading from top to bottom I saw – "Shaft" – "The go between" – "Up the chastity belt". Someone enjoyed setting that lot out.

Whilst on the subject of humour I must relate a true story of a pairs match play golf match which took place a few years back at our club. I was playing with a great friend, Ernie Harris, and one of our opponents had decided to use a brand new set of clubs for the very first time. As the game proceeded, this turned into a complete disaster for him and his partner virtually carried him round the course on his own. After we had won fairly comfortably we went on to complete the course and, standing on the last tee, and having hit another disastrous tee shot, he turned to his partner and said – "I've a good mind to chuck these clubs into the pond" – just to the left of the tee. His partner replied "I shouldn't if I were you – you'll probably miss!"

One rather amusing tale I forgot to mention concerned the Headmistress of the school where Jean first taught. They had a young Spanish boy whose proper name was Jesus. This created a real problem for the Head who was deeply religious and she insisted he be called "Sus" – is that really in the spirit of things?

In August 2002 Jean's consultant decided that the Aricept tablets she had then been taking for 5 ½ years were no longer effective. I heard that people coming off the tablets tended to deteriorate fast and I made strong protests to no avail. The dosage was reduced to half for 2 weeks, then one quarter of the original for a further 2 weeks and then stopped. As soon as I was aware that she might lose this support I kept a day by day account of our activities and was able to show just how quickly and badly she went downhill. This was so noticeable that I complained that although she was unable to answer a series of simple tests they gave her on each visit there were other very important points covered by a "quality of life clause" in the N.I.C.E. Report covering Alzheimer's. (National Institute for Clinical Excellence). For instance she became unable to manage the seat belts in our car. Fortunately I won the day and she was put back on the full dose after a week or so and she was able to resume as before and was often belted up before I sat down in the driver's seat. There were of course many other benefits to be had which may not constitute rocket science but can make life a lot more bearable.

Sometime during the summer of 2002 we had our Eucalyptus tree lopped as it was getting rather tall. In doing so a large branch dropped on top of the weather vane on the garage roof and broke it. The gardener took it away for repair and shortly after it returned I firstly noticed the E was beginning to sag and it eventually fell to the ground. I left it underneath the vane and phoned the gardener. A few days later before anything happened I was searching Jean's handbag, as I mentioned earlier, and I discovered 4 teaspoons which she had put there – but, to my amazement, I also found cast iron evidence that she had actually taken an "E"!!! As Bill le Sage said "You have to laugh to survive!"

After a time Jean's condition deteriorated further and when there was an announcement that a new drug called Exiba, aimed specifically at medium to advanced patients, would be on the market within a matter of weeks, I started writing letters to the consultant to try to get hold of this quickly. A lot of information was published on the internet and I soon discovered that the drug had been in use for similar purposes for 8 years in Germany and the makers gave details of tests which had been carried out in America over a 6 month period using both Aricept and Ebixa at the same time and the results were very promising. In fairness it had not then been approved in America.

Unfortunately although Jean had been with one particular consultant from 1997, who started her on Aricept the areas were divided in early 2002 and Jean was excluded from his list. This proved to be quite tragic in my opinion as the original consultant did prescribe the two tablets together, whereas our new man was completely against this despite my protestations. It does seem a bit much if a single hospital works independently on the postcode system. I appreciate I am just a layman in these matters but I was heavily influenced by my very detailed diary of what took place when she came off Aricept. To complicate matters further Jean was diagnosed to have a mild form of diabetes in January 2003 requiring me to re-work my culinary skills, such as they are. Eventually I asked for a second opinion and was given a very able gentleman, brought out of retirement to help with the shortage of people with his skills. Unfortunately he too refused to give the dual treatment I was after, the main obstacle being the fact that the N.I.C.E. Report on Exiba was not due until November 2003. Since then the date has been revised to May 2005 which is not very helpful for all the sufferers and a bit difficult to understand, unless the financial implications have a bearing on the matter. Notwithstanding this several consultants are prescribing the 2 drugs and I know that some people have found a considerable improvement in such cases. Certainly there have been no reports to the contrary and bad news travels very fast in this country. At the risk of being really controversial I cannot see why there should be any objections. My daughter Linda believes that it is some considerable time since Jean really knew who she is, although she accepts her just as someone who calls occasionally. On my own with her, which is a large percentage of the day, there is absolutely no hope of intelligent conversation – this really is not living as most of us know it!

Anyway, by March/April 2003 I had to concede there was no doubt her condition was becoming much worse and I was beginning to feel the effects of my role as carer and started to make noises about getting some respite care and other assistance. Our new consultant proposed that he would take her into the hospital from which he was based for assessment provided I would agree to her coming off Aricept and being put on to Exiba by him under controlled conditions. Very, very reluctantly I finally decided to accept and abandon my fight during which I had compiled quite a large file of letters pleading my case. From the information given the process would take some 6/7 weeks and I was rather taken aback when, after 3 ½ weeks, having only just completed the first 5mg. week, it was suggested that she could come home where I could deal with the gradual increase to a maximum of 20mg, in 5mg. weekly steps. I protested that surely this was too soon, realising that once she left there would be no way back if things did not run smoothly. It was then agreed that she could stay for one more week.

Once home I soon found out that certain things she had been capable of doing herself, with a little help from me when necessary, were now completely beyond her. If you have ever tried putting support stockings, or even tights on someone who has no idea how to help herself you will understand. Men were never intended to work in this direction! Nevertheless I was given a rest from being in almost constant attendance, for which I was grateful. The hospital itself was only built in 1997 and was very well appointed and in quite beautiful surroundings.

Once Jean was on the full dose it soon became apparent that there was to be no benefit from Ebixa. By this time we had to have a nurse to get her dressed every morning and when they had serious problems they reported back to the consultant and it was decided to take her off fairly quickly, and then put her back on Aricept. Bearing in mind that I had been told on several occasions that the Aricept was being of no benefit to her I found this was quite a revelation, and in some ways a vindication of what I have consistently said. Of course we will never know whether the combined drugs might have proved beneficial.

They had further problems with Jean and at one stage

309

prescribed a powerful drug to calm her down and this was much too strong and nigh on knocked her out. After this the consultant agreed to take Jean back for 2 weeks respite care, but the following week he suggested that I had done everything possible to look after her at home but the time had come to think about getting her into a Nursing Home. To this end he was prepared to keep her in hospital until a place became available. After the events of the last couple of months I had to agree that this would be in everyone's interest. I was advised to carry out a survey of the available nursing homes qualified to look after people like Jean and once again the Alzheimer's Society pointed me in the direction of the most likely ones. After several visits with the final decision made with both Linda & Gary present we decided on one not far from Dorking and after a very short time a place became available and Jean was installed in her new home, - still taking Aricept!! Fate then took a hand and Jean went into a diabetic coma as a direct result of an infection and was sent to The East Surrey Hospital who reduced her blood sugar levels and kept her in for 6 days during which she was not given Aricept. As I have to accept that it was never going to become a cure I suggested that perhaps this would be the time to see if she could survive without it and the consultant agreed.

From then on the diabetes became more and more of a problem and despite going on insulin injections the downward spiral continued until she mercifully died on 18th October 2003.

The service at the crematorium was packed – standing room only – with an estimated 115/120 people present. I was quite overwhelmed by the letters I received afterwards and I am quite certain that Jean did not realise what an impact she had made on all manner of people during her lifetime. Two friends of my son actually broke a holiday in Devon to attend and we had not seen them for ages. Two members of the Child Guidance Unit said she kept them sane when times were stressful!!

Since Jean's death I find I am frequently asked for advice in relation to dementia which seems to be constantly on the increase. I have several times referred people to the lady who has given me so much support for seven long years – Penny Weaver of the Alzheimer's Society.

It may therefore surprise you to know that a few years back the Council withdrew the funding that had been given for her and a colleague for a very considerable period which I think is scandalous. As it happens they had received an extremely large legacy from one of their patients which enabled them to continue. However I am quite sure that it was the intention of the donor to help to expand the service, not just to maintain the status quo. I really cannot understand the lack of thought involved here and have myself written to the Council in support of the efforts of the Branch to get the funding restored. I am pleased to report that they have finally agreed to resume for 2004/5 but seem determined to keep everyone on tenterhooks for the future which makes any sort of planning quite impossible.

After 51 years together life at home has become somewhat strange but at least I can now relax knowing she is no longer suffering from this terrible disease.

Early in 2004 I was invited by the Alzheimer's Society to put my name up for a meeting with the members of the N.I.C.E. Committee which eventually took place in October 2004 at which there would be around 40 people present – all I assumed to be carers or even patients. This was to bring them up to date with the thinking of the people at the sharp end. It should be borne in mind that treatments for Alzheimer's only became available in 1997, so this does not have a very long history. In the event I was not chosen and then I discovered that there were only 2 past carers in attendance together with a lot of their own experts in their own field. Quite a daunting prospect! In the December edition of the National Alzheimer's monthly newsletter was an article by the 2 carers in question. In it they mentioned having been sent a 1000 page document to read – 8 days before the meeting. Frankly I find it hard to credit such insensitivity – or was it a deliberate ploy to intimidate them? The whole purpose of the meeting was I thought to get their views. Fortunately one of these carers had had considerable experience at a very high level – but was it really necessary? Having had the meeting they then delayed publishing their findings pending the need for further cost evaluation.

Bearing in mind that the original report was postponed from November 2003 one would have thought this should have been cut and dried by now.

I was talking on the phone just before Xmas 2004 to Geoff Banks – former sax player in our group in Palestine and he tried to remind me of an incident in Palestine one Xmas. He assures me that he and I had to take a truck to Bethlehem to collect 25 WAAFs for a dance, possibly for the officers, and what's more – I HAD TO SIGN FOR THEM!!! I honestly have absolutely no recollection of this but – if I returned them – I do hope I got them - "SIGNED UNEXAMINED"! When the long term memory starts to go this is a really worrying matter – especially on a subject like this!

During Jean's illness we had quite a lot of contact with her cousin Eileen and I still see her from time to time and have already mentioned that she had worked on ciphers during the war. For her birthday I suggested taking her to

Bletchley Park to see the wonderful exhibition based on the wartime work carried out here with the Enigma machine and the very first computer. Like all people involved at the time she hardly ever spoke of her activities until recently and I was astonished to learn that she actually worked in the Foreign Office opposite No.10 for 7 years from 1942. I asked her how she came to be chosen for ciphers and apparently they picked anyone that could solve the Telegraph Crossword in 15 minutes.

In the course of her time there she met and shook hands with Ernest Bevin and Anthony Eden and I can remember her being quite agitated when the Burgess & McClean affair hit the headlines. What I did not realise was that she had seen him at the time he was in all probability gathering information which made it all the more personal to her.

In June 2002 we were in the throes of organising a big party to celebrate our Golden Wedding. As before it was to be musical, and once again the Queen had chosen OUR week – although not the actual day, as she did 25 years before. I know February is not a very good month but that was when she was actually married. I tried unsuccessfully to get some Golden Busy Lizzie's for the garden but apparently there was only one in existence!!!

On the day despite a lot of rain we had a whale of a time and collected a tidy sum for the Alzheimer's Society in lieu of presents, as we had done the year before my 75th birthday. After all how can you possibly buy something that is sensible for two people who have lived this long.

I of course invited our best man Allan Ganley to come, and, would you believe, he had a gig at Wavendon for which John Dankworth called for a 3 o'clock rehearsal – so no change there! Jean & I must be one of the very few couples who have never heard the best man's speech.

In January 2004 we had the Allan Ganley Big Band at Shepperton – 17 of the finest musicians in the country – unfortunately they can only be got together very infrequently these days but this was certainly memorable especially from my point of view. In the second half Allan mentioned that when he started out I was the first real musician he came across and he played Johnny Mandel's beautiful tune "Emily" in memory of Jean, this being the name of our granddaughter, and I found this very moving.

All that remains is to get this book published – I only hope it does not take too long – but in one of the thank you letters following the party, I was reminded that "The Cruel Sea" went through the hands of 40 publishers before being accepted.

It is now 2006 and the printing is going ahead at last. In the 3 years since I wrote the book the N.I.C.E. Committee has postponed the final decision on drugs for Alzheimer's, originally due in November 2003 for a third time and is supposed to report later this year. We must hope that public opinion will sway them in favour of giving everyone at least a chance of trying the tablets as soon as diagnosed. Once deterioration has set in it is surely pointless. Keep up the pressure!!

INDEX

Printed in the United Kingdom
by Lightning Source UK Ltd.
115077UKS00001B/112-333